Shifting Views

EDITED BY ANDREW LEACH, ANTONY MOULIS & NICOLE SULLY

Shifting Views

Selected Essays on the Architectural History of Australia and New Zealand

UQP

First published 2008 by University of Queensland Press
PO Box 6042, St Lucia, Queensland 4067 Australia

www.uqp.uq.edu.au

Designed and typeset by R.T.J. Klinkhamer
Printed in Australia by McPherson's Printing Group

This book was generously supported by a publication grant from the Society of Architectural Historians, Australia and New Zealand, and by a research grant from the School of Geography, Planning and Architecture, University of Queensland.

Cataloguing-in-Publication Data
National Library of Australia

Shifting views: selected essays on the architectural history of Australia and New Zealand/editors, Andrew Leach; Antony Moulis; Nicole Sully.

1st ed.

ISBN: 9 780 7022 3660 0 (pbk.)

Architecture – History.
Architecture, Modern – 19th century – Australia.
Architecture, Modern – 20th century – Australia.
Architecture, Modern – 19th century – New Zealand.
Architecture, Modern – 20th century – New Zealand.
Architecture – Australia.
Architecture – New Zealand.

720.994

Foreword

This publication marks twenty-five years since the first meeting of the Society of Architectural Historians, Australia and New Zealand (SAHANZ). Architectural history has been studied in this region for far longer by academics and independent writers who have published books still very much in circulation. Other more informal means of communication, like compiling personal archives, publishing editorials in professional magazines, giving talks and writing letters, have also all persisted; the tradition of the historical essay distributed to friends as an extended Christmas card comes to mind. All these activities have contributed to the ongoing building of a comprehensive archive of the history of architecture and places of significance in Australia and New Zealand.

Architectural history, in all its guises, is an integral part of what Crimp (1984) described as the 'archival' or 'stratigraphic' project of cultural production today: 'those processes of quotation, excerptation, framing, and staging that constitute the strategies of the work'. If architectural history, theoretical inquiry and heritage research are all cast as players in the creation of an archive of architectural knowledge, it is a short step to regard all these endeavours as fundamental to the representation and production of architecture today and into the future.

As Bernard Smith has continually stressed in his writings on Australian art, antipodean cultural history can be simultaneously different from – and also fundamentally a part of – other established sources and centres. Correspondingly, the geographical focus on Australia and New Zealand in this collection does not mean that their value is confined to an understanding of the immediate region. Many of the papers explore key issues of historiographical method and approach that are applicable to diverse time periods and contexts. Some deal with the colonial situation and engage in a dialogue of negotiation and exchange between the perceived centres of imperial cultural production and peripheral receivers. Other papers are quite specific in their focus, and through such specificity and detail they serve to clarify or bypass former generalisations and binary distinctions and generate broader perspectives.

Aside from the journal *Fabrications*, we hope this collection is the first of a number of substantial publications sponsored by SAHANZ. Through the keen eyes of the editorial team, *Shifting Views* draws together in one volume a selection of authors from across Australia and New Zealand, and across the disciplinary spectrum of empirical to theoretical approaches. Together the papers constitute a fascinating index of the state of inquiry into architectural history in the last twenty-five years. We trust that *Shifting Views: Selected Essays on the Architectural History of Australia and New Zealand* will prove an invaluable resource to researchers, students, architects and all those interested in the history of our built environment.

Hannah Lewi
President of SAHANZ, 2005–07

Contents

Introduction

In a paper first presented in 1984, Australian architectural historian Judith Brine tackles a question that resonates throughout the essays in this collection: by what means does our past become our history? Her example is Port Arthur, the former penal settlement in Tasmania, which she uses to identify those changing perceptions that affect the presence of building through time. As the nineteenth century gave way to the twentieth and the prisons and barracks associated with Port Arthur's past gradually fell into disrepair, the people of the town confronted their convict past – not without difficulty – and decided that it was important to preserve its artefacts in the present, for the future. Through the steps that Brine describes, what may have been the embarrassment of children and grandchildren on behalf of parents and grandparents became the town's heritage – a matter of pride, a patrimony that connects the present to its past by asking questions of it.

The Adelaide conference 'Australian Questions to Face', where Brine delivered her paper, was the first of a now twenty-five-long series staged by the Society of Architectural Historians, Australia and New Zealand (SAHANZ).[1] It is fitting that we begin this selection of essays, delivered at those conferences and across that time span, by invoking her contribution to the program. Brine's 'Charting shifting views', from which we borrow the title of this anthology, even now exposes several fundamental questions that historians of architecture face in Australia and New Zealand, and that still resonate with our present endeavour.

Architectural historians of this 'Antipodes' face regular reminders of the relative proximity of the first moments when these territories began to take part in the traditions of Western architecture. They also confront the recency of the evolution of frameworks that slowly but surely came to include Indigenous building traditions in response to the question: what is architecture? The more important question, upon which these conditions impinge, demands the modifier, what is architecture, here? These are the recurring questions of the region's architectural theory, criticism and historiography that run parallel to ours. Shifting to one remove, however, our concerns lie with the portrayal, historically, both of what architecture was and with what it *can be*, or *could have been*, from the fluid perspectives of the present moment – and of the present moments in which our authors wrote. These are issues of historical perspective, and of a self-reflective, critical historiography above all. The essays we present here share a determination to reflect on the conditions of writing architectural history in and of this region while they set about this very task.

This assumes, correctly, that the scope of what architecture is and has been in either Australia or New Zealand is by no means fixed. The job of defining what architecture, borrowed from Britain and Europe, would suit this part of the world, is embedded in the discussions staged by those who arrived – as they established the first missions, constructed the first houses for the governors of the numerous colonies, and raised courthouses, jails, storehouses and customs facilities. The relationships of the towns and territories in the region's numerous settlements in the eighteenth and nineteenth centuries to historical and contemporaneous precedents were likewise matters of deliberation. How to plan towns where there were none? To turn land into property and build thereupon? These questions all determined how far Britain's architectural history would extend to the far reaches of her influence. They also tested the frontiers of building for new conditions: from models of urban planning – symbolic, pragmatic and *laissez-faire* – to methods of construction responding to available materials, technologies and the environments in which they would be deployed. While some sought continuities with Britain, others differentiated the architecture and planning of the colonies from that of the seat of the Empire to which they were subject. Decisions that were rarely architectural in nature nonetheless raised or provoked the question already posed, namely: what is architecture, here?

Only recently, following marathon efforts of the last four decades, could we speak confidently of architecture in Aboriginal camps, on the Maori *marae*, or in the ephemeral and in the suburbs, beyond building into its representation, or as a form of evidence for the histories of ideas, culture, economics, politics, technology and religion.

This elasticity reflects changes to architectural historiography throughout the world. As a discipline, architectural history has long welcomed the interminable process of reinventing and contesting the values within which its scholars work. Yet part of the discussion we document here also considers the worth of sitting outside the main currents of anglophone architectural historiography. Just how far can perspectives developed in New York or Delft or London help us explain chapters in the architectural history of Brisbane, Wellington, Perth or Sydney? And how often does the location of architectural historians in such settings grant them licence to set the discipline's currency aside and to focus on the first principles of research and analysis?

Just as, for Port Arthur, the past became history and heritage by altering how its oldest buildings were seen from the present, the discussion of how and what to build in New

Zealand and the Australian colonies gave way to initial efforts to document early buildings and monuments in historical terms. Our libraries are replete with studies dating from the early twentieth century to today that make a plea for seeing various acts of building and settlement as architecture, using history as a way of legitimating new answers to old questions of authority and significance. Some of these books sought to establish a narrative for the architectural history of Australia or New Zealand, such as JM Freeland's *Architecture in Australia* (1968) or Peter Shaw's *New Zealand architecture from Polynesian beginnings to 1990* (1991), to become stalwarts of the two national canons.[2] However, next to these volumes are many besides who share their aim of claiming architectural history where there was once only a past, imbuing those pasts with values, and describing how they form part of a larger story – of Australia, of New Zealand, or of the history of architecture writ large. Scholars of architectural history in Australia and New Zealand would later build upon these foundational studies and react against them.

If Freeland, Shaw and others asked us to see architecture where others could not, then the terms of their histories became the targets of subsequent generations of architectural historians, who sought to challenge and recalibrate these accounts. Reconciling local definitions of architecture with imported frames of reference was undoubtedly a dimension of that long-term, multigenerational endeavour. So, too, was the effort of using the tools of architectural history to document and project overlooked aspects of our respective national pasts. Yet by demonstrating the different consequences of constructing architectural history according to the various premises available to architectural historians, later writers exposed the mechanisms at work in even the most straightforward accounts of the past. We can now witness, from our present point of view, a decades-old clash between documentary historians of architecture and critical architectural historians. The latter focused on minor figures as keys to disrupt set narratives and on the production of new takes upon major figures (to the same ends). They also sought to highlight works that fell outside the categories of high-culture architecture, bridging a gap between monumental histories and those figures, buildings and events that undermined them.

This critical approach has had the effect of a combined effort, even if it was not established as such, and it pays tribute to what Brine calls the 'salient characteristic of the greater part of Australian [and, we add for her, New Zealand] society,' the 'quality of "aggressive egalitarianism"'. As a value that finds a home in many of the essays we present here, it is worth elaborating. In 'Charting Shifting Views', Brine continues:

> It is constituted not so much by a strong belief that all are equal but rather by the obverse belief that no group should be accepted as more authoritative than the rest: in other words, by a widespread rejection of the legitimacy of elites. Such an ideological thrust is countered by actual powerful sections of the community including government bureaucracies and the professions who have a stake in maintaining their relatively privileged positions. Among the latter group are historians, architects and perhaps also architectural historians.

Shifting Views pays tribute to those architectural historians on both sides of the Tasman Sea who undermined the privileged figures of whom Brine writes by producing, from the 1980s, a new, critical forum for architectural historians. The common quality of the papers that follow is their exploration of chapters of architectural history while questioning the bases on which their work takes place. In some instances, such as Stanislaus Fung's 'The "Sydney School"?' (1985), Paul Walker's 'Kenneth Frampton and the fiction of place' (1991) or Julie Willis and Philip Goad's 'A myth in the making' (2000), the work enters more properly into the intellectual history of local architectural culture, addressing historiographical categories and calling their applicability into question through careful, detailed analysis of their foundations. They often start from the very beginning, rejecting 'isms' and the attendant conceptual structures that would shape research, and suggest starting points for historical reflection. As Fung asserts, the burden of proof was no longer on those who sought to break historical categories, but on those who had first asserted them. Some work in this book might be called theoretical, contributing to a critical history of the region's architecture in the spirit of the most advanced disciplinary developments of the moment. The writing of Judith Brine or Helen Proudfoot, which we would no longer readily describe as theoretical, was seen as such when their papers were first aired. Other contributions bring historiography's conceptualisation into play with greater subtlety: Duncan Richards's (1988) quiet assessment of 'Spanish style' as a category of architectural history through a study of a Perth architect; Robin Skinner's (1999) understated reflection on the way in which New Zealand's architects have been seen from a distance; and David Bridgman's (2004) reading of bungalows on the Northern Territory's north coast expose the interplay of complex cultural, procedural and technological relationships.

Writers such as Joan Kerr, in her classic polemic 'Why architects should not write architectural history' (1984), or Paul Hogben in 'The aftermath of "Pleasures"' (2003) astutely attend to the availability of architectural history to those who make buildings, and thus to the long-problematic moment in which architectural history is delivered up to its audiences. These essays ask: do historians bear any responsibility for the way in which architects know history, or instrumentalise it? 'Our architecture makes our history,' writes Kerr in conclusion, 'but the reverse is equally true'. Though many would rightly disagree, the perception that we, here, are 'short' on architecture is common. With what history we have, what is to be taken up? What left aside? What clues can architects find in history that will help them make good architecture? Some historians, it is fair to say, have been more conscious than others of the way their work is received by the profession. Some are themselves architects whose research into architectural history is only one aspect of their participation in architectural culture. Others maintain a cool distance that draws as much from circumstance as it does from a belief in the importance of a critical remove of the act of analysis from the uses to which others might put it.

Whether concerned with the interaction between a community of architectural historians and a profession that finds their work useful; or between generations of historians who disagree on the points at which historical analysis should begin and on the questions it should pose; these essays – and the conferences from which they are drawn – share a self-consciousness that sets them apart from the histories written by their disciplinary forerunners and those who believe that history begins and ends with laying down the facts as they are known. Indeed, in their earnestness to expose the scaffolding that holds up the histories of Australian and New Zealand architecture, the following writers point towards some answers to the question of why it matters to write architectural history in this part of the world. That these reflections emerge from a setting that allows for a trans-Tasman cross-fertilisation enriches both national lines of study.

We have alluded already to SAHANZ as an institutional setting for the essays presented here. Our selection of sixteen papers from more than 1,000 delivered over the organisation's quarter-century history clearly does not represent all the themes that these conferences have explored. We cannot describe the many topics that have received attention. Rather, we chart the way in which writers and researchers continue to exhibit a degree of 'aggressive egalitarianism' in their work, just as we note the ongoing appreciation of the need to balance documentary and critical historiographical modes. With this in mind, a few brief moments in the SAHANZ story help contextualise the selection of *Shifting views*.

The August 1984 conference in Adelaide at which Brine's and Kerr's essays were first presented had brought together a modest band of teachers of architectural history in schools of architecture, conservation architects, heritage specialists, and those architects and amateurs who had set pen to paper in building up a bibliography of studies on Australia's architectural history. The range of approaches displayed at this meeting spanned from empirical and descriptive studies of individual cases to openly reflective and provocative contributions on the state of the discipline's play. The meeting's convenor and the Society's first president, David Saunders, wrote in the conference's announcement that while 'in Australia fact-gathering has proceeded (and been published) with relative vigour for some years now … discussions about significance and interpretation are rare and in need of promotion.'[3]

This conference was not the first instance of an organised critical discussion of architectural history on Australian soil. The SAHANZ meetings, however, fast became the setting for the most sustained analysis of the bases and structures of architectural history writing, drawing on early efforts along directions that it would make its own and developing methods for keeping this local enquiry open and astute. In part, this drew on the Society's stated aims to hold established historical writers within SAHANZ accountable for their judgments, just as the earliest members held work of the post-war decades up to scrutiny. These conferences, consequently, witnessed a high degree of internal renewal among the discipline's protagonists. This change was not always welcome, and many shared the views presented to the 1987 Adelaide conference by Derek Linstrum, then Director of Conservation Studies at the University of York, who concluded his keynote address 'The uses of architectural history today' with a reflection on the 'current situation' for architectural history: 'when it settles down and the lunatic fringes have been cut or curled, it seems likely to offer a sane use of existing buildings, a reconciliation of old and new, and … a return to discipline that we all need.'[4]

What some saw as a lack of discipline – trading evidence for speculation – was for others a heightened sense of disciplinary responsibility. In no conference of the Society's first decade was this clash clearer than at Sydney in 1988, at a meeting themed 'Australian studies in architectural history'. With four years having passed since the first SAHANZ conference, its organisers could take stock of and contest the emerging character of the Society. Stanislaus Fung, introducing the conference proceedings, brings this relatively recent history into play: 'Looking back at these events, one is struck by the fact that architectural history is never as unitary and monolithic as some recent loose talk of "our discipline" might suggest, but is rather a complex of heterogeneous and sometimes contradictory practices conducted in a range of institutional settings.' He follows this reflection with a thinly veiled proposal: 'Against a background of the archival and empiricist interests that have been and are still shared by a substantial number of historians, new scholarly projects have emerged that attempt to bring architectural history into relation with developments in other fields of enquiry.'[5]

Although many have since regarded this moment as the seeds of a rupture between historians and theoreticians, or more correctly documentary and critical historians, it is clear from these remarks that the organisers understood the necessity to develop a form of discussion that could accommodate the breadth of scholarship being undertaken by the Society's blossoming, and increasingly diverse, membership:

> The current advance of 'foreign theoretical models' need not engender incomprehension on the one hand and a self-affirming autism of specialists on the other. Rather, it presents to members of the Society and interested persons generally, an occasion to enhance their sense of communality by considering and clarifying for themselves the aims and purposes that might inform a responsible response to the present state of diversity among Australian architectural historians.[6]

If Sydney's 1988 conference exposed camps that would become more pronounced in later years, before 'graduating' the Society's conferences to broad-based settings for discussion of architecture, it promoted the expansion of SAHANZ's territory rather than reinforcing disciplinary defence lines. If we have shrugged off Brine's value of 'aggressive egalitarianism' by singling out this early event, then we might redeem ourselves by observing that Sydney 1988 rendered explicit a potentially divisive tendency that was latent from the Society's very beginning. The theory of Brine, Kerr and Proudfoot would become the history against which others, who later adopted the mantle of theorists, would react. The historical instability of these definitions within a small community remains informative even today.

If we can speak of the 1980s as years within which the values of a regional, critical architectural history discussion were teased out, which asked as much of historians as it did of history, then the early 1990s systematically worked through the challenges of that initial trajectory and its first test. By 1996, and the Society's second conference in New Zealand (after Christchurch in 1991), the scope and tone of the meetings had become largely what they are today. From early meetings of fewer than two dozen speakers, the programs of SAHANZ conferences jumped to over 100 papers. With this boom came an attendant expansion of the Society's always self-determined remit. Themes once closely bound to architectural history and historiography became more abstract, offering less strict guides to delegations who saw SAHANZ as a forum not only for architectural history, but also for a broadly reflective discussion on architecture. This development, too, challenged the *raison d'être* of an organisation set up to promote the region's architectural history and historiography, but adapted to another need: promotion of the critical analysis of architecture, both within the contexts of its history and in the currents of ideas in which architecture dabbles and is implicated.

It becomes more difficult to defer to historical distance in considering this last decade, especially given that the long-term effects of shifts undertaken in the mid-1990s have yet to play out their full consequences for the architectural historiography of either Australia or New Zealand. Not the least of these considerations involves the 'property' of the Society's formal discussions on architectural history. Can we legitimately speak of the Society as a venue principally for the presentation and debate of scholarship in architectural history? Or is this an historical category belonging to the early meetings, now long since diffused into a much wider setting for the architectural humanities, including architectural theory, architectural philosophy, cultural and urban studies, intellectual history and design research? The issue, which the papers selected here describe, is one of continuity versus change within the local structures for architectural history research and its dissemination.

The paradox of SAHANZ is that its continuity is determined by change. It is an organisation that calls for a process of perpetual renewal through vigorous debate. This selection of essays, it stands to reason, offers architectural historians of the region a reminder of the recent history of their discipline, as it provokes, inevitably, some discussion of what comes next.

Andrew Leach
Antony Moulis
Nicole Sully

Editors' note

The essays included in this collection were presented at conferences of the Society of Architectural Historians, Australia and New Zealand across a period of more than two decades. The editors have made every effort to retain the papers as first published, making some editorial incursions to correct early printing and typographical errors and to ensure consistency of style across the collection. Some practices have changed within SAHANZ conferences over this time, leaving the referencing of some essays uneven in places. Where possible we have endeavoured to locate the original sources where referencing information has been scant; however, this has not been practicable in all cases.

Acknowledgments

We are grateful for the enthusiasm and support of the staff and board of the University of Queensland Press in realising this project. In particular, Madonna Duffy understood what we sought to do and helped us improve on our first ideas. Wendy Sanderson lent her keen eye to the task of editing the manuscript. The Editorial Board of the Society of Architectural Historians, Australia and New Zealand, chaired by John Macarthur, generously endorsed the project; and the Society's Committee, led by Hannah Lewi (President, 2005–07), matched their own enthusiasm for the book with a generous publication subsidy. The School of Geography, Planning and Architecture at the University of Queensland granted us funds to employ the assistance we needed to finalise the documents for publication. Hannah Lewi and Julie Willis helped us clarify our intentions about the table of contents; Geoffrey London's support was fundamental; many individuals helped us locate both proceedings volumes and the people whose work was in them. Alexandra Brown and Vanessa Rothwell lent valuable help at a vital stage of the production. We wish to thank the authors who have allowed us to reproduce their work here, and James Kerr for granting permission to publish the work of his late wife, Joan Kerr. Finally, we owe a debt to all the authors, convenors and editors who, for 25 years, have built up and sustained a setting for the advancement of architectural historiography in these two countries.

The Editors

Editors and Contributors

Editors

Andrew Leach is author of *Manfredo Tafuri: Choosing History* (2007), *Campus Confessions: Architecture and the Central Institute of Technology* (2004) and *Frederick H Newman: Lectures on Architecture* (2003). He is a UQ Postdoctoral Fellow in the School of Geography, Planning and Architecture at the University of Queensland. With Paul Walker, he edits the SAHANZ journal, *Fabrications* (UQP).

Antony Moulis is Head of Architecture at the University of Queensland, where he received his doctorate in 2002. His research interests include twentieth-century architecture, techniques in architectural design and the work of Le Corbusier. In *Fabrications*, he recently published 'An Active Silence: Le Corbusier's Art in Australia' (2007).

Nicole Sully is a Lecturer in Architecture at the University of Queensland. Her research is largely interdisciplinary and focuses on architecture and memory, in addition to the themes of architecture and exile, pathologies of place, and the history of Australian architecture. She has contributed to *A Guide to Perth Architecture*, edited by Gooffrey London (Watermark Press, forthcoming) and has published reviews in *The Architect* (WA) and *Fabrications*.

Contributors

After three decades teaching at the School of Architecture at the University of Auckland, **Mike Austin** was appointed Professor of Architecture at the School of Architecture and Landscape Architecture at Unitec, New Zealand, where he taught design and the history and theory of architecture. His doctorate (1976) was concerned with Polynesian architecture in New Zealand and his research has extended to the architecture of the Pacific Islands about which he has presented and published numerous papers. He is a life member of SAHANZ.

David Bridgman is a practising architect specialising in the field of heritage conservation and a Senior Lecturer in Architecture and Interior Design at Charles Darwin University, teaching architectural history and design. The Northern Territory's foremost architectural historian, he has undertaken significant research into the built environment of Australia's northern tropics with emphasis on the influences of colonial architecture of South-East Asia. His PhD examined Commonwealth Government housing provided for senior public servants in Darwin in the immediate pre-war period. He is currently examining the significance of the outback police station in the Northern Territory.

The second President of SAHANZ and one of its founders, **Judith Brine**, AM, has written widely on history and theory of architecture, urban conservation and education. She has served as Pro Vice Chancellor at the University of Adelaide, as Commissioner of the Environment, Resources and Development Court of South Australia and as an Adelaide City Councillor. She was awarded the President's Medal of the South Australian Chapter of the Royal Australian Institute of Architects, holds a Life Fellowship of the Royal Australian Institute of Architects and is a Fellow of the Planning Institute of Australia.

Deidre Brown is a Senior Lecturer in Architecture at the University of Auckland. Her contribution to this book was made when she was Senior Lecturer in Aotearoa New Zealand Art History at the University of Canterbury. Her research interests include Maori and Pacific art and architectural history. Recent books include *Te Puna: Maori Art from Te Taitokerau Northland* (2007), *Maori Arts of the Gods* (2005) and *Tai Tokerau Whakairo Rakau: Northland Maori Woodcarving* (2003; winner Best First Non-Fiction Book, 2004 Montana New Zealand Book Awards). She is currently preparing a new book on Maori architectural history.

Paola Favaro graduated in architecture from the Istituto Universitario di Architettura di Venezia (1984) and has lived in Australia since 1997. She has over 20 years' experience in architectural practice, education and research in Italy, Canada and Australia. Her current areas of research centre on the cultural and educational issues that inform and influence architecture through migration. She is completing her PhD on Enrico Taglietti at the University of New South Wales, where she teaches architectural design and architectural history and theory.

Stanislaus Fung is Head of History and Theory in the Architecture Program at the University of New South Wales. He has previously taught in the University of Adelaide (1989–99) and the University of Pennsylvania (1997–98). He was Founding Editor of *Fabrications* (1988–92). Among his publications on Australian architecture are essays in *Architecture Australia*, *Architectural Theory Review*, and *Voices* (Canberra), as well as papers in the conference proceedings of SAHANZ.

Philip Goad is Professor of Architecture in the Faculty of Architecture, Building and Planning at the University of Melbourne. A former editor of *Fabrications* and a contributing editor to *Architecture Australia*, he is author of *Melbourne Architecture* (1999), *New Directions in Australian Architecture* (2001), *Australian Modern* (with Rowan Wilken & Julie Willis, 2004), *New Directions in Tropical Asian Architecture* (with Anoma Pieris, 2005), and *Modernism and Australia* (with Ann Stephen & Andrew McNamara, 2006). He is an authority on modern Australian architecture, and with Julie Willis will edit the *Encyclopedia of Australian Architecture* (Cambridge University Press).

Paul Hogben is a Lecturer in Architecture in the Faculty of the Built Environment at the University of New South Wales. One of his research interests is an examination of the public relations practices of the architectural profession, for which he received a PhD in 2005. Among other things, this research considers the promotional politics that shaped architectural discourse over the twentieth century. Papers on these topics have been published in *Architectural Theory Review* and *Fabrications*.

Professor **Joan Kerr**, AM, FAHA (1938–2004), taught and researched Australian art and architectural history for over three decades at the University of Sydney, at the College of Fine Arts of the University of New South Wales and in the Centre for Cross-Cultural Research at the Australian National University. Among her fourteen books are *Gothick Taste in the Colony of New South Wales* (with James Broadbent, 1980), *The Dictionary of Australian Artists* (1992) and *Human Scale in Architecture* (with Jo Holder & Robert Freestone, 2003). With James Semple Kerr, she received a Jubilee Senior Heritage Award from the National Trust of New South Wales.

Miles Lewis, AM, is an architectural historian with special interests in the vernacular, prefabrication, the history of building technology and the principles of conservation. He is a Professor of Architecture at the University of Melbourne, a Fellow of the Australian Academy of Humanities, a Fellow of the International Advisory Council of the Royal Institute of Architects, and an honorary life member of the Comité International d'Architecture Vernaculaire. His books range from *Victorian Primitive* to *Suburban Backlash*, and he is editor of *Architectura* (forthcoming). He established the pioneering *Australian Architectural Index*, which is now being digitised for mounting on the web, and maintains existing web resources including the *Melbourne Mansions Data Base* and the *EG Kilburn Photographs*.

A Postdoctoral Research Fellow at the Aboriginal Environments Research Centre, University of Queensland, **Stephen Long** has expertise in the area of Indigenous environments and projects at the intersection of architecture and anthropology. He received a Dean's commendation for his PhD thesis, which examined Indigenous relationships with place and cultural heritage. Recent research includes a survey of Indigenous housing literature and field studies of Indigenous architectural traditions. His design work includes a project for a remote Indigenous community facility that received a commendation in the Royal Australian Institute of Architects North Queensland Regional Awards (2006).

Harry Margalit is Associate Professor and Head of Program (Architecture) at the University of New South Wales. He holds a BArch from the University of Cape Town, and an MA and PhD from the University of Sydney. He has researched and published on modernist and contemporary architecture in Australia in both the academic and professional press, and is a partner in the Sydney practice of Quinton-Margalit Architects.

Helen Proudfoot is an historian and heritage consultant who has maintained a special interest in the foundation and development of Sydney. She prepared the preliminary report on the First Government House site (1983) and has contributed to its conservation plan, as well as exploring various aspects of the site's development. Her books include *Old Government House* (1971), *A Guide to Historic Sydney* (1973), *Exploring Sydney's West* (1987), *Cadman's Cottage* (1988), *The Historic Buildings of Windsor and Richmond* (1988) and *Gardens in Bloom* (1989).

Duncan Richards is an architect and historian who has made a substantial contribution to the architectural and urban history of Western Australia. He has been a frequent contributor to *The Architect* (WA), and among his publications are the monographs *High Hopes: Marshall Clifton, Architect and Artist* (with Barbara Chapman) and *Donaldson + Warn: Crossing Midfield* (with Geoffrey London). With his wife Oline Richards, he produced two films: *Learning About Environment / Environments for Learning* and *Blowing in the Wind.* In 1994, he was named a Life Fellow of the Royal Institute of Australian Architects.

Robin Skinner is a Senior Lecturer in Architecture at Victoria University of Wellington, where he teaches architectural history and the architecture of the Pacific. Between 1999 and

2001 he lectured in the Department of Design Studies at the University of Otago. His recently completed PhD dissertation (University of Auckland) looks at the representation of architecture in New Zealand in mid-nineteenth century Britain. This is part of a larger project in which he considers architectural exchange within imperialism and colonialism.

Sarah Treadwell is a Senior Lecturer in Architecture at the University of Auckland, where she teaches in the architectural design studio and lectures on issues of architectural representation. Her research areas include analyses of nineteenth-century images of architecture in the South Pacific and New Zealand. She also writes on contemporary fine art practices that reference architecture. Her publications include 'Earthquake Weather' in *Drifting*, edited by Stephen Cairns (Routledge, 2004), 'The Motel: An Image of Elsewhere' in *Space and Culture* (2005) and 'Animation, the Cat and Escaping Drawing', with Paul Veart in *Interstices* (2005).

Paul Walker was educated at the University of Auckland and taught at Victoria University of Wellington from 1989–99. He is now Associate Professor of Architecture at the University of Melbourne. Walker has written widely on New Zealand architecture, and with Justine Clark is author of *Looking for the Local: Architecture and the New Zealand Modern* (VUP, 2000). Aspects of his current research on colonial and post colonial museum architecture are documented in 'Institutional Audiences and Architectural Style: The Napier Museum' in *Colonial Modernities*, edited by Peter Scriver & Vikramaditya Prakash (Routledge, 2007).

Julie Willis is an Associate Professor in Architecture at the University of Melbourne. Her research concentrates on Australian architectural history of the twentieth century. Recent publications include *Australian Modern: The Architecture of Stephenson & Turner* (2004, with Philip Goad & Rowan Wilken), 'In Australia, between America and Europe, Beaux-Arts and Modernism, scholarship and qualification: The Melbourne University Architectural Atelier 1919–1947' in the *Journal of Architectural Education* (2005) and, with Philip Goad, 'Invention from War: a circumstantial modernism for Australian architecture', in *Narrating Architecture* (Routledge, 2006).

Charting Shifting Views of Port Arthur and Associated Methodological Problems

1984

JUDITH BRINE

Introduction

In addressing the title of the conference 'Australian Questions to Face', one might begin by examining the nature of 'Australian'. If I ask myself what the salient characteristic of the greater part of Australian society is, I think I might postulate a quality of 'aggressive egalitarianism'. It is constituted not so much by a strong belief that all are equal but rather by the obverse belief that no group should be accepted as more authoritative than the rest: in other words, by a widespread rejection of the legitimacy of elites. Such an ideological thrust is countered by actual powerful sections of the community including government bureaucracies and the professions who have a stake in maintaining their relatively privileged positions. Among the latter group are historians, architects and perhaps also architectural historians.

If one was to admit the legitimacy of egalitarianism, neglecting for a moment its more militant aspects, what implications would there be for Australian architectural history? I think the answer must be a swing in emphasis away from history as histories of architectural objects and from history as histories of the producers of those objects and of their ideas incorporated into the objects and towards histories of another kind that give a new importance to history as an account of the changing appreciation of architecture. It is also consistent with a recognition of egalitarianism that such history would be primarily directed towards appreciation of those buildings that become important by virtue of the public interest expressed in them, and that the appreciation to be described should not be the opinions and experience of a critical elite but of people in general.

Precursors for this kind of history are not, I think, numerous, although Philippe Boudon's (1972) history of the houses built at Pessac comes readily to mind.[1] Because such histories are unusual, methodologies for dealing with them are underdeveloped. Further, if one again returns to consider the logical consequences of aggressive egalitarianism, it follows that the usual role of the historian and presumably also the methodology from which (s)he derives power must also be under attack. Some interesting problems arise in considering a suitable methodology for histories of appreciation, and it is to these that I would like to direct my attention at the conference. They are:

1. On what material is it appropriate to draw for a history of appreciation based on principles of egalitarianism?
2. How is such material to be processed, ordered and presented without introducing an elitist interpretive bias?
3. What is the significance of the kind of appreciation that becomes apparent from such a history?
4. What is the relationship between elite and popular modes of appreciation where they have coexisted?
5. Can an architectural historian develop a legitimate role in an aggressively egalitarian society?

In the meantime, what is offered here is a brief history of the changing nature of the public's appreciation of Port Arthur. It is a place that derives its importance from the visits that have been made to it over the last 100 years or so; that is, a place in which the public has demonstrated a clear interest. In addition Marcus Clarke's novel, *His Natural Life*, has become firmly attached to the site and the interplay of the reception of the site and the book is an interesting one to explore.[2]

The extent to which *His Natural Life* was formative in establishing a popular image of prison life at Port Arthur can hardly be overestimated. The process by which it did so is not an uncommon one; it might be described as the syndrome of the bestseller. Once a book achieves widespread popularity and engenders widespread comment, it in turn generates parallel works in different media. By this process its effect snowballs and the total reception of the novel and its adjuncts can be seen as an important cultural phenomenon. It imparts a new status to the book; the book's meaning is thus affirmed and an element of truth is conferred on it over and above that usual in a fictional work. It was in this way that Clarke's account of prison life at Port Arthur became so influential. The process also affirmed the importance of Port Arthur itself, including it, and the act of visiting it, within the same cultural phenomenon. It is unlikely, however, that *His Natural Life* could have exerted as strong an effect if it had not been a timely book that crystallised and dramatised widespread but latent attitudes.

Although *His Natural Life* has remained in print ever since it was first published, its popularity has waxed and waned. The book did not become a bestseller in the terms discussed above until after Clarke's death in 1881, when the book was reissued in Australia at a much reduced price. It continued to sell well for many years until, in the early years of the twentieth century, it gradually lost ground. This trend continued until the 1930s, when it became distinctly unpopular. It was slow to regain popularity, but by about 1970 it appears to have been once again appreciated and sales soared.

The work's literary reputation as a novel varied in a similar manner. It was critically well received when it was published in Britain. It gradually lost status until, in the 1920s, it was regarded as having few of the attributes of a good novel, although its historical importance was not denied. It was not until the 1970s that Clarke's work as a whole, including *His Natural Life*, was once again seen as being of high literary quality. It is notable that critical opinion, public opinion and general acceptance of the view that Clarke paints of convictism and in particular of prison life at Port Arthur have varied in harmony with each other. The process is obviously not only a simple one of cause and effect, but can also be seen as a symptom of widespread cultural changes affecting what constitutes a good novel, acceptance or otherwise of *His Natural Life* as a good novel and variations in opinion as to the veracity of the picture the novel presents of convictism.

To turn from the 'text associated with the place' to the 'place considered as a text', one must recognise that during the period under study the 'text' is not static because the building fabric – the buildings as physical artefacts – is subject to change. Such changes may not only influence people's perception of the fabric and affect their appreciation, but may also in turn affect the perception of the text's meaning. Hence a neglected fabric may be conducive to a gloomy picture being formed of the past associated with it. However, it is argued here that while changing appearance may be of some importance it by no means predetermines reactions to the buildings which are dependent, at bottom, on attitudinal stances derived from the world at large. It is not uncommon for people to take up radically different stances in relation to a building in spite of viewing it in the same state.

Nevertheless, changes in appearance should be considered relevant to this account, not only for their immediate effect on visitors, but also as being indicative of attitudes towards the buildings, since the appearance is dependent upon the regime to which the building is subjected and is the outcome of its ownership and policies for maintenance and presentation. Well before the prison closed it had become run down and dilapidated. Subsequently, the smaller buildings were sold and occupied and the site began to change its character. Successive fires in 1884, 1889 and 1898 reduced first the church and then all the major prison buildings to ruins, but it recovered its appearance as an attractive village in the early twentieth century. Later, as the government reassumed greater control of the site, it gradually lost its domestic character and took on that of an historic monument. The surrounding scenery has remained almost as impressive as when Clarke described it, and the place, although now much more readily accessible than it was, still retains a feeling of isolation and remoteness; it remains as Governor Arthur once described it, and to which Clarke added a dimension of irony, 'a natural penitentiary'.[3]

Viewing Port Arthur about the time of its closure

During the late nineteenth century it seems to have been widely accepted that convicts at Port Arthur were grossly maltreated: bullied by inhuman guards, frequently flogged and subjected to constant hard labour in irons. It was not, in fact, a very different picture from the one disseminated by Marcus Clarke in *His Natural Life*. Those holding such views who were directly influenced by the book probably visited Port Arthur as part of the cultural process of reification already described, while others went to use the site and buildings as a trigger in order to experience righteous indignation or to enjoy vicariously the horrors they associated with the place. Both the latter experiences may also be developed from *His Natural Life*, and both are expressed in Clarke's description of his own visit to Port Arthur. He writes of the first experience:

> In the folio reports of the House of Commons can be read statements which make one turn sick with disgust, and flush hot with indignation. Officialdom, with its crew of parasites and lickspittles, may try to palliate the enormities committed in the years gone by; may revile, with such powers of abuse as are given to it, the writers who record the facts which it blushes for. But the sad, grim truth remains. For half a century the law allowed the vagabonds and criminals of England to be subjected to a lingering torment, to a hideous debasement, to a monstrous system of punishment, futile for good and horribly powerful for evil.[4]

In the second vein he writes of the penitentiary:

> I pictured the many windows of that hideously square and practical structure crowded with heads; saw the open ground before us once more dotted over with chain-gangs, heard the cat hiss and swing, and caught the echoes of the awful mirth with which the doomed wretches cheered their lingering hours. How many sighs had gone up to Heaven from among those trim trees, how my tears had moistened those neatly chiselled flagstones?[5]

Such associations were at the time reinforced by the appearance of the site. Another visitor (Senior, 1880) wrote at about the same time:

> It oppresses you into silence to inspect the ruins of workshops, sawmill, tannery, and foundry and to know that the walls and windows of the houses and the fences of the gardens are tumbling to pieces. I cannot enter into many questions discussed during my visit; but if one-half of what was said in my hearing be true, Port Arthur will not crumble to hopeless decay a moment too soon ...

> The day may be bright, the flowers may blow, and the birds sing, but you will take leave of Port Arthur in decay with the remark that it is a gloomy place, gloomy in its present desolation, gloomy by the memories of bygone days.[6]

Viewing Port Arthur c. 1885–1900

Once the smaller buildings had been sold and the houses reinhabited the site assumed a more cheerful aspect; descriptions of the place changed accordingly:

> Port Arthur, the once dreaded and most vile spot of the tight little island, has now undergone a considerable change; instead of being the exile home of prisoners hundreds of honest colonialists live there now, clearing the bush, ploughing the lands, building up neat little cottages with a hope that before long they will reap the rewards of their labour. Port Arthur proper – the prison settlement that was – is called Carnarvon.[7]

This new encouraging appearance constituted at one and the same time a visual mismatch with the prevailing view of the place as a dreaded prison, but also reassured the visitor that the convict past was over. The same attitude presumably produced a change in name. Now the site's unpleasant associations could be enjoyed from a position of safety, underlining the vicarious character of this sort of experience. Hence Port Arthur is described as 'a spot as lovely in its position as it is ugly in its memories'.[8] The piece continues:

> There is even a 'proprietary school' in the heart of this scene of old-time horrors. The weed-grown prison yards, the open cells – 'sunshine and hope' everywhere where once reigned darkness and despair – the crumbling, flower-kissed walls, the sound of children's laughter – all these are fitter accompaniments for bright sky, blue sea, and wooing breezes than the clank of the chains, the curses of brutalised, lash-driven, hopeless men, the dismal tolling of the prison bell. Enough. 'Let the dead past bury its dead', and turn we to the contemplation of the 'living present'.[9]

Contrasting 'now and then' or 'here and then' was not only a process by which the present could be celebrated but also a process by which a general sense of the historical past could be developed. The use of quotations is endemic to the process:

> We were told that to stand in the old church ruin on a moonlight night and look seaward was worth a special visit; indeed, as we wandered by the water's edge, ... always looking gold through the pellucid mist of the gloaming; you might have said, as Lovelace did, on looking round,
>
> 'Stone walls do not a prison make,
> Nor iron bars a cage;
> Minds innocent and quiet take,
> Such as an hermitage.'
>
> Alas, how many were able to say it, we turn away in the thought, 'tis too sad,
>
> 'Tis cruel to remember,
> 'Tis wiser to forget.'[10]

In the same way, age in a building, or its apparent great age (for by now most prison buildings at Port Arthur were ruined by fire) was beginning to be appreciated:

> We in the colonies, unlike our more fortunate brethren in the nations of history, have but little in the realm of man's handiwork to which we can point as historical; all our buildings, stately though many be, are still possessed of that suggestion of new brick and fresh mortar, which ever-rolling time alone can remove. Had we anything the contemplation of which would carry us back in thought to the dim past, and bury for a while the present, had we any of those venerable relics with which England, with which Europe, abounds, what a craving it would allay, what a void it would fill, in the lives of many .... It matters little whether the object preserved ... causes sweet or bitter reflections, whether it leads to expressions of approval or detestation, it is sufficient that it is hoary with age, that it has played a part in history, that it is replete with thoughts of the past.[11]

Once a concept of a past was clearly established, the particular history of Port Arthur could be seen as only an episode in a wider historical continuum. JW Beattie, who produced the first guide book on Port Arthur, could, by using this process, view its history in a less fearful light. By establishing historical distance, Beattie (1892) is able to appreciate the historical nature of Port Arthur. He writes:

> Port Arthur was born in September, 1830, and during the long period of 47 years it passed through all the phases of a human existence – had its childhood, its manhood, and its old age, and it died and was buried in 1877. The wrecks of its great prisons are to-day, just like the ruinous tombstones of a neglected old graveyard, giving evidence of the magnitude of its past, and creating a longing desire in the minds of the curious to know something of its wonderful history.[12]

Nevertheless he acknowledges, 'to the majority [of Tasmanians] the past of Port Arthur is as a closed book.'[13]

The Mercury (1889) more closely expressed widespread public attitudes which crystallised, as is usual, on the prospect of the building's imminent sale and destruction:

> The old prison buildings at Port Arthur are to be sold tomorrow, and by this time most persons have, we think, reached the conclusion that the sooner they are cleared away the better. It is true, no doubt, that to a certain extent, they are objects of curiosity, visitors being attracted by their bad fame, and by a desire of being able to say that they have seen such things, just as they would go to any other place where the memories of a terrible past could be found. On the other hand, it must be remembered that the buildings themselves are fast going to decay, and in a few years will attract nobody, for they will be ruins without anything to make them worthy of respect, or even of remembrance.
>
> Apart from this, however, it is quite time that the colony was freed from the last vestiges of a system which was got rid of with some trouble, but with the hearty assent of all right-thinking persons.... We have received several letters on this subject, the preponderance of opinion being now decidedly in favour of the removal of the buildings, and the obliteration of a foul spot, which can only be remembered with regret, and which will be remembered quite long enough, without keeping up the buildings to recall it to our minds, and to the minds of our visitors, who, surely, can find many more things worthy of their attention, and more calculated to improve their understandings.[14]

The passage contains all the Tasmanian resentment of visitors' interest in Port Arthur. Most Tasmanians at this period were quite unable to accept convictism as part of their own past and could only come to terms with it via a process of obliteration. It was no wonder that they took no pleasure in the buildings, saw no value in them and wished for their actual demolition. Underlying such an attitude was the acceptance of the Clarke view of convictism and a belief that it was encapsulated in the buildings of Port Arthur. For them the buildings stood for a shameful convictism.

Viewing Port Arthur 1925–45

These attitudes continued in Tasmania well into the twentieth century. In 1926 the prospect of a film being made at Port Arthur of *His Natural Life* caused a furore. The following opinions are typical of those opposing the project:

> To our everlasting credit real Tasmanians have over-whelmingly blotted out the stigma produced by the convict system.[15]

> I have never read the book; the first chapter or two was enough for me. I wish every copy had been burnt, also that all the awful buildings at Port Arthur had been pulled down instead of using them for a sensational sightseeing tourist crowd.[16]

To gauge the importance of the opinions expressed we should take into account that at this time Tasmania was hard hit by the growing depression; it was not a time of general confidence; therefore, the widespread expression of anxiety might be for this reason over-stressed.

Nevertheless, a substantial group of Tasmanians were still bitterly ashamed of their past history and were most reluctant to have it displayed to others. Obvious anxiety was expressed by them about their convict origins; similarly, almost desperate attempts were made to differentiate between Van Diemen's Land and Tasmania and to ensure that others also did so, even though the images they presented of modern Tasmania were pitifully frail. Others were able to master their fears to the extent that they were able to adopt an alternative strategy – rejecting the picture Clarke offered of convictism as unreal – but were not sufficiently confident to be able to class it only as fictional and, therefore, not able to constitute a threat to them.

The linkage between rejection of the buildings and the desire to have them obliterated was also expressed by others:

> I would like to ask: are Tasmanians sincere in their desire to obliterate that portion of the history of this island? If sincere, why are the ruins allowed to remain to become a source of revenue or profit for the body who placed the 'toll gates'? Again, why did we allow our Government Tourist Department to parade this place [Port Arthur] as one of the chief attractions of this beautiful island for tourists? It would be hard to estimate the number of visitors to Tasmania who have visited this 'Port Arthur' (by the way, is it not now Carnarvon?) who go away and tell their friends of the bad old days, not forgetting to stigmatise the Old Country just as we maybe a hundred years hence will be stigmatised. These ruins serve no useful purpose; on the contrary, and surely in this island so full of beauty, so health-giving, and with its quiet old world atmosphere wherever one goes, it is hardly necessary to boost historical relics of a 'penal settlement' to attract tourists ... [I would like to] raze the buildings. I will give one week's work free.[17]

And also by this correspondent a little less drastically:

> I am sure the time has come to demolish all those dreadful buildings. The stones could be used to restore the really beautiful ruins of the church and let the rest sink into the oblivion it best deserves. Too long it has been a place of morbid interest to tourists. Though it is a monument of the wickedness and cruelty of the past, modern thought should see fit to get rid of such an eyesore to the beauty of this lovely island.[18]

Although both these correspondents saw little value in the Port Arthur prison remains and were advocating their removal, both also recognised that they stood as evidence of Tasmania's history and by their use of the word 'history' each writer reinforced the relationship he wished to sever. One can contrast the content of these two letters with the description that follows. In it the familiar device of 'now and then' is employed, and again visitors' 'morbid curiosity' is deplored, but in the last few lines there is an acceptance of an historical dimension and a consequent positive imaginative engagement with the buildings that would be quite impossible for those whose opinion is quoted above:

> As our party reached the township on a glorious autumn morning the beauty of the bay, with its setting of English trees and Tasmanian eucalypts, far outweighed the thoughts of the past. As a page of history the settlement of Port Arthur and the methods adopted are worthy of the deepest study, but as a means of satisfying a merely morbid curiosity as regards the dark cells and the other Early Victorian methods of prison discipline, such subjects are best left alone. Rather let one's mind dwell upon the natural beauty of the bay, with the reflections of the fringing trees mirrored in its placid surface and along the shore the signs of the present era as they displace those of the past. Time aided by fire, has done much to destroy the buildings of the old settlement. Many have been converted to other uses, whilst in place of the dull tread of the 'human centipedes' the old cobblestones of Champ-street echo to the honk of motor cars. Below the tall walls of the old penitentiary tennis parties are engaged in friendly rivalry, whilst out in the reclaimed area near the old slipyards the cricket ground calls its adherents.
>
> As one looks at the scene which this picturesque bay presents on this present Easter morn one recalls those lines of Browning,
>
> 'the past is in its grave,
> Though its ghost still haunts us.'
>
> The days of the old regime are over, although the mysterious influence of the old settlement grips one whilst within its precincts.[19]

Similarly, in a book which indicates the new mood in its title, *The romance of Tasmania*, M Hookey (1921) writes, 'at Port Arthur the ruined prison buildings still blot the landscape, bearing sombre testimony of the inhumanity of man to man. Existing records make gloomy reading, but here and there romance, undaunted by its grim surroundings slips through the prison bars.'[20] Another rather later quotation displays the same vaguely historic feelings: 'The architecture of the church, of the prison itself, and of the other buildings is essentially English; and arched doorways frame vistas of turreted walls and bold towers reminiscent of castles of Merrie England as pictured in the history books of our school days.'[21]

Almost invariably such nostalgic feelings are linked with thoughts of England. The following example displays a clear acceptance of Port Arthur as part of Tasmania's continuing history. It is, perhaps, a history more dependent upon historical legend than upon historical fact, which in itself insulates the viewer from too pointed a picture of reality. 'Romance', 'ghosts' or 'bad old days' are ideas that hold little real terror, as the slightly jocular quotation in the last extract showed. Even flogging receded into a past contiguous with that of 'Merrie England' and its medieval tortures. Once the sting had been removed from convict legend little harm was seen in Port Arthur remaining. Rather it was felt that it should be retained, for the feelings it engendered were far from unpleasant; they might even be described as faintly reassuring:

> Many of the [Tasmanian] villages, from their appearance, might have been lifted bodily from Old England. There are grassy lanes, village greens and buildings, some still in use and some derelict, that bear evidence of the solid work put into them in the days when labour was cheap. Port Arthur is the most celebrated of Tasmania's historic towns. When it was abandoned as a penal settlement in 1877 some of the buildings were pulled down so that the material could be used elsewhere, but after a lapse of a few years it was found that visitors were curious to see this relic of the 'bad old days' now happily long past ... [which] as a visiting journalist truly said, is 'Australia's only bona-fide ruin'.[22]

As such the site could be recognised as one of the class commonly valued overseas, and could engender a response proper to an important historic monument.

This shift in attitude and appreciation changed people's perception of 'now and then'; the tennis courts next to the penitentiary were no longer a reminder of a healthful present but were seen as an intrusion, detracting from an historical atmosphere. For the same reason the guide's out-of-date patter also jarred: 'With the indifference of the modern to our storied past the local authorities have erected a public tennis court in immediate proximity to the best of the ruins. This absurdity we enjoyed more than the tirade of the unsolicited local "guide".'[23]

Gradually, even for Tasmanians, historical appreciation bred acceptance of the importance of the site. It began to assume a new image as part of the development of Tasmania. On this basis convictism could be condoned: ED's analysis is an early expression of the new conceptual framework:

> England was not the cruel stepmother sending naughty children into exile, but a wise mother acting on the guidance of her wisest sons, sending her surplus population to the space they needed, the spaces that needed them. The convict system was established. It was a political move to people a new country, and relieve an overburdened population. Evils crept in as such will do into any movement, even as disease into the human system; but the big idea was there, and later, willing immigrants assisted and wealthier immigrants were assisted and wealthier ones encouraged.[24]

Or perhaps rather less tritely Clive Lord (1926) writes:

> To appreciate either the old buildings, or on a larger scale, the period of progress which they represent, it is necessary to place the ideas and ideals of a century's age in their correct perspective. To attempt to judge them according to present-day standards of thought will surely lead to a wrong interpretation of their place in the progressive history of not only our island home, but of the Commonwealth as a whole.[25]

From this standpoint Lord is able to reject past presentations of the prison and from a position of strength to recognise their mythical quality:

> It is an unfortunate fact that the popular historical books which have been written concerning the penal establishments of last century deal with the darkest possible aspect of the subject. Reams of records have been read by writers in search of tragedy in order that they might enhance their reconstructions of the past by tales founded on fact. The result is that a wrong impression has been created, and it is doubtful if this will ever entirely disappear.[26]

Instead, he develops a new image which was to persevere for a long time, gaining in strength as economic circumstances improved; it was the result of the adoption of an alternative myth of the history of Tasmania being one of purposeful industrial and social progress:

> Scanning the records of a century and more ago, one can realise the great problems which faced the statesmen of the Motherland. The loss of the American colonies, the cessation of slavery, and the dawn of a new era of

> thought as regards man's inhumanity to man were but a few of the greater movements which were serving to provide problems for those whose concern it was to guide the destinies of a great Empire.
>
> The colonisation of the Australian colonies was but one of the many matters to which attention had to be given, and gradually from small beginnings the great penal system was evolved, served its purpose, and gave place to a more enlightened period. The half century of 'the system' served to develop the young colonies in a wonderful manner, and with the great influx of free settlers it was but a short space of time ere these far-flung outposts of the Empire were entrusted with practically self-governing powers.[27]

Having thus invested the settlement of Port Arthur with positive rather than negative connotations, Lord opens the way for a new form of appreciation. He sees Port Arthur as a site expressing its former interesting function. His exposition begins with a quotation:

> *Simple en était la noble architecture!*
> *Chaque ornement, à sa place arrêté,*
> *Y semblait mis par la nécessité.*[28]

and continues:

> In his description of 'Le Temple du Gout' Voltaire wrote the above lines, and just as the form of the great architectural temple which he described was noble, and each part seemed placed there by necessity, so may we apply the feeling which lies behind these lines to the remnants of the old buildings which are now falling into ruin at Port Arthur and other places in Australia. The reason is not far to seek. These old buildings were designed in many cases by engineers of the Imperial Service, whose training and travels had made them masters in the art of building, and the structures erected were built with a strength which has defied the ravages of both time and other agencies of decay. Built as part of 'the system' – that great code which, despite its defects, advanced the initial and early colonisation of Australia in such a marked manner – the structures were meant to last. Moreover, each was a necessary item in the grouping of the settlement, and a little time spent in studying the planning and structures of such a settlement as Port Arthur opens up a most interesting page of early history.[29]

His positive appreciation of the purpose of the settlement is extended by a positive response to its buildings. In relation to the church, Lord (1926) exclaims: 'What tales the ruins ... could tell if the walls could but speak of all that took place within them!'[30] We might expect from earlier descriptions that tales of convict horrors will follow, but with one exception the description is of quite another kind and presents a different view of convict life and of the role of the convict:

> The foundation stone was laid by Colonel George Arthur on the 25th April, 1836, and the first service held on 24th July, 1837. When one considers that the church was capable of seating upwards of 1500 people its construction must have been carried out in an expeditious manner. Nevertheless, it was soundly built, for in spite of fire and neglect its walls still stand, and the ivy creeps upwards over tower and pinnacles. If any building of the old regime is worthy of reconstruction it is surely this edifice whose architectural qualities and picturesque setting render it well worthy of preservation. It was designed by an exile known as 'Mason', although this was probably not his real name. He afterwards secured his freedom and later practised his profession in Sydney.
>
> Lacking spire, roof, and fittings, yet the gaunt stone walls stand out, and the Gothic arches and pinnacles compel many a lingering glance. The old church well repays such examination, for it is built, as Keble writes, 'in a style of architecture which to me at least is, in comparison with all others, the most beautiful of all, and by far the most in harmony with the mysteries of religion'.
>
> Attractive as its ruins are, yet how much more so must the edifice have been when in use. Every care was taken of it, and the surround kept in perfect order. For almost forty years it remained intact, but in 1875 the long tapering spire was destroyed by a gale, and a few years later fire destroyed practically all but the walls – not only of this, but of many of the other structures within the settlement. The peal of bells which used to send their clarion calls across the waters of the bay are now heard in another part of the island.
>
> Tales are told of certain tragedies which took place during the erection of the church, and it is even said that one of the men whilst engaged at work fixing the flashings and spoutings was detected making spurious coin from the lead.[31]

The description can be described as self-referential. To Lord what was relevant to appreciation of the building was the way it was built, the way in which it was designed, and its subsequent fate as a building. Even the convict fable is tied into the building process. The fabric of the building is valued and its style appreciated. In short the description concentrates upon the building's architectural qualities – its form and the drama associated with the building process and the building's life. Such a view enables Lord to place value on the buildings for their aesthetic qualities and for what they mean; he writes of Port Arthur, 'its architectural relics represent, therefore, a rather wonderful lesson as to what was accomplished in quite a short space of time.'[32] In addition he notes they now have an increasing rarity value:

> Today, as one looks at the relics of this past page of our history and notes how they are giving place to more modern structures, one cannot help but realise how rapidly the old order is changing and giving place to the new. Yet, quickly as the structures of a past era are being removed, the process has been quicker in other places, and consequently Port Arthur has become a locality to which many people throng who desire to see the old ruins.[33]

Viewing Port Arthur 1940–60

It is likely that, although Lord's system of appreciation was a complete one and well expressed, it was not widely accepted at the time. However, its most obvious aspects were taken up and developed by J Coultman-Smith in the 1940s. They included recognising Port Arthur as a town that contributed to the development of Tasmania, the pleasure of imagining its past busy function by viewing its ruins, interest in the building process as typifying progress and an aesthetic appreciation of the building fabric that remained. Coultman-Smith's guide book to Port Arthur had a solid long-term success and its continuing sales and many imitations testify to the widespread acceptance of the myth of progress and its consequences.

Its acceptance enabled the author to eschew guilt and shame; hence there was no longer any point in being evasive about the details of convictism.

Convictism was now a concept about which fear had faded until it could be portrayed as a positively benign influence thus Smith (1941) wrote:

> The impression that is firmly fixed in the minds of the public is a picture of innocent men, women and youths torn from their cosy English firesides, herded like cattle into filthy transports, spewed upon the shores of Tasmania, insufficiently fed, weighed down with half a hundredweight of chains, flogged and kicked into inhuman labour, confined in small and unsanitary cells until they collapsed and died or became loathsome, savage animals.
>
> But that is far from the truth. Britain's transportation of felons to the Australian territories was a farsighted and, on the whole, successful colonisation system. The present prosperous position of Australia in general, and Tasmania in particular, is evidence enough of that.[34]

The preface to Smith's guide book written by Robert Cosgrove, the then Premier of Tasmania, exhibited the same kind of approach:

> It is a welcome departure that this book treats the convict days in a bright common-sense manner, with none of the morbidity and horror which have too often stamped such work. Students, the general public and tourists alike will here find interest and entertainment, adventure and revelation to absorb the most blasé and prejudiced reader.[35]

The press notices (Coultman-Smith, 1973), no doubt in part taking a lead from the preface, echoed the same theme; 'refreshingly new', 'an excellent corrective', 'surprising facts and figures', 'refreshingly bright, sensible and enlightened', and 'a common sense manner' were the kinds of key phrases used. Now that Port Arthur was seen to have a positive role in Tasmanian development, its conservation could be accepted and encouraged. We should note that the period at which this new myth was current was one of economic growth and relative prosperity, one in which it was easy to believe in a concept of progress and hence to find positive benefit from the settlement at Port Arthur. Once it had been accepted that progress was possible in an economic field, it seemed to have also been possible to believe in progress at the individual level, and anxiety about the stock from which so many Tasmanians sprung seems to have been alleviated. Coultman-Smith's (1948) view of Port Arthur in the past was a particularly sanguine one:

> The streets of the settlement were flanked by staunch and handsome buildings, its gardens a mass of profuse blossoms and squat, flowering shrubs. English trees adorned the roads, extensive harbour works thrust out into the port. At the north-eastern entrance to the town stood the finest church in the colony, with beautiful stained windows; prolific farmlands stretched out behind the sun-kissed sweep of Safety Cove. An artistically-designed hospital overlooked the town, soldiers in bright uniforms and lasses and ladies in crinolines and poke bonnets walked the cobblestones, semaphores flashed news and orders back and forth to Hobart, 80 miles away, full-rigged ships sailed into the harbour with convicts and merchandise, and out again with timber, produce, manufactures, and skilled tradesmen.
>
> It was a corner of Old England transplanted to the farthest outpost, a home beyond the Southern Seas, a workshop turning out the Colonies' finest craftsmen, a gateway to a new life and new hope.[36]

If we turn to the buildings themselves, we see here too the new form of appreciation, as they are regarded as being of interest in their own right. All in all Coultman-Smith (1948) concluded:

> The ruined town is full of architectural delights like the archway on the flagged verandah if the Courthouse and Administrative Offices, which might have been transported from among the relics of ancient Greece or the Roman occupation of Western Europe. Its beauty is enhanced by some indefinable quality coaxed from the stone in brown, golden, and cream tones to defy repetition by the architect and builder of to-day. To the craftsmanship of the convict masons have been added the tools of Nature in the hands of a hundred years of storm and sunshine, salt sea air, mosses, and tiny plants. Along the ancient streets and byways, among the foundations of the buildings long since levelled, across the hillsides and in the valleys are fragments of brilliant workmanship incapable of inspiration by the lash or noose. Brutality can drive man to work, but not to work as these men did – soundly, artistically, beautifully. Steps, pillars, walls, even gutters and drains, are carved and fashioned with the same worthiness and care ... the forgotten standard of the craftsman whose work was his life.[37]

One can note that appreciation of the ruins was focused upon the materials of which they were built and their natural textures and colours, upon the building process, including the manufacture of the materials, and upon the buildings' design and fabrication. Historical style excited little interest; instead interest was directed towards the fabric itself. Finally, it should be emphasised that the appreciation of buildings during this period is essentially visual. On the one hand, the abstract qualities of the architecture are enjoyed in what is an aesthetic appreciation; and on the other, the buildings are used as visual stimuli in order to 'picture' the settlement as it once operated.

Viewing Port Arthur 1960–80

The same kind of appreciation continued into the 1960s and 1970s. However, some changes in attitude gradually began to emerge, and for this reason the following quotation is still worth analysing in some detail:

> A saw-milling establishment in 1830, Port Arthur was established as a penal settlement in ... 1831 to replace the infamous Macquarie Harbour penal establishment, which was abandoned in 1833. The ruins of the institution affect visitors according to their varied temperaments ... The violence of the period and the evidence of man's inhumanity to man may still be conjured up, but there is much to be wondered at in the perfection of the architecture in what was then a very remote part of the world. However, this has its logical explanation in the role played by the military and its important quota of engineers, and the free labour provided by the convicts ....[38]
>
> The shame of the penal past was felt so heavily by succeeding generations that only the remoteness of the settlement and its economic uselessness explains the escape of what remains. Neglect took its toll and few cared. Fortunately as time passed into a more enlightened era the Scenery Preservation Board of the Tasmanian Government took care of the area, so that this most wonderful of Australian relics is being preserved.
>
> Some of the remaining buildings have weathered well, and in the process have assumed a benign appearance. The well-kept lawns and parklands with fine trees complement the beauty of the natural surroundings. Time seems to have brought all into a surprising unity. However, we must not forget the past. There is no more telling sociological document, no more revealing contrasts between the aesthetic capabilities of the past and the human degradation

> which accompanied it than these ruins, nor any more cogent reminder of the improvement in humanity which a process of slow evolution has produced.[39]

On the one hand, the quality of the building and the interest arising from this kind of architecture relative to its situation are commented upon, while on the other, the way in which it was produced is not ignored. The value of the settlement as a whole is recognised and provisions for its care noted. The aesthetic effect of the whole is described and the connection between the buildings and their purpose is acknowledged. All this follows the previously established patterns of appreciation and evaluation. The difference lies in the picture that is evoked by the buildings. Here it is not connected to the building process itself, nor to a picture of Port Arthur as Tasmania's third largest town, a domestic scene or an economic unit. Instead the beauty of the buildings is contrasted with a much harsher picture of convict life. The convict is no longer seen as a craftsman; here he merely provides 'free labour'. The tone in this respect is essentially ironic, contrasting Port Arthur as a place of value with a view of its past function as being reprehensible. The text represents a significant transition from one mode of appreciation to another. While it exhibits continuity with earlier texts it also contains within it the fundamental dichotomy of viewpoint, characteristic of the ironic mode, which is bound to arise when buildings are seen not to represent the life of the settlement but to be in opposition to it. It might be thought that this mode represents a return to that of the nineteenth-century appreciation pattern of 'lovely place, awful purpose', but here the 'lovely' is applied to the buildings themselves and not their setting; hence the irony is sharper.

Current views of Port Arthur

From this dichotomy two new modes of appreciation have emerged. The first arises from strong emphasis being placed on the value of the fabric and the importance of its retention. Such is now official government policy and large sums of money have been channelled into the maintenance of Port Arthur. The size of the federal government grants has been large enough to create widespread interest. The size of each successive grant has been regularly reported in the local press together with details of its disbursement on urgently necessary stabilisation work, historical research, scientific investigation, engineering testing, archaeological digs and architectural restoration. On reading these accounts it becomes apparent that the conservation process has become an end in itself. The drama of a wealth of professional activity concentrated upon the buildings and fighting their decay has its own interest and satisfaction, not only for the professionals directly engaged in the drama but, it is assumed, also for the public at large who can inspect the work in progress and participate vicariously in what is seen as the vital public enterprise of preserving Port Arthur. Such a form of appreciation might well be termed 'materialism'.

At the same time appreciation of the buildings' meaning is also seen as a professional concern by those in control of the site. The buildings are seen as an authentic historical document which, if subjected to sufficiently expert research, can yield information about the past. It follows that they should be interfered with as little as possible and that their form should be preserved for the benefit of future research. Since by now the buildings are decayed to the point where they do not readily convey their function, the general public is assumed to get its appreciation of the nature of the settlement in the Visitor Centre rather than in the buildings themselves.

Many people have expressed dissatisfaction with an arrangement of the site that prises historical meaning away from the fabric. Some have prepared an alternative management strategy and have advocated the restoration of the ruins in order to restore their explicit functional meaning. It is obvious that restoration to the point where a building appears much as a set for a television drama destroys the possibility of future alternative readings; hence such a policy might well be dubbed 'consumerism'.

It cannot, I think, be assumed that a policy of 'materialism' is being pressed by professional groups and that 'consumerism' is the public's counter response. The public appear to have enjoyed the drama of conservation at Port Arthur, but there is also evidence to show that projects which treat visits to historic sites as entertainment are exceptionally popular. Both 'materialism' and 'consumerism' have a degree of popular support. On the other hand, both are also supported by professional groups – though not by the same ones.

It is perhaps difficult to reconcile Port Arthur as a valued historic monument with the particularly grim picture of life at Port Arthur as it is now widely assumed to have been. In this sense 'materialism' can be seen either as evasion or as an unresolved schizophrenic view, while 'consumerism' can be seen as the more direct response to the historical message. The difficulty here is that by its explicit nature it perpetuates a functional message and, as such, precludes future use of the site as a cultural mechanism which is able to focus and reflect widespread attitudinal stances that change over a period of time. In fact, it denies the historical function of the site and precludes further histories of this type. A policy of 'materialism' at least allows this process to continue.

Why Architects Should Not Write Architectural History

1984

JOAN KERR

The title of this paper was inspired by a comment I have frequently heard from Australian architects, most notably from the convenor of this conference at the end of one of those enjoyable sessions spent dissecting a publication purporting to be architectural history written by – say – a journalist or a bishop. The comment that explains all deficiencies is: 'Of course, he (or she?) is not an architect.' I naturally believe that the word 'architect' should be amended to 'architectural historian', a term quite common in more developed countries. I noticed, for instance, when living in England, that architects there quite properly apologise for not being professional architectural historians when they dare to enter the field, in the (usually vain) hope that their work will not simply be dismissed with the phrase, 'Not bad for an architect'.

Countries such as Britain have acknowledged the profession of architectural historian for years. They have societies for them, a serious publishing industry, and the ears and eyes of at least a small informed and interested audience. Australia has not. For instance, I think that there are only three people lecturing on architectural history in the universities of Australia who were not originally trained as practising architects or engineers. There may, of course, be a couple of others, since we have no channels of communication to discover one another. This conference is therefore a most welcome occasion, even if it appears full of people who would define themselves as within the architectural profession rather than outside it. The major purpose of my paper is to suggest the advantages of redefining that position.

Because of the dearth of professional architectural historians in this country who are not architects, it would be pointless to analyse their contributions to Australian architectural history. Most architectural writing of any sort has, of course, been written by people who are, or have been, practising architects. Some have already realised that the two are incompatible. The rest, I believe, should not attempt to write history, despite Humphrey McQueen's opinion when I mention the title of this paper that, on the contrary, they ought to be encouraged since it keeps them from designing buildings.

McQueen is, however, a natural lateral thinker. Everybody else I spoke to – both architects and non-architects – agreed with my proposition, usually quite vehemently. The precise reasons differed, but all were based on the obvious premise that practitioners in any discipline are least capable of seeing the wood for the particular species of tree they happen to be growing amongst. Great painters, novelists, poets, politicians and so on have written great polemics, but would you trust them to produce a dispassionate view of their own subject, even if they believed themselves capable of removing those very blinkers that inspired their creativity?

I want to approach my subject rather obliquely, through analogy with two buildings that I believe are useful metaphors for major types of writing by architect-historians. The first is Philip Cox's revamping of the old Fruit and Flower Markets (opened 1911) in the Haymarket, Sydney, presently being converted for the Institute of Technology [now the University of Technology Sydney, eds]. This building seems certain to be a national award winner as a piece of contemporary design. It is, I am sure, already appearing in thinly disguised form and more modest scale on drawing-boards all over the country. Its obvious attraction is that it appears to be a splendid example of international postmodernism with a distinctively Australian flavour.

For the purpose of this paper Cox's building can also represent something else: a common sort of Australian architectural history methodology, appropriately typified by Cox's own books. The precise comparison I have chosen today is his contribution to *Australian colonial architecture*, the book he wrote with the restoration architect Clive Lucas, published by Lansdowne in 1978. Before embarking on this, let me first draw your attention to certain features of the Institute Building, particularly as they exemplify Cox's attitude towards the past.

What has become of the old Fruit and Flower Markets? As you can see, sections of the façades have been retained, to enhance Cox's work and to act as references for his motifs and materials. These surviving fragments are unquestionably local, undeniably 'Australian'. The tower in particular has been isolated and enhanced in its new setting to become a major justification for both brickwork and decorative detailing of the new design.

You might note, incidentally, that the fabric of this tower is almost entirely unchanged in its upper parts but stands on a base that is all 1980s, so the new paradoxically appears to have been built before the old – a complete inversion of the historical process. That is precisely my argument as to what architects do when they write history, although few results can be said to be as 'wittily' self-conscious as this.

More to my immediate point is the general status of the old components. They have lost their place within the general context of Edwardian market buildings, but they are not fakes (or replicas, if you prefer that word). Having recently been infected by the amazing 'Future Fall' conference in Sydney on postmodernism, where guest-star Jean Baudrillard managed to draw an audience of over 1,000 to the Mari Kuttna Memorial Lecture, I would like to appropriate a Baudrillard word, 'simulacra', to signify a status that is neither original nor imaginary re-creation. Baudrillard argues that the media have created a world of simulacra where nothing remains real, but I am using the term to signify those numerous progeny born of allowing contemporary architects to 'improve' the work of their predecessors. Such simulacra have not yet taken over our entire built or recorded past, although I sometimes feel that it will not be long before they do.

In this context Cox's simulacra have two distinct meanings, depending on whether they are read from their present or past context. They can exist solely in relation to Cox's dominant frame. His design identified and saved what was worthwhile from the past in terms of his present needs. He then created a hierarchy of values with these selected fragments by varying his emphasis. On the other hand, the fragments can still be identified as 'market' by comparison with the intact market buildings that survive beside them, although this is a most precarious identity. The retention of adjacent market buildings in unaltered form and use certainly formed no part of Cox's brief, although I would argue that they are vital to his concept. There is little hope that the old will survive the next phase of development in the Haymarket, unless the architectural historian can argue that the original is as important as the simulacrum in its modern frame.

Of course, every historian creates a new edifice out of fragments of the past and shapes them into some sort of hierarchy by his or her selection and emphasis. Yet the historian's frame need not be the intellectual equivalent of Cox's building. Value need not be assigned according to current taste; no hierarchy has to place the present at the top of the pyramid. And, above all, the theoretical values behind such selections and omissions need not be imported.

The Institute Building's ideological framework was clearly derived from the United States, particularly from the work of Michael Graves. Overblown motifs such as the keyhole windows might pretend homage to Australia's past, illustrated in the round window of that highlighted tower, but their real creator is Robert Venturi. Cox's stridently coloured bricks and stylish eclecticism speak with the smooth American accent of the Portland Building, not the rough Ocker of Sydney's Haymarket.

The theoretical language of Cox's contribution to the book he wrote with Clive Lucas, *Australian colonial architecture*, is also American, although behind this loud foreground accent an English voice can be discerned, just as Charles Jencks's English fluency sells American postmodernism to Australia. Cox, the historian, divides the architecture of colonial Australia into 'high style' and 'vernacular', a framework that comes directly from Peter Blake in the United States. Blake in turn derived it from Professor Brunskill's more convincing English dichotomy of 'polite' and 'vernacular'.

Since we are thought to need no architectural theory of our own, most architectural histories that go beyond the antiquarians' search for facts follow some imported ideological mode. Another very obvious example is Donald Leslie Johnson's *Australian architecture 1901–51: sources of Modernism* (Sydney University Press, 1980). The first illustration in Johnson's text, Ashbee's 'Little Coppice' (Bucks., England) of about 1905, is misleading only in the overseas direction it indicates. North America is the real arbiter of Australian architecture in this book, even if, chronologically, Johnson's first standards are English. Whether east or west, Johnson still judges every Australian building according to the way it measures up against buildings of the northern hemisphere. The two heads that emerge covered in laurels are Walter Burley Griffin's and Harry Seidler's, both of whom trained and practised in the United States before coming to this country. 'Modernism' is what happened overseas; therefore only overseas architects could do it well.

I hope this argument seems silly when put this way; I don't think it is unfairly perverted. It exemplifies a cultural provincialism that is not unique to Australia. In fact, both Britain and the United States indulged in it when the centre of architectural creativity appeared to be elsewhere. For instance, less than 30 years ago Sir John Vanburgh, that great eighteenth-century creator of the sets for 'Brideshead Revisited', used to be thought a failed Italian baroque architect when his work was compared to the paradigm baroque of Borromini. Vanburgh's variations, from this viewpoint, appeared flawed. But, once accepted as a player in a valid English game rather than as an alien participant in an Italian one, Vanburgh was awarded a high and honourable place in the history of the architecture of his own country. It might also be possible to present our early twentieth-century architects as Australians, not North Americans in all but location and ability.

More modest examples of changes in value judgments resulting from altering one's viewpoint might also be cited. Those eighteenth-century clapboard churches in North America with their sharp wooden spires deriving from James Gibbs's St Martin in the Fields in London were once viewed as no more than simple, flawed emulations of a 'correct' external model. They became accepted as a worthy part of the local European-derived heritage only when North Americans discovered they had a continuous internal history. In Australia we have half begun to realise we have an indigenous architecture, but we tend to think that only half our building stock belongs within it.

Because we accept that imported distinction between 'high style' and 'vernacular', we judge anything with stylistic pretensions against an overseas model, but accept the simple as exclusively our own, evolving from local needs. While the former has been excluded from any notion of 'indigenous architecture', the latter, being 'truly Australian', needs no wider context to explain it. This mistaken dichotomy really depends on seeing architecture as no more than simulacra, selected surfaces observed through alien ideologies. We cannot divide our built environment into 'high style' and 'vernacular' with the same certainty as God knows sheep and goats once we start to look beyond superficial similarities with indigenous buildings found somewhere else.

Let me cite a couple of examples from Cox's 'vernacular' chapter in *Australian Colonial Architecture*, selected, of course, to prove the inadequacy of this division. The Parramatta Female Orphan School was built in the Macquarie era and painted by the convict artist Joseph Lycett in about 1820 for use in his book of aquatints, *Views of New South Wales and Van Diemen's Land*, published in London in 1824. The building is plain and rectangular and its architect is unknown; it therefore becomes vernacular. But it looks suspiciously 'high style' when observed more closely. The design was modelled on Aird's House in Ayrshire – Mrs Macquarie's home when she was Miss Campbell – a paradigm Palladian composition of centre block, side pavilions and linking wings. Those linking wings were altered from curved to straight by the colonial builder James Smith and the building – being intended for convict bastards – was somewhat simpler than the original Scottish country house. Nevertheless, in this case (and, I suspect, in others), 'anonymous architect' equals 'female designer' and 'vernacular' just means simple.

In case this appears an unfair example to choose, let us look at a barn, a building Cox calls one of the most famous vernacular buildings in Australia – the barn at Tocal near Paterson, New South Wales. It was designed by Edmund Thomas Blacket, one of Australia's 'high style' architects. Blacket's surviving elevation for it is undated but stylistically it suggests a date nearer 1870 than the c.1850 Cox suggests, so it was not an innovative 'high style' prototype either; just a competent variation of an extant species. Nor is there any reason to believe that Blacket was responding to local conditions when designing Tocal barn. He probably drew it up in his office in Sydney, without necessarily having seen its proposed location.

Although architects are particularly fond of the 'vernacular' I do not believe it is a valid term for Australia, however relevant it may be in countries that possess centuries of isolated independent local building traditions. We need our own methodology to handle *all* aspects of our built environment. This distinction just imposes an imported model on top of selected simulacra.

The result is less valuable when used to manufacture history than when Cox uses it to create something new.

Perhaps you feel that selecting Cox's book and building was too loaded, so let me now turn to my second metaphor. This is an avowed Burra Charter restoration which has had over a million dollars spent on it to retain the original character of the place. (The official figure is $800,000, but that is thought somewhat understated.) This example should now be pure enough to stand for other aspects of architectural history by architects. The building is, of course, Elizabeth Farm at Parramatta, New South Wales, begun in 1793 and reputedly the oldest building in Australia.

Or is it now a simulacrum of Australia's oldest house? Can any modest colonial cottage have a million dollars spent on it to keep it looking original and still manage to be just that? We cannot describe the present building as an imaginary creation. Hundreds of thousands of dollars were spent on the roof alone; the original iron was taken off and a couple of bits that were not too badly rusted were re-galvanised and matched with perfect replicas that nobody could tell apart, once both processes had been carried out. Like an ageing Hollywood film star, silicon was pumped into the body for months, so the original structure could face the world in rejuvenated, but unaltered, form. All the shingles dating from the 1820s were inspected while the iron was off and a large number were replaced by exact (but cleaner and unbroken) replicas, especially where the public might be able to look into the roof and see them. Almost every door and window architrave was removed and cleaned up. Some were returned to a rather different position, but that did not really matter since they were all the same pattern. Gaps were filled with perfect replicas, absolutely indistinguishable from what used to be the originals.

When James Broadbent was appointed curator of this almost perfect simulacrum he cleverly emphasised its new nature by furnishing the house in a style that perfectly complemented it. Everything, or almost everything, was a replica – where possible a replica of a known object associated with the house; for example, John Macarthur's penholder and paperweight and his desk on which they stand. They too are almost indistinguishable from the original, but new and useable. Broadbent's furnishing seems a splendid example of postmodern italicising, even 'wittier' than Cox's isolation of the Flower and Fruit Market tower. It is perhaps rather a pity that the original house was not just left and an unashamed replica built next to it, or even placed in some new location more closely approximating Parramatta in the early nineteenth century than Parramatta does today. This would probably also have been cheaper.

You all know the story of George Washington's axe; how it is still the original one, despite having had seven new handles and five new heads. Just suppose someone found that first head and handle. They would not be like the original of George Washington's day, since they would be broken, chipped and certainly unable to fulfil the original function of an axe – chopping down cherry trees. The replica with all its handles and heads would be much more like that first axe than the real thing could be after the vicissitudes of all those years of use and neglect. Architects prefer the one; the architectural historian, the other.

Elizabeth Farm exemplifies this architectural blindness to history as a process. Part of the philosophy behind this restoration is the belief that architecture is what architects did. Architectural history then becomes the identification and assemblage of original facts. Who was the original architect? What are the significant additions? Who was *their* hero creator and what was their original state? It is, I suggest, a search for the eternally new.

The parallel with Elizabeth Farm in Australian architectural history writing is local, not imported. This time I cannot point to any books written by Ian Sansom, the architect in charge of the work for the New South Wales Department of Public Works, but I can trace his genealogy. Sansom was trained at the University of New South Wales under Professor Max Freeland, author of numerous architectural history books including the standard, *Architecture in Australia*, still our only attempt at a national architectural history. Freeland's architectural methodology, in turn, can be traced back to Morton Herman, whose book *The Early Australian Architects and their Work* (Angus & Robertson, 1954) had, and still has, great influence on Australian architectural history writing. This is particularly evident in dissertations on hero architects by students at the University of New South Wales – including Sansom's on William Kemp. It can also be seen in published volumes, such as the collection edited by Howard Tanner, *Architects of Australia*.

Herman's book was based on this same respect for the original architect as hero. It has the same enthusiasm for the isolated fact as Sansom had for the single shingle. Drawings take the place of photographs since Herman prefers the place as it was when first finished (minus service areas and setting) to the original marred by time. In Herman's case this passion for newness can be directly related to the writer's 'white Modernist' aesthetic, hardly surprising since he was an architect writing during the early 1950s. His preference for the purity and proportions of our so-called 'colonial Georgian' over the variety and historicism of Victorian architecture is another example of applying values drawn from one's own architectural era. It just seems surprising that this sort of writing persists today in the face of such changed architectural tastes. I assume it results from a feeling that if each part is perfect then the whole picture must be true.

Perhaps I should summarise the points I have made before concluding, since you may feel I have buried them in analogy and simulacra.

1. Architects put creativity before context.
2. They borrow theoretical models from overseas because they do not realise that Australia is not the same.
3. They believe that what you see is all there is.
4. They think facts are better than theory.
5. They add up parts and think they have a whole.
6. They think it is worthwhile and possible to recreate originals untouched by time.
7. They prefer to isolate a moment rather than understand a process.
8. They think that good and bad should not be interchangeable, but eternally valid.

No doubt some of you will claim that you don't do any of these things, and I have cunningly left myself the option of saying that you must therefore be architectural historians. If you are, then write Australian architectural history. If we had had an accepted body of architectural history of our own before now, based on an independent but globally-aware ideology, then I believe both Cox's and Sansom's work would have been very different. Our architecture makes our history, but the reverse is equally true.

The 'Sydney School'?

1985

STANISLAUS FUNG

Since the early 1960s, various well-known Australian architectural writers have been discussing an alleged regional architecture of Sydney, often referred to as the 'Sydney School' or the 'Nuts and Berries School'.[1] Although it has been more than 20 years now since the first publication on this subject appeared, there is no general agreement as to whether a Sydney School ever existed, and what its characteristics are. On the one hand, noted architects such as Peter Muller consider the whole notion 'ridiculous';[2] and on the other hand architectural historians, such as David Saunders and Jennifer Taylor, have discussed the 'Sydney School' in several publications. Although the issue remains contentious, only writings alleging the existence of the 'Sydney School' have appeared. This paper is an appraisal of these writings. It seeks to elucidate the nature and limitations of these writings and to suggest some directions for further study. The following discussion does not attempt to demonstrate the non-existence of the 'Sydney School'. The onus of demonstration is on those who allege its existence, and although the question of whether a 'Sydney School' existed or not is a curious and interesting historical phenomenon, the concern of the present paper lies in the implicit attitudes of the writers who first tackled this problem and unleashed much confusion and contention.

One important cause of confusion is inconsistent usage of the term 'Sydney School'. For Milo Dunphy, the Sydney School is a group of 'young'

Australian architects, alleged to have shared a 'unity of sentiment and aim'.[3] For Robin Boyd, the 'Sydney school [sic]' is an architectural movement which 'had no time for looking wistfully to a reluctant technological future'.[4] For David Saunders, the 'Sydney School' is either 'a very humanist style' or 'a very romantic approach'.[5] For Philip Cox, the 'Sydney School' is 'the architecture which used natural materials'.[6] For Jennifer Taylor, the 'Sydney School' is either a style or 'a romantic movement'.[7]

The 'Sydney School' sometimes means a group of architects, sometimes an 'architectural movement', sometimes a style; and at other times it can mean a romantic approach or a kind of architecture. And as Jennifer Taylor informs us, 'there was no "School" in the accepted sense of the word'.[8] 'School', 'movement', 'approach', 'architecture' and 'style' are neither synonymous nor interchangeable. The disparate meanings associated with the term the 'Sydney School' harbour untidy thinking, poor communication and fallacies of equivocation. But not only does 'Sydney School' mean different things to different people; the buildings, the architects and the dates involved also vary from one commentator to another. This will be made apparent in the following appraisal of publications alleging the existence of the 'Sydney School'.

Milo Dunphy appears to be the first writer to suggest the existence of the 'Sydney School' in a short article of 1962.[9] For him, the 'Sydney School' is a sign of the maturity of Australian architecture. He finds in the domestic work of some young Sydney architects 'a consistency and a consistent high quality'.[10] These architects show 'a unity of aim and sentiment' and work with a straightforward, just-solving-problems-in-the-best-possible-way approach. In Dunphy's view,

> A large number of ... young architects in Sydney are working in this simple vein. Bill Lucas, Bruce Rickard, Ian McKay, Peter Muller, Peter Kollar, Tony Moore, Russell Jack and Neville Gruzman are some of the more prominent names in what may soon be regarded as the Sydney School, one which is at least as distinctive as the Bay Region architecture of California.[11]

But Dunphy's 'unity of aim and sentiment' is created at the expense of proper distinctions. For instance, while Kollar, Muller, Jack and Ancher were all interested in Asian architecture, their aims and intentions were quite different. Muller and Kollar aimed at understanding the perennial principles and religious basis of Eastern architecture.[12] They did not aim at alluding to stylistic aspects of Asian buildings. Their attention was devoted to immaterial principles. Jack and Ancher, on the other hand, were not concerned with the meaning or symbolism and principles of Asian architecture.[13] They were interested, rather, in the physical appearance of mainly Japanese buildings. Also, Jack's aim in design was opposed to Moore's minimalist-brutalist 'simplicity'; so were the aims of Kollar and Muller.

Dunphy's choice of illustrations ranges from Muller's house at Pittwater, to Jack's house at Wahroonga, to Moore's house at North Sydney. These buildings reveal diverse qualities, and the illustrations do nothing to aid Dunphy's claim of 'consistency' in the works of the 'Sydney School' architects.

In spite of these oversights, however, Dunphy did have a case which, strangely, he did not present to his readers. The architects did share certain attitudes. They shared a commitment to modernist tenets such as anti-ornamentalism and the 'truthful' use of building materials. They were concerned with solar control through the use of shading devices and orientation. They generally showed a preference for natural materials. They shared a common rejection of the Internationalist idiom, and they all condemned the 'dreary bulk of Australian housing'.

Dunphy's neglect of these points, together with his unfortunate choice of illustrations, invites speculation on the seriousness of his claim of 'a unity of aim and sentiment' amongst the architects named above. But even considering the commonalities, the case for the 'Sydney School' is not very convincing. The commonalities are just too common to be useful for the identification of a 'Sydney' school.

Five years after Dunphy's suggestion that a group of architects in Sydney 'may soon be regarded as the Sydney School', his prophecy was nearly fulfilled in an article by Robin Boyd, published in 1967.[14] Whereas Dunphy suggests the existence of the 'Sydney School' by an attempt to show an internal coherence of the group in shared ideals, Robin Boyd proceeds by a contrast of 'the Melbourne school [sic]' and the 'Sydney school [sic]'.

Boyd admitted that his account of the state of Australian architecture was 'stronger on generalisations than … on names and examples'.[15] But for him, the 'Melbourne school' was 'forward-looking', 'adventurous and iconoclastic'. Its 'essential ingredients' were 'a great structural-functional idea carried out with an enforced austerity and a voluntarily cavalier technique'.[16] On the other hand, the 'Sydney school' was 'conservative and aesthetic', a 'passing flush of clinker brick and brown creosote' which 'began with domestic work' and was symptomatic of a 'local inbreeding of fashion'.[17] The 'Sydney school ... reveals in subtle romantic allusions to time or places unspecifically remote', recalling in particular the Californian Bungalow style of the 1920s.[18] 'Not quite capable of transplanting itself intact into the urban heart of Sydney', the 'Sydney School' remained associated with domestic work.[19] In time, its 'conceptual basis predictably was watered down by followers until practically all that was left were the rough dark bricks and the brown creosoted off-saw [sic] timber, a tamed Australian romantic kind of brutalism'.[20] Nevertheless, Boyd thinks of the 'Sydney School' as 'the nearest thing to a regional style seen in this country for more than a century'.[21]

In a later article, Boyd raises some new points about the 'folksy, crafty style' in Sydney.[22] This style, Boyd writes, was the architects' 'reaction against the tiny precision of the nonprofessional [sic] vernacular "contemporary" that unconsciously parodied the modern movement'.[23] Characteristic of this style is the use of off-form concrete and the use of 'fragmented forms with occasional nostalgic references, like arches and quasi dormers [sic]'.[24] Boyd notes the influence of British Brutalism and the Californian Bay Region style and, in public buildings, the influence of Japanese architecture. While a Briton or Californian may see little that distinguishes the Sydney buildings, Boyd claims the Australian 'who knows [the style] ... sees the subtle regional characteristics'.[25]

Boyd's article of 1967 'stimulated more discussion in Sydney than any other topic since the Opera House debacle',[26] but it is doubtful whether he is any more successful than Dunphy in the characterisation of the 'Sydney School'. Boyd's 'Melbourne school' and 'Sydney school' are general categories established by contrasting the different attitudes and concerns of some architects in these cities. Apart from the accuracy of his description, which has already been contested in print elsewhere,[27] it is clear that, in the context of architectural history, the Sydney scene did not have exclusive claim to be 'conservative', 'aesthetic', 'originating in domestic work', 'backward-looking' or allusive to 'times or places unspecifically remote'. As for the later article of

1971, it should be remembered that 'folksy, crafty' houses generally do not use off-form concrete, and that 'folksy, crafty' architects did not only react against non-professional parodies of the Modern Movement, but also against the Modern Movement itself. Furthermore, Boyd fails to identify the 'subtle regional characteristics' which he claims Australians in the know are able to discern.

Notwithstanding these minor failures, Boyd managed to be more firm than Dunphy. Whereas the latter had merely suggested the possibility that some Sydney architects might be regarded as the 'Sydney school', Boyd called his 'Sydney school' 'the nearest thing to a regional style'. In 1969, Professor David Saunders was able to outdo both Dunphy and Boyd.[28] Instead of discussing 'the nearest thing to a regional style', Saunders proclaimed that 'Sydney does have a lively architectural theme or style'.

Saunders refers to this phenomenon as 'the backward-looking avant-garde'.[29] Whereas Dunphy refers to pre-1962 buildings, Saunders discusses post-1960 buildings. The earliest house in Sydney's regional style, Professor Saunders thinks, is Donald Gazzard's house of 1960 at Hunters Hill.[30] This style went through a development, and Tony Moore's house at North Sydney of 1961 'was part of the development', together with Peter Johnson's house at Chatswood of 1963 and Ken Woolley's house at Mosman of 1962. Generally, the style does not extend to large projects, but Saunders mentions three examples: Gazzard's Wentworth Chapel at Vaucluse, the terraced town houses overlooking Rushcutters Bay and the Newcastle University Union Building, both by Ancher, Mortlock, Murray and Woolley. Stylistically, for Saunders, all these 'backward-looking avant-garde' buildings may be related to a 'Mediterranean or perhaps an alpine Italian image', to 'brutalism', to 'Griffin's Castlecrag, and to Californian Bungalow time'.[31]

Buildings of this style are: 'essentially romantic', 'delight in tricky splitting of levels ... in glimpse views, in unexpected sources of light, and in cheeky roof forms with sharp sky-light-holders. In the project house versions, a favourite device is that the house bears a flush-ended asymmetrical gable roof over a wall split vertically into alternating brick and glass, one of the dividing lines reaching into the apex'. Typical materials are clinker bricks or white-washed brickwork, 'lots of wood', and 'a roof of brown terra-cotta tiles'. The variety of materials used is small, usually handwrought or looking handwrought.

> The range of structures is small, not favouring difficult spans or adventuring with non-conventional ideas. Small enclosed gardens are to be found within and around the plan, thick with native trees and shrubs but freely admitting bamboos and ferns; outcrops of Sydney sandstone come to look as if that is what they always belonged to, and water seepage is artfully diverted to Japanese-typed ends ...
>
> It is an architecture which gives people strenuous exercise, injects mysteries and a touch of disorder, and tears clothes'.

In addition, Saunders feels a casual mood is evident.[32]

In his one-page article, the most important and cogent account available at the time, Professor Saunders presented his personal impression of what he believed to be a regional style in buildings of Sydney. In a *tour de force* of such brevity, Saunders understandably concentrated on a synchronic analysis of Sydney's 'backward-looking avant-garde'. The question of development was raised without elaboration and without the opportunity to pursue comparisons the uniqueness of Sydney's architecture could not be established. Some comparison of the 'Sydney School' style with other styles can be found in Saunders's discussion of modern Australian architecture published in 1981.[33] In this article, Saunders revived Boyd's category and discussed both the 'Melbourne School' of the fifties and the 'Sydney School' of the sixties. The discussion on the latter is here quoted in full:

> The kind of house referred to as 'Sydney School' is essentially a brick house, using rough, variegated bricks of a kind which a few years earlier had been treated by brickmakers as rejects. There is a great deal of exposure inside as well as outside the house, of those bricks and that roughness. Timber is also treated in this bushcraft way – exposed structures, stained or untreated wood, sometimes not smoothed in any way. So much it shares with Brutalism, and up to a point is a domestic component in that larger story. It is, on the other hand, a very humanist style, with surprising divisions of space by way of changes of level, and with small alcoves and bays, and unexpected windows. Steep red-brown tiled roofs are used, in complete contrast to the Melbourne house of a

> decade earlier, which preferred sheet materials and low pitches. Within the roofs some spaces become virtually attic spaces. It is a very romantic approach, unpredictable in plan, trading in small hidden delights. It is not really very far from the Queen Anne of sixty years before, but delighting in sloping sites as that did not.[34]

While Saunders related the 'Sydney School' to overseas styles such as the Californian Bungalow, as we have noted above, Philip Cox saw in the 'Sydney School' a 'return to the vernacular'. In an article on 'The Development of Domestic Architecture in Australia', published in 1972, Cox attempts to discuss his subject in five pages.[35] His discussion of the '"nuts and berries" school' is short enough to be quoted in full:

> Today there are many young architects exploring the same problems of form and space as the architects of the last two hundred years. In timber, brick and glass a return to the vernacular – commonly known as the 'nuts and berries' school – was experienced in the late fifties and sixties. Upon the foundation of truthful structural expression and use of materials a new thinking was directed towards the exploration and interpretation of space within the house through the use of the open plan and varied sections. Materials used today are generally in their natural state but have lost their initial austerity. There has always been a strong nationalistic feeling to develop an Australian architecture just as there appears to be an eagerness to create an Australian art.[36]

Apart from the loathsome effusion of sweeping generalisations which Cox has not substantiated, the 'return to the vernacular' involves no unique Australian characteristics. It is not the exclusive claim of the '"nuts and berries" school' to use timber, brick, glass and 'open plans' to practise 'truthful structural expression' and to incorporate 'varied sections' in the design of houses.

In another discussion, 'Housing over the past 10 years', published in 1973, Cox hinted at an evolutionary or developmental view of the 'Sydney School':

> For 'high style' domestic architecture, as opposed to general housing, much has occurred. The Sydney School of 'Nuts and Berries' (the architecture which has used natural materials such as common bricks painted or unpainted,

> with stained timber windows [sic], exposed structure and tile roof) rose to its zenith and many excellent examples of this expression were built to whet the historian's appetite for the future. Through this school of thought, the cleavage between the classicists [Harry Seidler et al.] and the romantics [Ken Woolley et al.] has continued unabated.[37]

Although Philip Cox failed to contribute a single iota of insight to the study of the 'Sydney School', he managed to outdo Professor Saunders as far as confidence is concerned. Whereas Saunders's affirmation that 'Sydney does have a lively architectural theme or style' still presupposed a question, no hint of question or doubt remains in the articles by Cox.

Both the question of development and of the distinctiveness of the 'Sydney School' so glibly raised by Cox are dealt with in detail by Jennifer Taylor, who has in fact contributed more than any other person to the study of post-war domestic architecture in Sydney. Since Taylor is an internationally recognised authority in this area, her works demand to be examined with a different set of standards from the one applied so far.

The first major publication by Taylor is a monograph entitled 'An Australian Identity: houses for Sydney 1953–63'.[38] Nineteen architects and 41 buildings from 1946 to 1968 are mentioned or discussed in the text, which consists of an introduction, an epilogue entitled 'After 1963' and two main sections. The first of these is a discussion of the characteristics of 'Sydney School' houses, and of the early houses of Sydney Ancher and Harry Seidler. The second main section is entitled 'The Development of a Regional Architecture 1953–63'. In this section, themes such as 'Organic Architecture', 'Neo-Brutalism' and 'The Natural House' are discussed in relation to the architects who had contributed most to them.

The thesis put forward by Taylor in this book may be summarised succinctly thus: There was a development of a regional architecture in Sydney during the decade 1953–63.[39] 'The gestation phase of the movement – sometimes referred to as the "Sydney School"' – was over with the building of the Woolley House and the Johnson House.[40] The architects involved in this 'School' shared 'common attitudes and aims' and 'were independently arriving at related and similar solutions for local domestic architecture'.[41] They aimed at creating houses which were harmonious with the landscape.[42] They were concerned with climatic control, and they used exposed natural materials which were locally available.[43] The result of the 'Sydney School' movement was 'an Australian house'.[44] In particular, the John James House, built between 1967 and 1968, 'appears to gather together all that had gone before and resolve the different tendencies into a single unified statement'.[45]

The most important of the claims made by Taylor in her monograph concerns an alleged development of a regional architecture in Sydney. In Taylor's 80-page publication, no less than 49 pages have been devoted to this topic. Her views may be outlined as follows.

Taylor begins her discussion by introducing the houses designed by Peter Muller. For Taylor, these houses, constructed of exposed natural materials, demonstrate 'a complementary balance of shelter and site' and 'became the catalyst for much which followed'.[46] Taylor then puts forward the claim that the year 1957 was 'a turning point for the residential architecture in Sydney'.[47] She introduces the Jack House at Wahroonga, the Ancher house at Neutral Bay and the Lucas House at Castlecrag in relation to the aims and concerns of their architects.[48] Taylor suggests that Muller, Ancher, Jack and Lucas 'could have agreed on a common manifesto that spoke of sympathetic materials, economy, simplicity and an appreciation of the beauty and harmony of nature'.[49] She claims that the attitude of these architects 'soon found far wider adherents'.[50]

Further on, Taylor asserts that 'the initial expression in physical terms of the coming together of the work of the 1950s is to be found in the houses designed by Bryce Mortlock'.[51] Having discussed three Mortlock-designed houses, Taylor then turns to houses designed by Bruce Rickard and Ross Thorne.[52] She indicates that 'it is difficult to determine the place of Rickard in the development of Sydney residential architecture',[53] but she claims that the same qualities of Frank Lloyd Wright's work which Rickard implanted in Sydney 'reappeared during the mid-1960s though in another guise'.[54]

Taylor next focuses on the houses by Moore and Gazzard, which were influenced by Brutalism. She notes that in contradistinction to houses previously mentioned, Moore's house is 'compact', 'closed and vertical'.[55] After a brief discussion of architect-designed project houses (circa 1961), Taylor asserts that 'a house with a distinctive local character was beginning to emerge in the Sydney area'.[56] She claims that:

> The general exterior character of houses became more rugged and dynamic. Internally they became more complicated. In particular, natural light was introduced as a strong design factor through the fracturing of the mass of the building and the use of skylights and other forms of high lighting. The articulation of units and parts of units became more and more clearly defined.[57]

Immediately after making the claim of an emerging regional identity, Taylor announces that the Woolley House and the Johnson House mark the end of 'the gestation phase' of the 'Sydney School'.[58] After discussing these houses, Taylor asserts that 'by 1964 the image for a whole family of related houses was fully established'.[59] Finally, Taylor claims that the James House gathers together 'all that had gone before', and presents 'a single unified statement'.[60]

A number of key points in Taylor's account of the alleged development of Sydney's regional architecture stand as unsubstantiated conjectures. The year 1957 as a turning point remains unexplained. It is not clear what the architectural changes that occurred in this year were. Taylor's assertion that Mortlock's work constitutes a 'synthesis' of the 'work of the 1950s' also stands without justification. The post-gestation phase buildings, particularly the Woolley House, the Johnson House and the James House, show common characteristics similar to those described by Taylor when she writes of the emerging regional character of the houses in Sydney. They have sloped, tiled roofs and multi-level layouts. Their interiors give a strong sense of enclosure, often showing Brutalist influences, and so on. In contrast to these houses, the earlier houses described by Taylor are mostly single-storey buildings with flat roofs. These houses emphasise a strong sense of continuity of interior and exterior spaces by using large expanses of glass under deep eaves. Often these houses are carefully detailed, unlike some later Brutalistic houses with 'crude detailing'.[61] These earlier houses are presumably gestation phase buildings. Taylor has not explained why the clearly discernible change in stylistic traits of the early houses of 1953–59 and the post-gestation phase buildings occurred. She has also not explained why the Woolley House and the Johnson House should be considered as marking the end of the gestation phase and therefore, by implication, be regarded as 'more mature' than earlier buildings. The special position of the James House in Taylor's account stands unsupported by scholarly reasoning.

It is clear, then, that at key points in Taylor's outline of the alleged development of a regional architecture in Sydney between 1953 and 1963, necessary arguments have not been advanced to support her assertions. The lack of argumentative support for Taylor's claim that a development occurred, however, does not in itself negate the possibility that a regional architecture existed. The identification of a unique set of characteristics common to a group of buildings does not necessarily depend on the notion of development. Therefore Taylor's claim of the existence of a regional architecture needs to be appraised separately.

In her monograph, Taylor has made a series of remarks on the common aims and concerns of the architects mentioned, as well as on the similarities of the houses these architects designed. These remarks are put forward to justify considering these architects as a group, and to support Taylor's claim that there was a 'distinctive local character' in some of the houses in the Sydney region. In her discussion of the common characteristics of 'Sydney School' houses, Taylor merely asserts the existence of a 'distinctive local character', but does not demonstrate how this 'character' is distinctive from other established regional architectures.[62]

The common aims and concerns of the 'Sydney School' architects mentioned by Taylor include the intention to create houses that harmonise with their environment, the common preference for materials such as brick and timber, the aim to create 'functional' designs, the concern for 'truthful' expression of structure, the concern for climatic control and 'economy', and the rejection of the International Style and what Dunphy calls 'the dreary bulk of Australian housing'. These intentions and preferences, while useful in distinguishing the 'Sydney School' architects from those elsewhere in Australia around the 1950s and early 1960s, are not sufficient to identify the 'Sydney School' architects as a unique group of architects in the history of architecture. The commonalities identified by Taylor are very general, and are not exclusive to the Sydney architects mentioned by Taylor.

In sum, both Taylor's account of the development of a regional architecture in Sydney, and her characterisation of this architecture in her monograph of 1972, remain unsubstantiated and inconclusive. In appearance, Taylor's monograph attempts to answer the questions raised by Saunders earlier. In reality those questions remained unanswered. But in 1979, in an article by Taylor entitled 'Looking at the Sydney School', the assertions and conjectures in the 1972 monograph are taken as constituting an established historical account, and are summarised by way of introduction to the subsequent discussion of the rapid acceptance and diffusion of the 'Sydney School' style.[63] The 1979 article by Taylor therefore has unsupported conjecture as the basis of its discussion.

In this article, Taylor again presents the reader with quite arbitrary and unjustified statements. This is evident in the manner in which she conducts her discussion. Instead of identifying common stylistic traits as argumentative support for the categorisation of 'Sydney School' buildings, she assumes the existence of a 'Sydney School' style and asserts that the post-1963 buildings she has in mind exhibit characteristics of the style.[64] This is particularly evident in her discussion of medium-sized and large buildings. Taylor claims that certain buildings 'took their place quite happily in urban and suburban streets', that 'the style was even comfortable on tight city sites'[65] and, by such personal judgments, bypassed the question of what the specified schools, baby health centres and so on have in common with the pre-1964 houses. Taylor's view that the Ku-ring-gai College shows 'affinity with ... the concerns of the Sydney School' because, in her opinion, the building relates harmoniously to the site, suggests that she is drawing relationships between buildings with exceedingly general concepts.[66] The concern for harmony of building and site is not exclusive to 'Sydney School' architecture, but is shared by the architecture of many other places and periods.

In recent years, several of Professor Taylor's works mention the 'Sydney School'.[67] The discussions are brief and do not add substantially to our understanding of the subject. The alleged evolution, maturation and development of the 'School' are mentioned without detailed discussion.[68] Behind the adoption of an evolutionary scheme for the study of the 'Sydney School' are a series of assumptions and attitudes which are of crucial importance to the direction of future studies.

Recently, a number of leading scholars have condemned the use of evolutionary models in the study of art history.[69] The reasons behind this anti-evolutionist stance are summed up well by Professor Joyce Brodsky:

> In nature, the organic process insures constant replication rather than change, except through a complicated and still little understood process of mutation. In the application of the model to art, the mysterious birth of a new pattern or style out of the death of the previous cycle in regular, frequent, and predictable ways, is already a radical departure from the natural process. The biological model needs even more severe alteration in order to account for the unpredictable, but regular change that characterises the history of art. The model is also suspect because it is not specific to human structures but applies to all of organic nature. As an animal, man certainly shares in this nature but as he produces forms that differ from other living creatures, one needs a theory able to account for his making of unique things. The biological model does not do that primarily because it overlooks the changing human cultural context as well as the structure specific to humans. While appearing to be developmental and therefore a change oriented analysis, the model is, in reality, static, because it is a-temporal and even a-contextual.[70]

In addition to these considerations, it may be pointed out that the evolutionist model involves the assumption of cumulative, usually irreversible change. Now, in architectural design, architects are not obliged to adopt any stylistic innovations of their predecessors. Every architect has the possibility of adopting previous innovations, rejecting them, or simply being oblivious to them. The application of the evolutionist model to architectural history therefore involves the imposition of a deterministic model on a process which is not necessarily deterministic.[71] The 'Sydney School' may or may not have evolved or developed, but the assumption of its evolution and development is dangerous.

The development of the 'Sydney School', particularly in Taylor's major study, proceeded uni-linearly and chronologically. Short-term changes, well-publicised events and well-known architects engaged her attention. The discussion of the 'development' is more an account of a series of events in time rather than a series of changes in time. Taylor's account is a history of events, *l'histoire événementielle* in French Annalist terms.

The intention to write this type of history influenced the use of evidence. The writers promoting the 'Sydney School' mainly relied on their own personal experiences and impressions, reminiscences of architects in Sydney, a few published sources and photographs of buildings. They appear to regard empiricism as the main, if not the sole, source of knowledge. The writers gave voice to that part of the past of which their architect-contemporaries were conscious, and tended to neglect the silent majority – the commonplace, inarticulate past which was the context of these 'glamorous events'. Now, historical change is not uniform. Short-term changes or events are quite easily noticed and remembered, but long-term changes and trends tend to elude contemporary participants and tend to be overlooked. A historical study exclusively reliant on contemporary sources emphasises the conscious motivating forces in history and tends to neglect these long-term changes, as well as the presuppositions and the unconscious limitations of the mentalities that determined what was thinkable or conceivable for a given period. Future studies would profit by a close juxtaposition of medium- and long-term economic and social trends with architectural developments.

In the writings appraised above, writers have mainly presented their personal opinions with little argumentative support. Issues of development and influence are treated by means of assertions and personal conjecture rather than rigorous demonstration. Often the articles are too short to allow chronological treatment of their subject and the pursuit of necessary comparisons. The brevity of discussion forces the writers to direct their attention to characteristics common to buildings. The resultant discussion emphasises the communal rather than unique aspects of the buildings, thus giving undue credence to the existence of a style.[72] In the end, the writings did not establish the uniqueness of the 'Sydney School' conclusively.

This inconclusiveness of the writings appraised above is in part due to a lack of methodological discipline. The writers, interested only in presenting their own views, did not identify a historical problem and then choose a method of inquiry to tackle it. Here the selection of a method of inquiry is closely related to the definition of 'Sydney School'. It is meaningless to ask 'Was there a Sydney School?' without specifying the meaning of the key term.

If the 'Sydney School' means a certain group of persons, the above question implies an inquiry as to whether there was a group of architects practising in Sydney and united by a general similarity of principles and methods that distinguishes them from any other group of architects in the history of architecture.

If the 'Sydney School' refers to an architectural movement, the question inquires whether there was a series of buildings in the Sydney area which, when examined sequentially in the chronological order of their design or construction, demonstrate that there was a group of architects whose actions and endeavours were directed more or less continuously towards a special end either in the performance of their buildings, or towards a distinctive architectural expression. Furthermore, the question inquires whether the alleged 'movement' is a distinctive, unique trend in the history of architecture.

If the 'Sydney School' refers to a style, then the question 'Was there a Sydney School?' inquires whether there were constant elements, qualities, and expressions discernible in buildings in the Sydney area, which distinguish the group of buildings in the history of architecture. Also, the question inquires as to whether there were any special ways or methods involved in the design and construction of a group of buildings in the Sydney area, which in themselves and in their effects distinguish the group of buildings in the history of architecture.

These questions, and others, remain to be answered by future studies. Among the more important tasks is the comparison of 'Sydney School' buildings with similar examples of buildings, such as Dutch houses of the 1950s. This would provide a much-needed indication of the degree of uniqueness of the Sydney buildings.

This interest in the unique in modern Australian architecture, however, is not only an historian's concern for stylistic categorisation. The writings appraised above shared with the architects mentioned the same interest in regionalism. The writers are not only 'historians' but also aesthetes, concerned with the promotion and popularisation of 'nice' buildings. Most of the writers are also qualified architects, interested in drawing lessons from the past and in the maturity of their regional architecture – all this is very fine. But these personal commitments have led to highly selective accounts of domestic architecture. The 'Sydney School' is discussed in isolation, apart from all the nasty 'featuristic' and otherwise 'dreary' housing that formed a part of its context. Future studies should beware of such an a-contextual approach.

It has been the intention of the foregoing discussion to show that the confidence in the existence of the 'Sydney School' is disproportionate to the amount of serious study given to the subject. From Milo Dunphy's first suggestion in 1962 to the acceptance of the 'Sydney School' in recent architectural publications overseas,[73] the initial tentative suggestion grew to a widely accepted notion. The progressive acceptance of the concept of a 'Sydney School', however, is based only on inconclusive, relatively short discussions, characterised by a lack of methodological discipline.

The 'Sydney School' was an interesting notion probably because the writers were searching for an aesthetically pleasing Australian architecture. The 'Sydney School' was accepted as a label, despite insufficient study, probably because the readership and the writers both shared this search for a modern Australian architecture. The meaning of the 'Sydney School' as a term was left conveniently vague, and the personal viewpoints of the writers appealed to the readers' instinctive judgment rather than to rigorous thinking.

Between a full stop and a question mark, the difference is great. Both have their rightful places in scholarly discourse, but the 'Sydney School' should go with a question mark for the time being.

Attitudes and Evidence: The View from the Government House Verandah

1988

HELEN PROUDFOOT

Since I began work on the history of the Government House site in Sydney, I have been interested in the various ways that the building and, after 1845, the site, have been perceived. In this paper, I shall try to relate these perceptions to certain preconceptions contained both in the study of Australian history generally as it was emerging at the turn of the century and as it has developed, and to the study of the more specialised field of architectural history. I also want to point out the association that the site has enjoyed with the Royal Australian Historical Society, especially in the days of its early formation. The Society has had a physical association with the Government House site, as some of its preliminary meetings were held in a terrace in Phillip Street which happened to be built on pan of the site. It has also had an intellectual association, which has been important to the site's understanding.

Governor Phillip's house, the construction of which commenced on 15 May 1788 to replace a prefabricated tent dwelling that Phillip had brought from London, was the first major building of significance constructed on the continent of Australia. It was of two storeys and built in the vernacular Georgian style familiar to Phillip and his company, straightforward but distinctive in its form. It was built with painstaking difficulty, with untried materials and without the benefit of sufficient lime for its mortar. The governor took possession of it in June 1789.

The governor's house became a symbol of stability and authority in the colony and the focus of the seaport town that then began to grow up around it. It was the centre of government and administration as well as a house. It was gradually extended, with each of the governors from Hunter and King to Macquarie and Darling building onto and adapting the original nucleus. It was adapted to the climate and to the social roles of the governors. It was in the centre of things, the keystone of the town, which grew, much as the house did, in opportunistic ways.[1]

Hunter added a verandah; King made the first major extension of the house alongside; Macquarie remodelled the rear of the house and added an eastern wing; Darling raised the roof to accommodate additional bedrooms and extended the back of the main block. The archaeological investigation of the site, carried out in phases since 1983,[2] has revealed the importance of the outbuildings to the workings of the house and, more generally, to the history of the colony, for it was in these rooms that the first printing press was set up and the *Sydney Gazette* began publication.

The building complex was recorded by Mortimer Lewis in 1845 before it was demolished. The governor had moved to another, grander house which rose 'like a moon among its lesser luminaries'[3] among gardens in the Government Domain, withdrawn from the bustle of the town. The quayside was being reclaimed again and formalised, and the town's streets, paradoxically arranged in a pattern that had previously converged upon Government House, were then pushed through its site to the new quayside.

The site then lay derelict and unkempt. It became part of a city block contained between Young, Bridge and Phillip Streets. Parts of it were sold off and two banks of substantial terraces built. A carter's yard in the centre was occupied by a temporarily public building from 1912 to 1970, and then the site became a car park.

A copper foundation plate was dug up in 1899 by chance, under the footpath of Bridge Street, by a workman digging a service tunnel for the Postmaster-General's Department. It was inscribed by a hand that stirred a strange emotion in the reader.

> His Excellency, Arthur Phillip Esq. Governor in Chief, and Captain General, in and over the Territory of New South Wales. &c, &c. &c. landed in this Cove with the first Settlers of this Country, the 24th Day of January, 1788, and on

> the 15th Day of May, in the same Year being the 28th of the Reign of His present Majesty, George the Third, the first of these Stones was laid.

The story today begins with a diversion. In 1864, less than 20 years after the building complex begun by Governor Phillip had been demolished, a local legend about an early 'government house' on a different site from the Bridge Street one emerged. It was claimed in an article in the *Illustrated Sydney News* of 16 July 1864 that a tiny cottage with one door and two windows in Pitt Street was the first government house to be built. This information was repeated several times, with variations of the 1864 depiction appearing as woodcuts in the newspapers. It was given a degree of credibility with a mention in J Henniker Heaton's *Australian Dictionary of Dates and Men of the Time*, published in Sydney in 1879,[4] where it was claimed that the copper foundation plate was for a temporary government house and that the site of the first true Government House was in Pitt Street, and the remains had been pulled down in 1868. This is the first known and rather puzzling mention of the foundation plate, which was not rediscovered until 1899.

This piece of information was represented as an antiquarian curiosity. No historian came forward to refute or deny it when it surfaced. It is curious indeed that this idea persisted, off and on, for several decades, especially when the first government house had been demolished only within living memory. Andrew Houison, in his inaugural address as president of the newly-formed Historical Society in Sydney in 1901, remarked on the loss of exactness when even well-known landmarks were remembered. 'In the newspapers of to-day,' he said:

> allusions are constantly being made to Forgotten Sydney ... Quite recently there has been considerable discussion in the papers as to the locality of certain buildings and the dates at which others were erected. If there be so much difficulty in these matters, so soon after their demolition, even while there are still among us many who have visited them, how much greater then will be the difficulty in future years in identifying some spot around which history throws a halo, when the 'old folks' have passed away.[5]

Houison quoted an article from the *Sydney Morning Herald*, where the formation of an Historical Society had been advocated. Such a society would, it was hoped, 'have the effect of stimulating the habit of research. It would accumulate a mass of detail, from which the historian of the future would derive much valuable information ... It would rescue from oblivion many valuable records ... It would enable us to know more about the country in which we live.' These were the impulses that had prompted its formation. At that point, Houison felt, drawing an analogy from one of Macaulay's essays, the Society should try to produce 'maps' rather than 'painted landscapes'; that is, collect exact information rather than devise philosophies of history or imaginative reconstructions. He felt that, to make the past present and to bring the distant near, painstaking collection of information was the first step, and it was with this that the members of the Society resolved to concern themselves.

Thus by 1899, and with the discovery of the foundation plate of Government House under the footpath at the corner of Bridge and Phillip Streets, there was, in the air, a recognition of the need to begin some enquiry on a modest, local scale and to collect material so that information would not be lost or recorded incorrectly. Some serious public-sponsored historical work had also begun in the preparation of the *Historical Records of New South Wales*, a collection of documents relating to the early settlement period held in the Public Records Office, London, which began publication in 1893. By 1899, six volumes had appeared under the editorship of FM Bladen, a Sydney barrister.

It was Bladen who came forward and identified the copper plate as undoubtedly belonging to the first Government House. He pinpointed the spot where it was found in relation to the surrounding streets: 'Forty-five feet in a west-south-west line from the kerbstones on the west side of Phillip Street. It was directly under the pavement of the southern side of Bridge Street, seven feet six inches in a south line from the kerbstone.'[6]

This measurement of Bladen's was invaluable in the confirmation of the position of the footings when work began on the excavation of the site. The kerb today is in the same position as it was when Bladen measured it. Both the plate and a number of bricks were deposited in the Australian Museum, at the time considered the most appropriate place for them. After the Mitchell Library was founded, the plate was transferred there. The bricks went to Vaucluse House some time after 1910 but disappeared there in a miscellaneous collection of old bricks and artefacts.[7] One, however, from the 1899 discovery of the footings, was given to Mrs AG Foster, a founding member of the Historical Society, and she later deposited it in the Mitchell Library where it has remained, useful for comparison.

The nineties were the years of exciting archaeological discoveries in Egypt and the Near East, and in reporting the find of the plate, the editor of the *Herald* could not resist a comparison.[8] He draws a parallel with the discovery of the tomb of Romulus in Rome and speaks of 'the permanency and the immense appeal of the past', as if this was something that happened elsewhere but not in Australia. Against this, he sets 'the curious interest that attaches to the men who built their houses and lived their lives here where we live ours, a generation that has pulled down their buildings or hid them'.

From a reading of the reports of the event, it seems that the full significance of the discovery, and of the building it came from, was not fully appreciated in 1899. The fact that the foundation plate was from a building that was the centre of the first European settlement of the continent was not acknowledged. It was regarded more as a curiosity than a significant relic from a highly symbolic building.

At the time of the discovery of the plate in 1899, and despite the impending formation of the Historical Society, Australian history was barely recognised as a proper subject for study. Academic historians, in the shadow of their English universities and only few in number, suffered from the feeling that Australian history, like its culture, was inferior and derivative. By the end of the nineteenth century, historians had lost the boldness and freshness of approach that men like WC Wentworth, JD Lang and John West had brought to their writings on Australia early in the century.[9] A sense of inferiority was to persist for many decades; indeed, until well into the 1960s, reinforced by the appointments of Oxford-trained historians to chairs in Australian universities, who tended to take a British Empire bias as their starting points.

Nevertheless, if the academics remained diffident, the grassroots historians were not. The Australian Historical Society, later to assume a 'Royal' prefix, was determinedly antiquarian in bias, and it played an important role in Australian studies at that time. Its articles established the tone of the enquiry into the founding period and there was considerable interest shown in the early colonial years by its lecturers and writers.

Some important articles describing Government House and its builders, locality and uses were written in this early period and published in the pages of the Society's *Journal*. JP McGuanne began in 1902 by publishing a detailed account of the building of the house and its use by the early governors.[10] This remained the seminal article on which many of the accounts in the following years were based. It was followed by several articles by the educator and engineer Norman Selfe an important and lively figure in the technical education circles of the day. He wrote about Circular Quay and the activities around Sydney Cove and included Government House in his range of interests.[11]

In 1910, David Scott Mitchell's bequest of a great library of Australiana to the state resulted in the opening of the Mitchell Library, making a specialised collection of documents and books readily available for the first time for researchers, and producing a surge of popular interest in the early foundation years of the colony.

Older colonists began writing down their recollections of earlier times. In his reminiscences, Captain WAB Greaves remembered Bridge Street as it was in the mid-nineteenth century, an unfenced, unformed rough track with grass margins; a favourite spot for public meetings protesting about the continuation of transportation, with the platform consisting of a bullock dray drawn up under the shade of the old stone pines.[12]

There were other articles on Government House and its vicinity published in the *Journal*. John Weingarth, a surveyor, wrote on the old Tank Stream and the then-vanished profile of the stream's entrance into Sydney Cove, drawing up a useful map in relation to the streets and quayside of the 1920s. Mrs Foster wrote an informal article on old homes and epitaphs in 1925 and 1926. In 1928, William Dixson, later the benefactor of the Dixson Library, wrote of his collection of early Australiana, which included some important pictures of Sydney Cove and Government House and its location, discussing various aspects that had arisen since McGuanne had published in 1902.

In 1917, too, in a gesture designed to draw attention to the site of the Government House and the importance of the building that had once stood there, the Royal Australian Historical Society erected a ceramic memorial plaque on a concrete plinth on the corner of Bridge and Phillip Streets, near where the copper foundation plate had been found.

Interest in the history of architecture in the Australian context began to stir at about the same time. The architectural profession, still feeling the effects of the collapse of the 1880s boom and the 1890s depression, nevertheless maintained publication of its magazine *Art and Architecture*, and a few articles about past Australian architecture and buildings began to appear. Among them was one by Frank Walker on the vice-regal residences of New South Wales.[13] It was in the Walker Papers, in the Library of the Royal Australian Historical Society, that the plan showing the subsequent street pattern imposed on the demolished Government House site was found before the commencement of the archaeological investigation. This plan proved crucial, in conjunction with similar plans located in the State Archives and the Lands Department, for the firm establishment of the location of the foundations.

While this amateur historical activity was going on early in the century, the academic historians made little impact. In 1891, George Arnold Wood became Challis Professor of History at the University of Sydney as a young man of 25, and single-handedly founded the history school there. He had no assistant for another 25 years so he was able to do little writing or research, even though he developed an interest in the early colonial period and contributed a number of papers to the Historical Society *Journal* and published *The Discovery of Australia* in 1922.[14]

Interest in Australian architecture quickened in the twenties under the influence of W Hardy Wilson and Sydney Ure Smith. The latter was editor and publisher of the journal *Art in Australia*, which began publication in 1916 and intermittently included articles on Australian architecture. Both espoused Georgian colonial architecture as an ideal, regarding this early period with some nostalgia as a sort of innocent architectural golden age.

It has been pointed out by the historian DR Hainsworth in the introduction to his book, *The Sydney Traders*, that these pioneer historians were restricted in three ways: by their own early twentieth-century preoccupations, by the nature of the evidence available for their use, and by what he called, interestingly enough, the 'view from Government House Verandah'.[15] The period was seen through the eyes of a succession of harassed governors, mainly because these governors supplied much of the documentary evidence in their dispatches and official papers. Hainsworth maintained that, though the view was elevated, the true historical form of the period could not be discerned from it.

There was little theoretical basis underlying the research and output of these pioneers of Australian historical writing, apart from a commonly accepted linear evolutionary model whereby change was viewed as a causal process in time, directed towards a predetermined goal, where each step on the way could be seen as a further development in the progress towards a better situation. Political events were seen as pointers in this progress and political figures as the major participants.

The first biographies of Governor Phillip were produced using this method in the 1930s, by George Mackaness and M Barnard Eldershaw, a composite name adopted by two women historians, Margery Barnard and Flora Eldershaw, and HV Evatt wrote his account of the Rum Rebellion. Lachlan Macquarie and John Macarthur received attention from MH Ellis in 1947 and 1955.[16] It is interesting to note that these writers were outside the academic stream of historians, who still remained largely aloof from the field of Australian studies, despite the fact that they were the only publicly funded historians in the country at the time, preferring to reinforce a dependence on English methods and European subject matter, while seeming inhibited about the writing of biographies by both Marxist and Collingwood theories. Brian Fitzpatrick, looking at Australia, saw it in terms of British imperialism.[17]

The first architectural histories produced in Australia also followed a linear chronological approach, notably those by Morton Herman and JM Freeland.[18] Both discussed Government House and its important place in the history of Australian architecture. Herman, in particular, recognised its symbolic value, calling it 'the tap root' of Australian architecture. As pioneers in the field, these two books made an impressive beginning but, as Bernard Smith was to point out in his review of Freeland's work,[19] this linear approach had very real disadvantages when architecture and aesthetics were being discussed.

The results of the linear approach to history were that historic sequences could be introduced without context as part of the narrative progression and that assumptions of influence could be made from immediately preceding events, with one event seeming to lead to or cause the next. Causal links could be implied without evidence being clearly established. This was a particularly popular way of interpreting Australian history about the time of Federation, when the national bias could reinforce the narrative method with the goal of Federation forming a suitable climax.

With respect to the history of architecture, the linear method as practised in Australia in recent decades has certain dangers, depending upon the writer's bias. If he or she were a champion of modern, functional architecture, rejecting historicism as debased and irrelevant, then the changing progression of architectural styles characterising the different decades of the nineteenth and twentieth centuries – each exhibiting influences from outside sources – could be seen to lead on through the 'confusion' of nineteenth-century eclecticism to the purer light of twentieth-century technical rationalism. Even though Australia could boast only a meagre number of these pared-down, rationalist buildings, and even though these were synonymous with post-war austerity and tended thus to make a virtue out of necessity, simplicity and functionalism, they could be extolled as a desirable goal.

On the other hand, a writer who admired the elegant simplicity and predictability of the Georgian and Regency architecture that was transported to the colony, could then structure their account on the 'progressive degeneration' theory, whereby the fine qualities of Australia's first crop of buildings were seen to be progressively corrupted by ever more extravagant eclectic influences as the nineteenth century wore on. Both Herman and Freeland subscribed to this latter view of architectural history, idealising the early period – though Freeland also saw merit in the post-1960s architecture, seeing in it a sort of re-emergence after a long period in a stylistic wilderness. This view appeared to be shared by Robin Boyd in Melbourne, who skilfully lampooned the preferences of Victorian suburban dwellers.

Subsequent writers on early Australian architectural history such as Howard Tanner, Phillip Cox, Clive Lucas, Robert Irving and Miles Lewis, in attempting a broad, all-Australian sweep, have not yet broken away from this linear approach, but they have made a concerted attempt to trace back stylistic and technical influences to their sources in Europe. However, a more critical appraisal of the subject has begun to emerge with Bernard Smith and his students, such as Joan Kerr and James Broadbent, making enquiries aimed at more specific aspects of Australian architecture, linked to a wider theoretical framework imposed by the study of art history.

It is difficult, however, to abandon 'periodisation' as a framework in the study of architecture, as change, and the gradual evolution of style, is a distinguishing characteristic. It provides, in fact, part of the fascination of the subject. As techniques and taste change, so do buildings and they reflect these changes in a most obvious and emblematic way. Taken together, they reflect their times in a curiously coherent manner, so that even revivals are recognisable as such, and the mainstream of a building period seems to gather an inexorable stylistic momentum, each example absorbing influences both from overseas and from the structures currently being built around it.

The linear approach to history in Australian historical studies generally has been under several fronts of sustained attack by academic historians in recent years. The first front was mounted by the followers of Hegel and Marx, who adopted the view that historical explanation should have an organising principle and suggested that this should be the dialectic between the economic system and the organisation of society into contributing economic groupings or classes. Marxist historians have had a strong influence in academic history schools in Australia, and their approach contributed to the neglect of local and regional historical studies at the academic level and the downgrading of much-needed Australian biographical studies for many decades.

A second front of attack on the linear evolutionary model of history-telling was launched by the social scientists and geographers. The first were acceptable to the Marxist stream and espoused the study of minority groups such as Aborigines, convicts and women; the second began to fill the breach at the local and regional level left vacant by the historians. They studied the evolution of, and relationships between, cities and towns and their hinterlands. They also studied the arrangements of land uses within the city structure and their changes, directing attention to the heart of Sydney and the area around Government House. Articles by KW Robson, GP Walsh and Norman Edwards have discussed land use changes in the area.[20]

Another influence on the historians is the impact of anthropology and archaeology, which has been especially influential in the conservation field.

These disciplines have been particularly valuable in focusing attention on the role that the study of sites can play in the reassessment of the study of history in the Australian context. Techniques for finding, listing and interpreting material remains have been developed. Historical archaeology in Australia, however, still suffers from an inadequate database and finds difficulty in escaping the confines of the specific. The evidence is being collected but it still needs to be organised and used to illuminate our knowledge and interpretation of the Australian experience.

Yet another explanation of attitudes to the early period in Australian studies was recently put by Geoffrey Bolton at the Australian History Association Conference held in February 1988. He drew attention to the fact that the period before 1850 has been treated, by the influential Melbourne school of academic historians, like a 'picturesque footnote' to the more serious and important period after that date – a view that the Bicentennary celebrations did little to expel. We have, alas, fallen victim to the old inter-city discriminatory rivalry. The foundation years were linked to antiquarianism and tended to be dismissed, instead of being seen as the seminal period of foundation.

Thus, it may be seen that preoccupations in the study and pursuit of history in Australia in the last 50 or more years have had implications for the way in which the Government House site has been regarded. They may also help explain why academic historians, with a few notable exceptions, have been absent until the last few years from the debates and considerations of the site and from the heritage field generally.

Because of its historiographical background, it appears that Government House has been seen as a relic of the 'view from Government House Verandah,' described by Hainsworth, a view that he dismissed seventeen years ago as inadequate. Other historians may have seen in it a revival of the old antiquarian tradition, the examination of an artefact in detail without reference to its context or its relationship with other, wider themes. Others again may have dismissed it as irrelevant to the Marxist dialectic of conflict over resources, production and class.

But the view from the Government House Verandah has changed and the vantage point itself is perhaps now better understood. Our preoccupations have certainly changed: Aborigines have re-emerged, there is less emphasis on the great men and more on the poor; women have begun to be acknowledged, both collectively and individually; the dynamics of environmental change are beginning to be explored.

The evidence available now has been reworked and reassessed and made more accessible with republication of most of the early journals, the publication of other manuscripts and books, and the closer examination of other early documents like the Bigge Report and its appendices. It has been extended, with work like that done by Alan Frost in the Public Record Office and other English libraries, by Hainsworth himself and Brian Fletcher, Margaret Steven, Hazel King, John Hirst, Tom Parsons and others. New perspectives have been brought to bear on the colonial experience from other disciplines: Robert Dixon and Paul Carter, Isabel McBride and John Mulvaney have extended our perceptions. Imaginative reconstructions, whatever we may have thought of them, have coloured our vision. Urban history has emerged as a sub-discipline with historians such as Graeme Davison, Tom Stannage, Jill Roe and Peter Spearitt. This field of enquiry has been fostered by many heritage studies of specific areas.

How has Government House fared? Rollo Gillespie, another writer outside the academic history stream, wrote a useful account in his *Vice-Regal Quarters*, published by Angus & Robertson in 1975. He emphasised the social roles of the governors and also their complaints about the condition of the building, linking these to their disillusionment of office. 'It was a house of frustration', he wrote, 'a house of little ease', unhealthy and inconvenient. These much-quoted sentiments had for some time coloured popular perceptions of the building, clouding its primary significance.

Cox and Lucas noticed it only in passing in their *Australian Colonial Architecture* (1978), using it as an illustration of what they called 'the vernacular process', whereby the building passed from unadulterated English model, to verandah-ed house, to extension 'horizontally' into the landscape. Particular attention was given by Robert Irving to it in his unpublished thesis 'The First Australian Architecture' (1975) and in his chapter on Georgian Australia in a recent book on the Australian house in 1985.[21] My own unpublished report, 'The First Government House, Sydney, and the Subsequent History of the Site after 1845', was submitted to the Department of Environment and Planning in 1983 as a preparation for the commencement of the archaeological investigation under Ann Bickford and her team.

This site of Government House in the city of Sydney has drawn together many strands of historical enquiry. It has been the subject of various articles and accounts since 1899, and since 1983 has itself been subjected to one of the most intensive archaeological investigations yet carried out in Australia. In some ways, the enquiry has been disappointing: it has not been like recovering a ship full of treasure. There were no great and valuable finds. But the investigation has offered a vantage point from which the first settlement can be viewed and it has allowed a significant focusing of attention. It also recaptured an excitement of a most immediate kind. Here were the stones laid and the governor's house built; here was the tangible evidence of the first colonists' endeavours; here in the heart of the great city they founded was the enduring substance of their beginnings, lost and then found again. Who could fail, whatever theory of history they espoused, to be impressed?

The Spanish Scene: Some Houses of the Thirties by Marshall Clifton (1903–75)

1988

DUNCAN RICHARDS

> A strong feeling has been growing in Australia that we ought to be developing a characteristic type of architecture of our own. As in all ages one country has borrowed ideas from another, and adapted them to its own requirements, we should be doing the right thing in borrowing from Italy, Spain and South America.
>
> ARL WRIGHT[1]

It has long been recognised that a significant group of houses in what is termed the 'Spanish style' exists in metropolitan Perth, dating from the thirties. Beyond this recognition not a great deal is known about these buildings. Not all the designers have been identified,[2] nor has the correct sequence of development of these buildings been established. The nature of any influences and models, whether they were local, national or international, remains conjectural.[3] Even an appropriate descriptive terminology is uncertain. Terms such as 'Spanish', 'Spanish Mission', 'Hollywood Spanish Mission', 'Californian', 'Mediterranean' and even 'Early Western Australian Renaissance'[4] have been used and continue to be used loosely and often interchangeably. Most importantly, no assessment has been made of these buildings in terms of the meanings ascribed to them by their designers, their owners, or the general public.

Given this ill-defined situation, what is surprising is the importance attached to this group of buildings and the significant role they play in what is best described as the architectural folklore of Western Australia. In this interpretation two architects, Rodney Alsop and Marshall Clifton, stand out with an almost mythic clarity. The story begins with the Hackett Memorial Buildings at the University of Western Australia (1927–31) which, it has been suggested, were 'to have a profound influence on later buildings on the campus and in the state'.[5] Influenced by Professor Leslie Wilkinson,[6] Rodney Alsop in the Hackett Memorial Buildings, and in the later houses he designed during the early thirties, introduced the concept of the 'Mediterranean' style as an ideal type for a 'British community' living in Western Australia.[7]

Impressed by these buildings, the young Marshall Clifton travelled to Europe and Spain, returning to Perth in the mid-thirties to build the two 'classic' Western Australian examples of the genre in the Clifton House (1937) and the Day House (1939). These works by Clifton have been assigned a complex and pivotal role in the architectural history of post-war Western Australia. On the one hand, they are identified as significant examples of the romantic and eclectic design tendencies of Perth architecture in the inter-war years, largely due to the correct manner in which they conform to accepted criteria for the 'Spanish style'.

> Italian or Southern European style may be recognised by the free use of circular arches in colonnades and entrance porches, together with broad wall surfaces of tinted plaster of varying textures, shuttered windows and deep shadows into which sun can never penetrate. Roofs [that] are flat and should, strictly speaking, be of the pan-tile type.[8]

Stressing the correctness of this stylistically-oriented design process in these examples places the process in a reasonable light, while at the same time drawing the *orientation* to a close – a closure reinforced by the architectural hiatus that resulted from the Second World War.

On the other hand, by interpreting these works in terms of climate and function it was possible to view them quite differently and argue a case for their being the first tentative steps towards modernism. As Ian Molyneux remarks:

> [Clifton's] own house in Johnson Street [sic], Mosman Park, was designed in about 1937, soon after his return from a tour of Spain. Despite the anti-rationalist, romantic act of selection of an identifiable style, and despite the picturesque, artful manner in which subjective criteria of design are met, the house is quite modern in several ways. The white reflective walls, shuttered small openings, and T-shaped plan (casting shade onto terraces in reveals of the T) are all conscious devices in response to climatic conditions, and the main functional areas of the house are clearly zoned. The stylism of the house simply moderates the expression of these zones whereas a more 'modern' house might have aggressively asserted them.[9]

While this interpretation of the role of the 'Spanish style' in Western Australia's architectural development before and after the War possesses a powerful dramatic order, it is not factually sustainable.[10] The 'precursor' reading fails to grasp what the 'Spanish scene' represented for the young architects who were concerned with its development during the late twenties and thirties.

The Spanish scene was not a stylistically-inhibited fumbling towards the plain truth that modernism represented, but an intuitive critique of modernism and the exploration of an alternative architectural model that was felt to be better suited to Western Australia's environmental conditions and social aspirations. But were Western Australian architects in the late twenties and thirties aware of architectural events in Europe as this concept of a critique suggests?

It appears that the architectural profession was well aware of architectural ideas and events in England, Europe and America, even if they did not always favour what was happening. In 1927, the Royal Institute of Architects of Western Australia (RIAWA) President, Mr ARL Wright, commented somewhat uncharitably: 'In Germany, Holland and France, many young architects have *put aside all precedent* in an endeavour to invent something absolutely new and modern, and have succeeded in producing monstrosities such as the world has never seen before. Oh! for a plague to cut them all off!'[11]

During the period that we are focusing upon, most significant Western Australian architects travelled both nationally and internationally. Also, due to the importance of boat travel and the stays in Fremantle required to refuel and reprovision, as well as disembark and take on passengers, it was possible to interview and entertain anyone with architectural interests and opinions who passed through Perth, most of whom were reported in the local newspapers and in the architectural and technical press. Figures as different as Sir John Sulman, Professor Wilkinson and the young Best Overend all contributed to the local architectural debate in this way. If the weekly trade publication *Building and Construction* is representative, then it would be reasonable to suggest that Western Australian architects were indeed aware of the impact of the modern movement and the work of the major architectural figures of the day. Even Richard Buckminster Fuller and his Dymaxion House project were reported, somewhat sceptically it is true, in September 1931.[12] It is with this awareness in mind that the development of the 'Spanish style' in Western Australia needs to be explored.

The first *clearly defined*[13] examples of the 'Spanish style' in Perth were not the works of Rodney Alsop, but of the 'glamorous' 29-year-old Perth engineer/architect Reginald Summerhayes (1897–1965) who returned to Perth in 1926 to become a partner in his father's well-established practice. Reginald Summerhayes had already experienced an extraordinary early career that included service with the Royal Engineers during the First World War and, subsequently, a period of years as an architect in Singapore with the firm of Swan and McLaren.

Almost immediately on his return, Summerhayes designed two houses based upon Spanish precedent; the first for his friend, the solicitor RD Forbes (1927), and the second for himself (1928). There is no evidence to indicate that Summerhayes was aware of, much less influenced by, Professor Wilkinson's house designs of the twenties and the first of his own projects predates the announcement of the Hackett Memorial Buildings competition results for which a Summerhayes entry was awarded a creditable fourth prize.[14] If these 'Spanish style' houses have any physical, rather than intellectual, models they would appear to be the housing designs that Summerhayes undertook during his Singapore stay.[15] Thus, at least in its Western Australian mode, the 'Spanish style' appears to have enjoyed a hot-humid Singapore stopover during its journey to Perth.

Building and Construction reported on the first of these projects in December 1927. In an article that appears to be a collaboration between Summerhayes and the editor, the background and design rationale of the 'Spanish style' is so succinctly identified that it is worth quoting at length:

> The Spanish style [is] becoming popular in domestic architecture and threatens to become the vogue so far as Brisbane is concerned. It is a simple adaptation of *rural Spanish* architecture, a style that has become known in Florida and other American states as the 'Mediterranean type' on account of its similarity to dwellings which may be seen on the shores of the Mediterranean. This style should be eminently suitable to adoption to Western Australian homes, as it has proved to be so successful in countries whose climatic conditions are identical to those of this State. For this style to meet with a degree of success, the architect must treat his building on very definite and simple lines; for the general effect is dependent wholly upon general mass and simple roof lines. For interesting colour notes, the characteristic 'Spanish' tile is used which should possess a blending from light buff to mulberry. Window openings are usually emphasised by wrought iron grilles designed upon lines of restraint and refinement and such features as entrance doors and other openings should be provided with deep recesses, rough textured stucco [should be used] for external wall finishes, combined with glazed tiling, in the form of panels where interest is required.[16]

What were the issues embodied in this design that seemed significant and justified the heading 'A new design in architecture for WA – an excellent example of Mediterranean design'?[17]

Firstly, the evocation of a Western Australian architecture. The use of the 'Spanish style' and, possibly even better, its American or Californian derivative, was seen as appropriate architectural borrowing, or 'doing the right thing', in ARL Wright's phrase. However, it is important to understand that this value was argued only in local terms. For the editor of *Building and Construction*, Spanish and Spanish Mission were understood as regional, not national, styles and their adoption in Western Australia was justified in regional rather than national terms.[18] Professor Wilkinson contributed to this view in his Perth pronouncement of 1934 in which he said: 'There could not be a distinct Australian type of architecture.'[19] Wilkinson was in this case arguing for a regional approach to the development of architectural form in Australia.

Secondly, the 'Spanish style' was justified on social grounds by its appropriateness to the Western Australian social milieu. The courts, loggias and other forms of partially enclosed outdoor rooms that resulted from the preferred plan forms were seen as ideal settings for the casual, relaxed, suburban lifestyle that was, and still is, characteristic of Perth.

Thirdly, the adoption or adaptation of these forms was justified on the basis of observable and objective parallels in climatic and environmental patterns.

All these justifications for stylistic adaptation are, of course, well-known and have been advanced in other Australian circumstances. However, one final argument is possibly more unusual. It was proposed that the forms possessed value because they were *new*, at least in Western Australia. As *Building and Construction* puts it, 'the home when completed; will strike quite a new note in domestic architecture in this state'.[20]

The Forbes House was never completed as initially proposed. The 'shock of the new' put forward as one of the virtues of the 'Spanish style' was to prove a difficulty and the Forbes House and the later Summerhayes House, when built in 1928, did not match the original stylistic vision. In order to realise these projects they had to be *conventionalised*, both visually and constructionally, but I will return to this later.

Marshall Clifton (1903–75) was a recently qualified architect in 1928 when the Forbes and Summerhayes houses were built; he received his architectural training in the Western Australian Public Works Department, possibly the only Perth practice whose work reflected the influence of the ideas and example of Professor Wilkinson.[21] That Clifton knew of the Summerhayes projects is certain; after all, the architectural profession in Perth was then a small group and Summerhayes had become a successful, influential and dynamic member of it. Whether Clifton ever read the initial report of the Forbes House is not known, but he visited Summerhayes socially on occasion and in the thirties was to become a friend and, for a period, an architectural associate.

Whether these projects and others that Summerhayes built in the 'Spanish style'[22] were influential is not clear, but in 1930 Clifton set out on a three-year odyssey to England and Europe. During his travels, he visited Russia to 'investigate the latest developments in architecture and the new social conditions under the socialist regime'.[23] What impressed him was not the new architecture, but the social programs it sought to satisfy. He rarely spoke of the modern architectural works that he visited in Russia and elsewhere then, or in his later life. At the time he felt that they were based on 'a wrong interpretation of functionalism'.[24]

On the other hand, what he saw and experienced in Spain was to nurture him for the rest of his architectural career. It was not the romantic imagery that was central, despite its obvious charm, but the power of so many environmental examples that confirmed the value of his early farming experience and emphasised the value of a simple, direct, precedent-oriented approach to architectural design. Clifton's 'design touchstone' became what he called the 'peasant Spanish home' and others have termed the 'rural vernacular'. The sort of functionalism seen in this architecture seemed for Clifton to be more an embodiment of the social environment, revealing patterns of architectural form that seemed to evolve out of common and well-understood social rituals.

On his return to Perth in December 1932, Clifton first accepted a partnership with a well-established older architect, George Herbert Parry (1882–1951), and then in 1937 started his own practice. With the Clifton House (September 1937) and the house for his friend Dr J Day (June 1939), he produced a pair of works that form an interesting parallel with the Summerhayes projects of a decade earlier.

In the case of the earlier projects the houses, in their initial form, were not compatible with the usual Western Australian home building practices and traditions, and a number of difficulties arose. In comparison to more typical building forms, 'Spanish style' buildings tended to be costly to build and more difficult to maintain. For this reason Summerhayes had to modify the design of the Forbes House and build what was, to all intents and purposes, a traditional house with Spanish touches. The sectional drawings in the built versions of both houses make this conversion process clear. A decade later

Marshall Clifton was able to build what he drew without the necessity to re-design using more conventional forms and constructional methods. To this extent, over the decade there had been a change in local design awareness and constructional practice. It is difficult to perceive today, but these Spanish villas in Western Australia, proposed by young architects at the beginnings of their careers, are 'ideas' buildings that were both conceptually and constructionally new to their designers and the public. Because they were new, and a little shocking, they could initially only be proposed with certainty for the architects' families, or for close and trusting friends wealthy enough to pay the price of the new.

The Spanish villas designed by Summerhayes and Clifton were experimental buildings that embodied a social vision of a comfortable, generous and safe suburban lifestyle, coupled with a regionally appropriate physical environment to support and make this social vision possible. These projects may appear to be worlds apart from the villas that Le Corbusier was building in Europe during the same period and they are. Where they differ is in their objectives, values and techniques. These Australian villas are alternatives to and not precursors of modernism.

In 1932, one of Perth's many visitors, the Melbourne architect JH Butler, optimistically remarked that 'it is unlikely that we [Australians] would adopt the cold modernistic architecture of central Europe'[25] when we had the option of the 'Spanish style' before us. He was wrong of course, but it is a point of view that Clifton would have endorsed. Marshall Clifton was the only Perth architect to carry this pre-war vision on into his large body of post-war housing and to achieve an extraordinary transmutation of the 'Spanish style' into a simple housing vernacular. This body of work is so typically and essentially Western Australian in its social and physical aspirations and forms that it has become virtually invisible, neither recognised nor valued by the architectural fraternity but only by owners and users.[26]

Finally, it must be recognised that there has always been another aspect to the 'Spanish style', the dark side of The Force perhaps! This involved an emphasis on the flamboyant, exotic and cosmetic application of stylistic elements. This has not been a significant aspect of the 'Spanish style' in Western Australia, but it has been evident.[27] For example, Sir Bernard Evans created a 'Med' fantasy for the entrepreneur Claude de Bernales at Cottesloe in the mid-thirties.[28] In recent years, this tendency has re-emerged in Western Australian architecture. Possibly the best example (or worst, depending upon your point of view) is 'El Caballo Blanco', a successful tourist facility and hotel situated in the Darling Ranges outside Perth. It is intellectually and visually appropriate that the facility offers daily visits by Zorro to entertain the guests – undoubtedly to make his mark! The source of this side of the 'Spanish style' in the hype of Hollywood is clearly revealed.

If there was anything Marshall Clifton would have disliked more than the modern movement it would be this devaluation of forms and symbols; for he believed, both architecturally and socially, that 'simplicity is the first effort in the direction of order'.[29]

Kenneth Frampton and the Fiction of Place

1991

PAUL WALKER

Reviewing Kenneth Frampton's *Modern Architecture: A Critical History*, Alan Colquhoun notes that in the introduction to the book Frampton 'points correctly to the difficulty of deciding where to begin a history of modern architecture, but he does not mention the equally difficult problems of how to end it'.[1] I will be using the position at which Frampton problematically ends the 1985 edition of his *Modern Architecture* as my starting point in this paper: the idea of a critical regionalism in which history, critique and advocacy become inextricably entwined. But critical regionalism, Frampton points out in the preface to the book, is not a clearly defined school of architecture, movement or group of designers. It is a 'critical category' – a product of historiography – which he uses to 'draw attention to the fact that a regionally inflected but critical and "revisionist" form of modern architecture has been in existence for the past forty years or more'.[2]

What characterises critical regionalism? At the end of the book Frampton makes seven points.[3]

1. Critical regionalism is critical of modernism, but while eschewing modernist utopianism and the 'big plan' it abandons neither modern technology nor the emancipatory sociopolitical intent of the modern movement. Critical regionalism is not a revival of the vernacular.

Embracing what Frampton has called universal civilisation (the instruments and techniques that modernisation affords), this regionalism nevertheless inflects the accoutrements of such civilisation so that local culture is extended rather than replaced.

Jorn Utzon's Bagsvaerd Church is frequently cited by Frampton as a case of such an inflection of universal technique: arranged upon a grid, it employs rationalised modular building systems, but conjoins these with the idiosyncratic form of a sinuously profiled concrete shell vault on the interior. But surely this is what architects do with technology all the time, more or less successfully. And how, we might begin to wonder already, can such inflection of form and detail have social or political bearing?

2. Critical regionalism conceives of architecture not as the free-standing building, but rather as a bounded domain or a 'place-form'. Paradigmatic is Mario Botta's dictum that in building we should 'build the site'. The architecture should be configured onto and into the site such that it defines or gathers a locale around it, which entails also that each building task be thought of as discrete.

With this notion Frampton signals his allegiance to the Heideggerian notion of *Raum*, which he interprets as place in contradistinction to space.[4] He also has in mind Hannah Arendt's views on the *polis* and political life, for the polis is the 'bounded place-form' in its public mode.[5]

3. Critical regionalism emphasises architecture as a 'tectonic fact' rather than a semiotic system. 'We may speak here of the presentation of a structural poetic rather than the representation of a facade.'[6]

Frampton disparages much postmodern practice – that of Venturi, Moore, Graves and Portoghesi – insofar as it is scenographic. This is to say that in postmodern architecture the expressive 'system' of the building and those systems that hold it up and keep it watertight and so on, are considered quite distinctly. To be fair, Frampton sees Venturi's position in *Complexity and Contradiction in Architecture* as almost all right in its advocacy of a judicious borrowing of elements from commercial culture. But *Learning from Las Vegas* is beyond the pale.[7] Further, Frampton's attack on scenography could be sympathetically read as an implicit criticism of the narrativisation of architecture that has occurred in the wake of postmodernism and which continues apace even without the borrowed, historic attire. Such criticism is necessary.

However, on the other hand, to be fair to the postmodernists and their apologists in turn, it must be pointed out that Frampton does not generally acknowledge that the impetus for scenographic postmodernism – misdirected, perhaps – came from genuine social concerns about most of the population having been disenfranchised from any kind of identification with their built environment. People do not like architecture now. But Frampton would rather continue with the empty sign of modernism.[8] He sees the postmodern as nothing but a further commercial commodification of architecture, an appeasement of capital. 'In contradistinction to Critical Regionalism, the primary vehicle of Populism is the *communicative* or *instrumental* sign. Such a sign seeks to evoke, not a critical perception of reality, but rather the sublimation of a desire for direct experience through the provision of information.'[9] Is there any such thing, though, as direct, unmediated experience, any apprehension of the world that could not – however churlishly – be characterised as the provision of information? Frampton believes there *is* a fundamental distinction between 'intellection' and 'the phenomenological perception of built form'.[10]

In dismissing the populism of the postmodernists, Frampton has overlooked another significant point often made from within their ranks: that public architecture (which is to say all architecture in some degree) addresses itself inevitably to more than one cultural group. This is a particularly pertinent idea in New Zealand. Where would the discourse on biculturalism that exercises architectural thinkers and historians here now belong in this regionalism?

The answer is 'nowhere'. For Frampton's advocacy of a local poetics of the tectonic is a retrieval of architecture for high culture. This is a retrieval for which I might personally *feel* some sympathy – I have never felt comfortable with the equation of architecture with social work – but I find it hard to *think* about it sympathetically in view of Frampton's claim that critical regionalism is to be an architecture of cultural resistance. For I do not see how the return of architecture to some sort of aesthetics as its formative base can be thought of as anything but reactionary: 'the primary principle of architectural autonomy

... is embodied in the revealed ligaments of the construction and in the way in which the syntactical form of the structure explicitly resists the action of gravity'.[11]

Disturbing as this elevation of an architectural aesthetics based on a connoisseurship of construction may be, in the political-cultural discourse in which it is proffered, equally disturbing is the result of the application to pre-modern architecture of the tectonic alone as a criterion of aesthetic value. Out it all goes. For what is the baroque if not scenographic? (Here one would like to ask of Frampton whether or not the curvaceous interior treatment at Bagsvaerd might not, itself, be a remnant of baroque scene-setting.) And can the idealised coding of construction in both the classical tradition and the gothic (Viollet-le-Duc aside) be seen as anything, in Frampton's eyes, but a scenographic misrepresentation of the 'tectonic facts'?

4. Critical regionalism stresses site-specific factors – topography, light, climate. Place characteristics are properly derived from landscape. Culture is rooted in the soil.

Of course this carries the corollary that cultures that are not so rooted, that do not have land, are somehow improper. Certainly they cannot have proper place forms. The 'Gypsies', whom Suzanne Langer describes in her *Feeling and Form* taking their 'place', the camp, with them wherever they go, are only deluding themselves.[12] Peripatetic academics might seem to be another shifty lot.

5. Critical regionalism emphasises the tactile and other sensuous characteristics as much as the visual.

Connected with this idea are Frampton's complaints about the impact of photography on architecture. These are made in *Modern Architecture* and elsewhere.[13] 'The veil that photolithography draws over architecture is not neutral. High-speed photographic and reproductive processes are surely not only the political economy of the sign but also an insidious filter through which our tactile environment tends to lose its concrete responsiveness.'

Buildings come to be made to be photographed rather than to be touched. Frampton is right. But I cannot feel as outraged about this as he does, for do not those of us on the periphery, the regions, gain from the photographic representations of buildings extant at centres remote from us? 'Authentic experience' of this architecture simply isn't feasible out here at the edge of the world. We might draw the conclusion, uncharitably, that Frampton thinks only of his own pleasures. Less charitably still, we might wonder how he comes to know all the buildings about which he writes.

6. Critical regionalism occasionally uses 'reinterpreted' vernacular elements, both local and imported, to further inflect its use of contemporary technology. 'In this regard, [critical regionalism] tends towards the paradoxical creation of a regionally based "world culture", almost as though this were a precondition for achieving a relevant form of contemporary practice.'[14]

I am not sure just what this means but suspect that it may open an abyss down which the whole project of critical regionalism may disappear. Consider the piece that Frampton wrote about the Riverside Centre in Brisbane, a forty-storey office tower on the edge of the Brisbane River designed by Harry Seidler with all his usual *élan*. Frampton gushes:

> With its arbitrarily placed 'facade-terraces' and its lush tropical landscaping and outriding organic forms (the curvaceously profiled restaurants and terraces that flank the river) and above all with its rationally articulated central structure, Riverside may be read as a tectonically rigorous but topographically inflected work; as a building that consciously mediates between the demands of universal civilisation and the constraints of topos, between the received standards of a global practice and a critical commitment to the cultivation of a local identity and culture.[15]

However, he goes on to write of a resistant culture and acts of defiance. But what is it that Riverside is resisting? What is defied? The reflective glass of the AMP Building down the road? Certainly Riverside does not defy those principal adversaries of the locally inflected cityscape that Frampton points to elsewhere, 'the freestanding high-rise and the serpentine freeway'.[16] It *is* a freestanding high-rise. Or does that correspondence suggested by Seidler for the sunshades on the tower to the awnings of the vernacular Queensland house, and the Burle-Marx landscaping at the base, compensate for the participation of the tower in 'megalopolitan' development (it is a big building) and even overcome that participation to such a degree that the whole can be fairly seen as 'an act of defiance or as a lucid challenge to the juggernaut of consumerism'?[17]

I do not believe so. Nor do I believe they are even symptomatic of some general cultural condition that desires to resist. Rather, Frampton's aesthetic judgments, sympathetic to the forms and procedures of modernism, have overcome his political stance. The 'phenomenology of experience' has been allowed to usurp intellection. It is only with this kind of slippage that regionalism and world culture can be seen as the same thing.

7. Critical regionalism 'suggests that the received notion of the dominant cultural centre surrounded by dependent, dominated satellites is ultimately an inadequate model by which to assess the present state of modern architecture'.[18]

It is, of course, for this reason that we are interested in regionalism here, not only because much of the building fabric that surrounds us is in some way regionally inflected, but also because discourse on regionalism surely belongs most properly to the regions. Our readings of the flood of books that arrive from the metropolitan centres might not be the canonical ones because we cannot readily participate in the interpretative community wherein such material is produced. But we do know what it is to think and experience at the margins.

There are further things to say in regard to Frampton and the reputed dissolution or diminishment of the dominating role of the centres of Western culture in the postmodern moment. I will return to these issues further along. But having laid out and partially criticised Frampton's seven features or attitudes of critical regionalism, I want now to offer some more general discussion, for the points raised thus far in critique might be criticised themselves for exploiting paradoxes that Frampton acknowledges in his work, and for selecting atypical cases.

There are three questions I wish to ask. Firstly: is a general theory of the specific possible? Does such a question have an answer? Maybe a logician could tell us if there is a Cretan paradox lurking here or not. But perhaps a way of answering would be to say that a metacriticism or a metahistoriography is indeed conceivable, within which general statements about the nature of the specific, global statements about the regional are viable. Such statements would not have bearing on particular critical occasions, which would retain their individuality, specific terms of reference, precedent, cultural context, and so forth. But what is striking about Frampton's writing (history or criticism – who knows?) is that when it addresses the specific instance – always for Frampton a building – the uniqueness of the situation slips away. This quality in Frampton's critical discourse on buildings has been noted also by David Dunster.[19] It shows in two ways. On the one hand, there is a tendency always to see buildings as symptoms of some cultural condition (and therefore not actually an integral part of it – Frampton castigates Portoghesi for suggesting that we think with buildings as well as about them)[20] and, on the other hand, a tendency to see them all in relation to a common repertoire of ideas and precedents. Thus are a building in Japan by Fumihiko Maki, a building by Alvaro Siza in Portugal, and Frank Lloyd Wright's Johnson Wax administration building, all related by Frampton in some way to Pierre Chareau's Maison de Verre in Paris of 1932.[21]

Less incidentally than this (Frampton obviously likes the Maison de Verre!) it is necessary to observe that criticism and history are, like buildings, produced in specific situations and might therefore be expected to have their own regional inflections, their own specific attributes.

This kind of specificity is not found in Frampton's texts. To my knowledge Frampton has published the following, more-or-less alike, papers: 'Towards a Critical Regionalism: Six Points for an Architecture of Resistance,' 'Prospects for a Critical Regionalism', 'Modern Architecture and Critical Regionalism' (1983), 'Critical Regionalism: Modern Architecture and Cultural Identity', 'Critical Regionalism: Speculations on an Architecture of Identity' (1985) and 'Ten Points on an Architecture of Regionalism: A Provisional Polemic' (1987). Closely related is another piece published in 1988 called 'Intimations of Tactility: Excerpts from a Fragmentary Polemic'.[22]

All but one of these (the piece published in 1987 in a journal called *Center*) begin with a quotation from Paul Ricœur's essay 'Universal Civilisation and National Cultures'.[23] Six of them refer to Heidegger's famous essay 'Building, Dwelling, Thinking' and the idea of *Raum*. Four of them cite Luis Barragan on a memory of his childhood village. Three of them relate the story of Lucio Visconti's insisting that the floors of the main set he used for filming *The Damned* be clad in real parquet so the actors would assume a proper gait and posture, and then go on to mention that a similar tactile sensitivity is found in Aalto's Saynatsalo Town Hall. In another, Saynatsalo appears immediately followed by Visconti. The point here is not to reflect on Frampton's repetitiveness as some kind of fault. Rather, it is indicative of a position (a carefully bounded textual place) that has been thoughtfully assumed and confidently proselytised. Of course there are differences in these papers: one lists six points towards critical regionalism, another seven; one makes ten points in a 'provisional polemic'; another consists of 21 polemical fragments. Nevertheless, all these different hands have been dealt from the same rather limited pack of shuffled cards. They constitute a single game, a single universal argument.

This brings me to my second question. Does Frampton play out the very dominance of the regions by the metropolitan centre, universal civilisation, that his critical regionalism repudiates? What comes to mind here, of course, is Frampton's own location at one of the supreme metropolitan centres, New York.

How can it be that the home of the principal current theorist of regional architecture is at the centre, given that, as was suggested earlier, the proper locus for making such theory is the regions themselves. There is a sense, then, in which the discourse on regionalism has been appropriated by the centre, with Frampton as agent of this appropriation. This kind of claiming of positions, which in the postmodern world have been theoretically elevated, has apparently occurred in other fields too. Craig Owens, in his essay in the book *The Anti-Aesthetic*, which includes one of Frampton's earlier critical regionalism texts, writes about an interrogation of binarism occurring after modernism, an interrogation that would reject the critical value of paired oppositional terms such as presence/absence, nature/culture, male/female, signified/signifier ... and, we could add, centre/margins (and in New Zealand, Pakeha/Maori).[24] But such oppositions are not, in fact, overcome or disregarded. Rather, what has happened is that the second term in each pair has apparently assumed the privilege formerly enjoyed by the first. Further, though the distribution of privilege among these signifiers has changed, the discourses in which they are employed have not. Commenting (rightly or wrongly) on how few women have participated in the modernism/postmodernism debate, Owens suggests that 'postmodernism may be another masculine invention engineered to exclude women'. This exclusion is engineered by the appropriation of the feminist voice to play a role in the discourse of male critics.[25]

Reconsidering Frampton's regionalism in light of this discussion, it is interesting to consider the geographical distribution of the locations that he investigates. In the piece with which I began they are: Denmark, Catalonia, Mexico, the Napa Valley, Greece and Japan. Mostly they are not so far from the main metropolitan centres physically, politically or culturally. (Frampton's map of the world must look like one of those distorted ones the surrealists drew.) Most telling is the treatment of the Swiss cantons as paradigmatic regional enclaves. Writes Frampton:

> Switzerland, with its intricate linguistic boundaries and its tradition of cosmopolitanism, has always displayed strong regionalist tendencies. The cantonal principle of admission and exclusion has favoured extremely dense forms of expression, with the canton favouring local culture and the Federation facilitating the penetration and assimilation of foreign ideas.[26]

He goes on to discuss the architecture of the canton of Ticino in particular. But is not Switzerland, like other Western European countries, a chief beneficiary of the universal civilisation, the capitalism that it helped to invent? Prosperity is among the factors leading to the emergence of regionalist architecture, notes Frampton.[27] Perhaps critical regionalism is, then, not so much an inflection of universal civilisation as a reflection of where the capital it produces is accruing. 'Authentic' experience is only for the wealthy.

Not all the places Frampton mentions are, of course, as affluent as Switzerland. But the discussion of Ticino is given many paragraphs, while Brazilian regionalism, for instance, is covered by a passing mention of the early work of Oscar Niemeyer and Alfonso Reidy, work carried out in the 1940s.[28] Is there nothing to say of building in Brazil now? In Frampton's mental map of the regions, Ticino looms larger than Brazil; Switzerland is more important than the whole of South America. This is a reflection of economic facts rather than phenomenal ones.

The final question I wish to address is that of whether critical regionalism is viable as a general strategy for configuring and reconfiguring the whole built environment, or a formula for limited resistance only. A project like Seidler's Riverside Centre is a model for mainstream architectural practice. It has qualities we would like to see in all such buildings, assuming that they are an inevitability. But, suggests Frampton, critical regionalism is fragmentary only, not a general model. 'It flourishes sporadically within cultural fissures that articulate in unexpected ways the continents of Europe and America.'[29] Important here is the idea that regional architecture will be manifested as the bounded domain – in a sense as a *hortus conclusus*. (The image of a garden is not incidental. Frampton has said that 'any kind of critical practice worthy of the name would have to concern itself with a new relationship between human artifacts and nature.'[30] In the garden these come together.)

Frampton contends that such closed architectural configurations can maintain 'an expressive density and resonance', opening the inhabitant or visitor to experiences that are potentially liberative. They are liberative insofar as they are a reminder that things can be other. In such enclaves the 'ceaseless inundation of a place-less, alienating consumerism will find itself *momentarily* checked'.[31] These enclaves are small (even the exemplary Swiss cantons cannot sustain a critical architecture past the scale of a Mario Botta house[32]). They intimate a redemption of the material world, but do not make the means of any general redemption apparent. It remains a matter of (good) faith. Perhaps this explains the importance of Bagsvaerd to Frampton; it is, after all, a church.

The idea of the redemptive enclave, interesting as it is, does not, however, entail the idea of regionalism. Can not a liberating aesthetic experience be had in such a piece of picturesque but regionally inappropriate fakery as a walled Chinese garden in Vancouver? Or an art gallery? It is also unclear as to whether such experience, though it be enjoyed at Bagsvaerd or among mock rocks, might not just as well be characterised as mere respite from or compensation for the daily life shaped by capitalism, which, surrounding the garden, underwriting it even, continues unabated. Politics and phenomenal experience are, then, the terms we are left with after this explication of critical regionalism.

With respect to the experience of place, 'authentic', unmediated experience is not possible. Our minds are never empty. In his calls for the authentic, Frampton implicitly invokes the *genii loci* that Norberg-Schulz calls on directly. Thomas Schumacher has commented in regard to this that 'the "spirit of place" is to contemporary architects what the "spirit of the age" was to the architects of the modern movement. *Zeitgeist* has been replaced by *genius loci*.'[33] The latter is as misguided as the former. Frampton is caught in a trap described by Derrida in his writing on representation, the trap of a surrender to a returned desire for presence, for a plenteous reality.[34] But such authentic experience can be postulated only when there is a general experience of *inauthenticity* from which it can be projected and represented as a theory.

If this investigation of Frampton's arguments has resulted in the rejection of much, nevertheless the ideas of region and enclave or place are important ones still for any discourse – historiographical or critical – that address architecture now. But I want to suggest as a concluding point that these are terms that refer not to essences but to political entities. Places are formed through politics and not the other way round. Frampton does allude to the political dimension of the region: 'an aspiration at least to some form of cultural, economic and political independence' is a contributing factor to the emergence of a regionalism.[35] But in a slight, though suggestive, piece Colquhoun has written of another kind of regionalism than Frampton's:

> This regionalism exists as part of the unconscious ideologies underlying current practice and is connected with the actual political economic situation whose modalities are only indirectly related to any supposedly indigenous culture. It is the result of a complex interaction between modern international capitalism and various national traditions ingrained in institutions and attitudes.[36]

The sharpest differences between any two architectural cultures – those of Australia and New Zealand, for example – are not to be explained by climate or topography or any *genius loci* but rather through their different institutional and political contexts, their different social and cultural histories, their different *fictional* landscapes.

The Imperial Technology Cringe

1996

MILES LEWIS

Architecture and building in the British Empire was in many respects not so much colonial as simply British. So far as Anglo settlers were concerned there was not a relationship of ruler and ruled, or exploiter and exploitee. They were British citizens in a greater Britain. The status and facilities of Melbourne were comparable with those of Manchester. Manufacturers of building materials were more likely to send their sons to represent their company in an Australasian colony than in a British provincial town.

Impressions of the Antipodes

British visitors to the Australasian colonies in the nineteenth century commonly reported on how like home the towns were, and how well established they seemed to be. But as the century drew on there was less emphasis on the surprisingly British appearance of these outposts in the wilderness, and more acceptance of them as being simply British towns. Their inhabitants saw themselves as British citizens, and many Australian natives even after the Second World War still spoke of Britain as 'Home'.

Melbourne was a little different, for by the 1880s it was the third most populous city in the Empire, excluding India. In his *Victorian Cities*, Asa Briggs treated Melbourne, along with Manchester, Middlesborough and others, as Victorian cities, and like other writers before and since, he quoted GA Sala's reference to 'Marvellous Melbourne'. There was a period of about 40 years when some visitors at least could regard Melbourne as being as good as or better than an English provincial city. Some saw it as a bit brash and American, but even the Americanism could be a matter of surprise only because the place was otherwise assumed to be basically British.

I by no means wish to confine myself to Melbourne, or to the four decades of Melbourne ascendancy, but it is true that that city and that period are key to the wider situation. Melbourne was the centre of technical development and manufacturing. Patents would be taken out first in Victoria, and subsequently in the other colonies. There was no British city other than London that played such a focal role. It was a role that began quite abruptly in 1853, when the scale of gold discoveries and the scale of the resultant immigration became apparent.

In 1854, one of those immigrants wrote to his friends in London, bubbling over with excitement, describing a whole range of public and private buildings in progress. They were explicitly compared with their London prototypes – a shopping arcade that resembled the Lowther, another arcade even better, and a horse bazaar that far excelled Tattersall's in London: 'We have a very fine arcade – something like the Lowther – cost a little over £30,000 and another erecting which for elegance of design far outstrips the other: it is estimated to cost £180,000. Tattersall's Grand Horse Bazaar outdoes anything I have yet seen for horses: Tattersall's at home a mere shed to it.'[1] Puffery, perhaps, but when cable trams appeared ahead of all English cities but London, there was something more to it. Even that was hardly proof of Melbourne's importance, as GS Duncan, who did the job, had already built the first line outside America – in Dunedin, New Zealand. Dunedin, Melbourne, and a dozen or so colonial cities were rivals, not satellites of the great provincial centres of England.

Intercolonialism

Even more important than the boom episodes, like that created by the gold rush in Melbourne, was the enduring intercolonial culture. From the first days there had been troops and traders and administrators whose world was intercolonial. They may still have thought of England as home, but the reality was that they had long been garrisoned in Canada, or grown indigo in India, or been in government service in the Caribbean. England knew little of their clapboard houses, jalousies, ventilating monitors, flat roofs, evaporative cooling devices and *chunam* plaster.

James Broadbent first drew my attention to Robert and Helenus Scott, settlers at 'Glendon', New South Wales, one or both of whom invented 'Scott's Oixianathumator or House Cooler'. The Scotts were of Indian colonial background, and seem to have drawn upon an established Eastern tradition – forms of evaporative cooling had been regularly used in the royal palaces of Persia and India.[2] In colonial times in India, doors and windows were fitted with tatties or screens made from the fibrous roots of sweet-smelling khai grass, and in hot weather servants splashed these with water.[3] This was the principle of the Scotts' invention.

In Scott's Oixianathumator, as Broadbent describes it, 'a curtain of calico suspended before a window was kept moistened by a controlled flow of water fed from a cistern to the rod holding it'.[4] Almost precisely the same thing was suggested in 1859 by the Victorian architect Francis White as a way of cooling Parliament House, Melbourne. White speaks of hanging coir matting over the windows of the building and keeping it saturated with water by means of a perforated copper tube over each window, this being fitted with a stopcock to turn the water on and off. His proposal was in effect to turn Parliament House into a giant Coolgardie safe. There is no suggestion that White had any knowledge of the Scotts' invention, and indeed he freely acknowledges his source, referring to it as 'the Indian method'.[5] He was drawing directly upon the same Indian tradition as the Scotts.

It was also in 1859, and it may well be connected with the work at Parliament House, that TW Badham of Richmond, Melbourne, obtained a patent for a method 'by which air entering the room is saturated by being made to pass over wet surfaces'.[6] What these methods do, of course, is to achieve evaporative cooling at the expense of humidification, which is quite different (pace Broadbent) from the modern concept of air conditioning, in which both the temperature and the humidity are controlled.

By 1888 the oixianathumator reappeared with Chinese overtones at Hay, New South Wales, where 'Czar Lodge' had 'Chinese curtains' hung in front of the verandah in hot weather, 'surmounted by a perforated pipe from which water is allowed to drip upon the curtains, thereby rendering the atmosphere within delightfully cool as well as shielding the brick walls from the sun's rays'.[7] In the 1930s at Thylungra station in western Queensland, the main house had projecting from it a semi-enclosed room known as the 'birdcage' clad in hessian over 42 × 1½ × 17 rabbit netting[8] with taps at intervals around the top, from which water dripped onto the hessian.[9]

Evaporative cooling is satisfactory only in a hot and very dry climate, and would be quite unsuitable in a humid climate such as that of Sydney. In a drier climate it can be very effective, and the Adelaide Club is cooled to this day by tatties, which are wetted with a drenching apparatus. The first tatties appear to have been ordered in September 1893 through the secretary of the Madras Club, two of 2.25 × 4.95 metres, two of 3.45 × 2.78 metres, and one of 2.7 × 3.13 metres, with the bottom cut away in a large upward-pointing V rising 2.1 metres, presumably to allow for walking underneath. The arrival of these was acknowledged in January 1894 and a further set were ordered to arrive in September-October 1895; then a further order was placed in February 1897.[10] The material of the original blinds, which were replaced from India every year or two, is not known, but it may have been sisal. In recent times coir matting from South Africa has been used, and at the time of inspection the current set had been in place for eleven years.[11]

The punkah was known in Mogul India, and was first adopted by Europeans in Bengal in the 1780s.[12] In 1830, it was specifically advocated for use in Australia by an old India hand, TW Maslen, who suggested that 'it might be kept in motion by some simple machinery' (rather than being operated manually by a punkah wallah in the traditional fashion).[13] By the mid-nineteenth century the device was well known and was discussed by Charles Tomlinson in his *Warming and Ventilation*,[14] where he refers to those of the Nabob of Oude, which were indeed worked by a steam engine imported from England. The government resident at Roeboume, Western Australia, in the 1880s fitted his house with punkahs, consistent with what was seen as its 'semi-Indian' architecture.[15] The punkah was fairly widely adopted in the tropical parts of Australia and in the south in hotels like the Imperial and the Southern Cross in Adelaide, until it was replaced by electric fans at the turn of the century.[16] It was also used rather self-consciously, and in many cases still is, by the Melbourne Savage Club, the Mildura Club, Tattersall's Club in Brisbane and other such institutions.

These aspects of ventilation and cooling are quite arbitrarily selected. There were many other aspects of borrowing from India – flat roofing and *chunam* plaster as has been mentioned, the bungalow form, and to some extent the verandah. India in turn is only one of the intercolonial sources, and there were many other building practices common across a number of colonies but unknown in Britain. It will suffice merely to mention the use of stumps. Within Australia they have a complex and interesting history which I will not pursue here, and they have a sort of European precedent in the form stone steddles and rick stands. But essentially they are to be seen as a device of tropical origin that becomes part of the colonial *lingua franca* and surfaces even in such untropical locations as New Zealand. In 1866, Lady Barker was dubious about the use of 'small rough-hewn stone piles' for her homestead in the Malvern Hulk, but reported that it was in accord with local practice. They were prepared in Christchurch, transported 80 kilometres inland and placed at 1.8 to 2.4 metre spacings beneath the house floor.[17]

Prime markets

In general Australians, New Zealanders and other colonials consumed the same goods as did Britons at home, and sought nothing better. However, there were practical problems when British standards did not suit colonial conditions such as a hotter climate or tougher native timbers. The colonial market did not warrant any special exertion by British manufacturers, so colonials were forced to improvise or look to other sources, and both approaches were taken in the case of axes. In Australia Governor Arthur Phillip complained from the first that 'bad tools are no kind of use', but the problem was more the fact that the Australian timber was so much harder than the British. Four years on, Phillip was still asking for saws and axes, as those from England had worn out and some attempts were being made to forge tools from scrap iron, but with very little success.[18]

By the 1820s, distinctive local tools had begun to develop and Peter Cunningham stated: 'Edge tools require to be particularly well tempered to withstand our hard woods. Our felling axes are long and narrow, to penetrate our iron woods more readily, and with one somewhat larger and narrower still, the mortices are cut in the posts.'[19] This implies that axes different from the English standard were used, but it may be that this was a question of selecting one of the less usual English types rather than redesigning the implement entirely. Robert Irving has explained that the English felling axe, though unsuitable for the job, remained the norm in Australia until the American axe was imported, probably in the 1860s.[20] A German observer commented that the American axe would fell and smooth logs in the same number of hours as the German axe would require days.[21] It was likewise superior to the English one, which had a large but light head, a straight cutting edge, straight tapered cheeks and a straight short handle. The American axe, 'a steel version of the Red Indian axe', had a small, heavy head with fat cheeks and a curved cutting edge and a long, tough hickory handle that could absorb shock: it was swung wide and thrown into the wood, whereas the English axe was used like a chopper.

Hard timber presented similar problems for nails, but in this case it seems that the British makers developed a specific response. Even the American nails could not be driven into Australian hardwoods without breaking, as was admitted by the Melbourne merchant GF Train, himself an American.[22] The Ewbank pressed nail had resolved this problem but it was still under patent, and the exclusive product of one British manufacturer. It was a resilient nail that was much liked and widely used in Australia, in sizes from one to six inches (25 to 150 millimetres), but its origin and its relationship to other British developments remain somewhat obscure.[23] Amongst these, TJ Fuller had received a patent in 1834 for mechanically hammering the points in such a way as to resemble hand forging, and John Jackson received a patent in 1845 for forming nail heads.[24] Higgs & George's patent wrought nails were available commercially in Britain by 1845,[25] but it appears that these were one of the American types, for which Higgs & George were the British licensees.[26]

The eponymous Ewbank was presumably the patentee of the Ewbank nail, and his company is credited with introducing it to Australia in about 1838.[27] In 1860 Ewbanks were said to have been the first to produce nails which could compete with those forged by hand,[28] but subsequently Ewbanks seems to have been succeeded as manufacturer by JJ Cordes & Co. of Dos Works, Newport, Monmouthshire in Wales. Cordes's Ewbank nails were described as flatpointed rose nails and flatpointed strong wire nails. The former were made in sizes from 1 to 3½ inches (25–89 millimetres) long, the latter from 1¼ to 4 inches (32–102 millimetres).[29] However, a large proportion of the Ewbank nails found in Australia seem to be very considerably larger.

The earliest reasonably authenticated Ewbank nail in Australia seems, in fact, to be earlier than 1838 and of a larger size than those described. It was recovered from the cottage prefabricated in Sydney by the Royal Engineers for Captain William Lonsdale and erected in Melbourne in 1837. It is a 6 inch (150 millimetres) nail, which is severely corroded but undoubtedly of the general type and, as it seems correctly dated to 1837 when the patent was still in force, it must be by Ewbank rather than one of the later imitators.[30] Ewbank nails have also been found at 'Pontville', a house of the 1840s at Doncaster, near Melbourne,[31] and also it appears (for they are not identified as such by the investigators) in the homestead at Matanaka, New Zealand, also of the 1840s.[32] Ewbank nails have also been found in the shingle roof of a Melbourne cottage of 1853[33] and by 1862 they were listed in Mayes's price-book.[34] They were still being advertised by McEwan's of Melbourne as late as 1886[35] and apparently still in use in England at the turn of the century.[36]

Another British response to the colonial market was the prefabrication of buildings, an activity carried out on so enormous a scale that it is hard to know where to begin. I have discussed elsewhere the first European house in Australia, made of oilcloth for Governor Phillip's use by Nathan Smith, the patentee of the material.[37] This was a response to a market need rather than to any specifically colonial physical constraint, for Smith and Baber were also making oilcloth garden structures for home consumption and Phillip's house in fact performed very badly in Australia. Nonetheless, other such buildings were exported, not least of all to Sierra Leone.[38] Soon afterwards the London architect Samuel Wyatt developed a 'moveable hospital' specifically for colonial use, the first of which was sent to Barbados,[39] whilst another came to Australia and has been discussed in detail by Robert Irving.[40]

Easily the most important of the English manufacturers was the carpenter and builder Henry Manning,[41] who was not only the most prolific and influential maker by far, but also developed a distinctive system of construction specifically in response to the Australian market. He can possibly be regarded as the first system builder in the modem sense, as opposed to those other prefabricators whose work differed little from traditional carpentry. However, Manning manufactured traditionally carpentered houses as well and had allegedly been the builder of Napoleon's house at St Helena, to which his house for Governor Hobson of New Zealand was subsequently compared.[42]

Manning claimed to have begun supplying emigrants' houses some time about 1823[43] but he seems to have invented and begun making his panelled houses towards 1830, possibly for his son who was reported to have gone as a settler to the Swan River in Western Australia.[44] The panelled houses, which he referred to in 1843 as 'skeleton houses', were made of standardised modular components and did not have to be custom-built in London, but he also continued to make larger, more conventional and substantial buildings.[45] Who the son in question may have been is unclear, but there was a Charles Alexander Manning who settled in Fremantle, having been formerly a West Indian merchant. His marriage certificate gives the father's occupation as 'architect', which seems promising enough, but the father's forename is given as John, and he has elsewhere been reported as William.[46] He may of course of been JH or WH Manning.

At the Swan River colony, which was to become Perth, it was said that:

> These cottages were found to be of the greatest service to settlers, both in protecting their families from the weather, and their property from theft. Many persons who took ... only tents, suffered severely in both respects; their tents being frequently blown down in the middle of a stormy night, and their goods being thus not only exposed to weather but to pilfering. Provided with

a cottage of this description, an emigrant might land from a ship in a new country in the morning and sleep in his own house on shore at night.[47]

At any rate Manning was claimed, by 1833, to have made many houses for the Australian colonies and particularly for the Swan River. A single room at Hobart Town was said to be let for £1 a week, while one of Manning's portable cottages with two rooms could be bought in London for £50.

The Western Australian connection is somewhat elusive. A photograph survives of one house built in the 1830s in what is patently the panellised Manning system, 'Mona Cottage', Perth, which is slightly unusual in that it has attic rooms under the roof, and the side walls are extended with a row of small additional panels, about 0.9 metres high, to create the necessary roof space.[48] Manning's customers appear to have included the Western Australian Company, proprietors of the Australind Settlement at Port Leschenault. The journals of the Chief Commissioner, Marshall Waller Clifton, name the window sizes most useful to settlers and indicate that these can be obtained from Manning of High Holborn. In 1842, Clifton's son was building a new house and mentions taking Mrs Clifton's cottages down river. These, which may have been Manning cottages, appear to have been very small structures with gothic windows (inviting comparison with 'Jolimont', Melbourne). They formed the basis of the first Leschenault house, which was destroyed by flood in 1862.[49] A surviving house at Kalamunda, thought to be a Manning structure, has been identified by John White.[50]

Many more Manning houses reached the other Australasian colonies and a number survive at least in fragmentary form in South Australia, where they have been studied by Paul Stark and Gilbert Herbert, and in Victoria. A puzzling example in New Zealand is the former Pegasus Press building in Christchurch, the first stage of which appears to have been built in 1852 very much on Manning's panellised system, though when investigated in 1989 it was believed to be made entirely of local timbers. Further probing or sampling is currently impracticable because the building has been completely refurbished.[51]

British timber buildings arrived on a large scale in response to the gold rushes and continued to reach the colonies in fluctuating quantities throughout the rest of the century. However, from the 1860s American houses came in increasing numbers, and they continued to arrive even after the British imports ceased. Most other types of prefabrication, such as zinc and 'portable brick' houses, are far less important, but it is arguable that at least *papier mâché* and slate houses were specifically developed for Australia.

The important new market was in iron, and British manufacturers had exported iron structures of one sort or another to West Africa, India, the West Indies, and even to Van Diemen's Land, before the Californian gold rushes created a mass market. In this case British manufacture was not, in the first instance, in response to the demands of Australia, New Zealand or any of Britain's own colonies. That having been said, however, there were many custom-designed buildings and many new standard models developed specifically for the Australian market in the 1850s, and some new manufacturers who sprang into being specifically to export to Australia. The major instance is Samuel Hemming of Bristol who, according to one slightly vague account, actually began, like Manning, by making a cottage for a son who had emigrated.

Cadets and tourists

Making houses for sons who emigrated was one thing, and sending one's sons out to the colonies as agents was another. Examples are not easy to document, but it appears that even so important a firm as Doulton & Company, manufacturing potters of London, Liverpool, Birmingham and Staffordshire, sent out a Doulton family member to advance their interests. J Doulton and Company of 91 Flinders Lane West, Melbourne, imported from the parent company: 'stoneware drain pipes, water closet pans, square and angular urinals, glazed and unglazed paving tiles, 12 inches, terra cotta chimney tops ... the segmented block pipe (for large sized drain pipes)'.[52] Both the chimney tops and the segmented block pipe were the subject of Victorian patents in the name of James Doulton himself.[53]

In other cases family members, including principals, came to récon-noitre the colonial market but returned home to exploit it. John Lysaght was a significant British manufacturer, but he repeatedly visited the Australian colonies and they became his biggest market, with Lysaght iron being by far the most widely used in Australia. Ultimately Lysaght's began to manufacture in New South Wales, and were the only Australian makers. John Lysaght began manufacture in Bristol in 1857 in the factory previously established by one Clarke,[54] and it is claimed that he used the well-known Orb brand from the outset.[55] The Lysaght works at first galvanised black sheets obtained from producers in the Midlands, but in 1880 Lysaght acquired the Swan Garden works at Wolverhampton and the nearby Osier Bed works, with a total of twelve rolling mills.[56] By 1876, John Lysaght was listed in the *Post Office London Directory* as a portable house builder, and by 1889 the company claimed to specialise in iron roofs and buildings and operated from the St Vincent's Galvanized Iron Works in Bristol, the Swan Garden works and the Osier Bed works at Wolverhampton, with an office at 36 Gracechurch Street, London.[57]

John Lysaght himself made three separate visits to the colonies and the success of his business was attributed to this assiduity.[58] In 1879, he decided to establish a central selling agency in Melbourne and it opened in 1880 under Thomas Davey as the Victorian Galvanized Iron & Wire Co.[59] Branches followed in the other southern colonies, but Sydney and Brisbane were handled by the apparently quite independent firm of Lysaght Brothers. In exchange, their wire products were handled by the Melbourne agency. This arrangement lasted until 1899, when the Melbourne-based operation became Lysaght's Galvanized Iron Pty Ltd, with a newly established branch at Sydney under HR Lysaght, responsible also for the Queensland market. The new company became the largest customer of the manufacturing company in England.[60]

Lysaght's galvanised iron was well established in Australia by 1887, when the contract for a giant order of 500 tonnes for the Melbourne Exhibition Building went to Lysaght's 'Orb'.[61] At some stage the 'Guinea' brand was established for Lysaght's second quality iron, and this was being imported to Australia by the 1880s.[62] By 1895 the firm's total output had reached 40,000 tonnes a year, three-quarters of it destined for Australia.[63] It is interesting to compare the 'Adams-Mars' brand, which had also come on the market by the 1880s.[64] It was made by George Adams & Co of the Mars Iron Works at

Wolverhampton, who were able, by 1903, to claim that theirs was the best-known brand in the South African market, whereas in Australia it ranked well after Lysaght's.[65]

In 1883, a Lysaght wire netting plant was established on the Parramatta River under the management of John Sandford, formerly the director of an ironworks in Bristol.[66] By 1904, the Australian branch had become a distinct company, with headquarters at Sydney controlled by Arthur Lysaght as managing director and Robert Wilkinson as general manager. It had extensive works on the Parramatta River, a Melbourne branch with a large wire netting works on the Yarra at Footscray, further branches in Queensland and New Zealand, and sub-agencies in South Australia and Western Australia.[67] However, as a wire netting manufacturer the company's relevance to the building industry is slight and all the galvanised sheet iron continued to be imported from Britain.

From 1914, Lysaght's in England devoted more and more of their activity to the war effort until by 1918 they were producing galvanised iron at just seven per cent of pre-war levels, and exports to Australia were slashed. However, just after the outbreak of war the company had prudently bought a site at Newcastle with a view to establishing Australian production. Nothing more was done until 1917, when the government sought to encourage the establishment of a local sheet rolling, corrugating and galvanising industry by offering bounties and tariff protection as incentives. Now the company set about establishing a factory on another site at Newcastle, which had been swapped for the original one. The land required considerable reclamation work, but the sheet rolling and galvanising works of the company, now known as John Lysaght (Aust) Pty Ltd, were able to commence production in 1921.[68] In 1936, rolling mills and a galvanising plant at Port Kembla were bought from Australian Iron and Steel Limited and seem to have been in production immediately, but a major new factory was also set in train for completion in December 1938.[69]

Another British traveller was Robert Boyle, patentee of the 'air pump ventilator', but he differed from Lysaght in that he travelled everywhere, though he took a special interest in this region. He was a London manufacturer who produced an extensive range of extract ventilators, many of which appear to have been used in the Australasian colonies. The first known local reference to Boyle's products is by one of the competition entrants for the new Public Offices ('Treasury') in Brisbane in 1883, who proposed a system of vents leading to the corners of the roof 'surmounted with Boyle's air pump exhaust'.[70]

Apart from his range of individual ventilators, Boyle had apparently developed an integrated system of ventilation for workhouses and hospitals in 1882, using his 'air pump ventilator' (perfected in 1887) and 'air inlet brackets', to ventilate cheaply, efficiently, and without draught.[71] Boyle actually visited Australia 'in the interests of sanitary science and of the well-known ventilating and sanitary appliances of which he is the inventor'. An account of the trip appeared in the *Building News* of 2, 9 and 16 September 1892 and was then reprinted as a booklet.[72] He later produced an extraordinarily handsome and self-consciously artistic catalogue-cum-treatise, in which a number of the products look familiar in relation to Australian examples.

Incorporation

Colonial successes, like provincial Roman generals in their own empire, were able make their way back into the British mainstream. Hugh Childers reached Victoria in 1850, became Inspector of Denominational Schools in 1851, Auditor-General and a nominated member of the Legislative Council in 1852, and Collector of Customs and a member of the Executive Council in 1853. After this meteoric rise had slowed slightly Childers returned to England in 1858, was elected to the House of Commons in 1860 and resumed his upward march, becoming Financial Secretary to the Treasury in 1865, First Lord of the Admiralty in 1868, Chancellor of the Duchy of Lancaster in 1872, Secretary of State for War in 1880, Chancellor of the Exchequer in 1882 and Home Secretary in 1886.

The building industry does not offer quite such dramatic instances, but there were many who made their fortunes in the colony and returned 'home' to live as gentlemen. There were a few who continued their trades or professions, and one was E Alexander Rippingille. He emigrated from Plymouth to Adelaide in 1850 but soon afterwards moved to Melbourne, where he set up as a platemaker and subsequently fabricated what he claimed was the first quartz crushing machine in Victoria, for the Mount Blackwood Mine. He had works in La Trobe Street where he manufactured guttering and other products, until 1861, when he returned to England a wealthy man. He established himself as a stove manufacturer with great success, and died in 1894.[73] His patent kerosene stove was advertised in *Dr Holbrook's American Cookery*, published in Melbourne in 1888.[74] The architect Robert Haddon exemplified was another way in which colonial success could be parlayed into empire status. He had published his *Australian Architecture*, the first local text on the subject, in 1908.[75] He was then invited to contribute to Middleton's *Modern Buildings*, an encyclopedic text of imperial scope published in about 1910, which also had as South African section by Herbert S East (formerly of Melbourne).[76]

Conclusion

This paper has been about technology as culture – as a reflection of society, economy, history and ethnicity – not as the inexorable advance of science, or the achievement of firsts and biggests. However, technology is not so easily researched as architectural style, or indeed painting or music. Much of it is invisible. Even when it is visible few students understand it or feel impelled to record it. Primary sources such as patents, where they exist, are recondite and difficult to access. Within these constraints, however, it has been possible to demonstrate a different relationship – or at least a differently *slanted* relationship – from that normally assumed to have been obtained between Britain and her colonies. Britain, if at first reluctantly, began to manufacture goods to meet the special requirements and the extreme market demands of the colonies. The colonies began to take initiatives that placed them in advance of provincial English centres. Colonial achievements began to count in Britain itself. All this would have been taken for granted at the time, for it is what imperialism meant in the nineteenth century, just as it is what it meant in Roman times. But today, when 'empire' and 'colony' are dirty words, it has been worth re-establishing.

Heavenly Groundings: Missionary Architectural Practice in Nineteenth-Century New Zealand

1997

SARAH TREADWELL

An elaborate tradition of timber architecture already existed in New Zealand when the missionaries arrived. For those with church building on their minds, stones would anchor the missionary endeavour and would lodge the religious institutions heavily on, and into, the ground. Their dream of stone churches, however, was to be renegotiated through contact with the Indigenous architecture and the nature of the land. This paper examines the architectural negotiations effected by missionaries faced with a land and architecture resistant to fixity, through the writings, drawing and practice of the Reverend Richard Taylor.

The Rev. Richard Taylor was sent to New Zealand by the Church Missionary Society in the early years of the nineteenth century. He worked in the Whanganui area on the western coast of the North Island from 1839 to 1873. During his missionary time, Taylor kept journals recording his extensive travels, the people and architecture he encountered, geological, ornithological and vegetative forms, the climate and even the state of his own body.

His journeys were extensive and repetitive; up and down the winding Whanganui River, along the west coast of the North Island from South Taranaki to Wellington. He crossed the high country past smouldering volcanoes and journeyed far into the north. The distances were large and trips frequent; he wore out his body through repeated immersion in icy rivers and nights on fern-covered ground. There seems, looking back from the convenience of the late twentieth century, something obsessive about his journeying. He stands out even among well-travelled missionaries, as if he had to criss-cross the land with paths to bind, patterning persistently his, always transitory, presence.

Constantly reiterating lines of passage and communication intersecting with other patterns of movement in the country, it seems that standing still, putting down roots, would make apparent a certain tension and detachment. By keeping on the move over the land that in its volcanic and seismic aspects was signalled as a site of contention, Taylor could tread more lightly. His gentle repetitions wore their own designs into the surface. Torn by a commitment to the permanence of his God, his restless, rootless movements formed layers of stories and accretions across the earth.

In 1853 Taylor, in the company of Governor Grey, climbed up Mount Taranaki to the source of one of the frequently traversed rivers. In his journal he drew the scene of their encounter with the source.[1] Perhaps Grey was the man depicted with the staff, master of all he surveys, standing back from the edge? Taylor, however, lay tentatively, peering into the chasm, awkwardly prone on the ground. Stretching towards the void he would have been aware of the undercut nature of the edge. Imaginatively reliving the moment in his drawing, he recorded a rhythm in the land; it approached the edge in waves like prows of ships.[2] The figure clung to the surface aware of the undercurrents and turmoil that boiled beneath.

The drawing in his sketchbook is an image that epitomises missionary dilemmas with the land. Pictured is an absence of firm footings, a collapse of clearings into the void. Fissures and rifts and the necessities for bridging rend his journals.[3] Taylor recorded at Putiki on 5 August 1843 an architectural consequence of fissures in an unquiet earth: 'In July we experienced a severe shock of an earthquake which threw down many chimneys, cracked the walls of our church causing several bricks to fall and opening the earth in deep fissures one in the bed of the river being several hundred feet long and of great width and depth'.[4]

Later at Putiki, in 1851, Taylor recorded an instance when the foundation of the missionaries' work, as well as their architecture, was undermined by the nature of the ground:

> I went to see the man who is putting fresh blocks under the church. The former were quite perished and it is wonderful the building has stood so well on such an insecure foundation. It presented to me a picture of ourselves and God's mercy towards us in not allowing the storms and tempests of life to cast us down to the dust although we have no real foundation to rest upon.[5]

Taylor did not see foundational security as achievable through human agency. While his writings expressed some dismay at this lack of permanence, in his day-to-day life he utilised the possibilities of a local, lightly-founded architecture. In his journal in 1846, Taylor recorded preaching in a highly unstable church: 'We had thunder and [lightning] with very heavy rain in the night, this morning very high wind ... Whilst I administered the Sact. the church which is a native erection of light and unsubstantial materials rocked to and fro in a most fearful manner. I fully expected some of the rafters would come tumbling down every instant.'[6]

This 'native erection' moved with the prevailing conditions, accepting the possibility of structural collapse. Taylor, although fearful and expecting failure, continued to preach within the shaking structure. Commentaries recorded numerous collapses of buildings and the desperation that the fallibility of structure evoked with its casting of the missionary project into doubt.[7]

Where permanence was geologically impossible then anticipation or precedence – the idea of the past repeated, refigured, in the future – could be substituted for a lack of persistence. Repetition and rebuilding was a characteristic of existing indigenous patterns of architecture in New Zealand, but architectural repetition and remaking has been resisted by European architectural histories of the country.

One such transient building that Taylor often visited was a church/ meeting house built in the early 1840s, located in the Waikanae pa near Wellington.[8] It was a building that combined patterns of the indigenous architecture with ecclesiological forms and was one of a series of quite substantial constructions.

The Waikanae 'church' is of interest in its historical and physical effacement.[9] The literal instability of its grounding on the coastal sand dunes is repeated in the way in which it has been positioned historically. The

Waikanae church has always been discussed in conjunction with the near-identical and more famous building, Rangiatea. Neither now exists. However for many years, until it burnt down in 1995, Rangiatea was discussed as a unique instance of harmonious race relations. At the same time, the Waikanae church was referred to as the predecessor or ancestor of Rangiatea. Yet in order to maintain notions of the unique historic object that positions Rangiatea within New Zealand architecture, the building at Waikanae – although acknowledged as a precedent – had also to disappear. It is not discussed in any architectural publication.

In 1843, Taylor recorded his pleasure in the Waikanae building.[10] He described it as woven and beautiful; the beauty contained not only in the interior but also in its categorisation as religious and exotic.[11] Taylor reflected on the effort put into the building, mentioning both the size of the structure and the presence of ornament, in an attempt to place the building as 'noble' and therefore enduring. He also connected the church to an enduring, but non-English, strand of building – Islamic architecture. Taylor saw the Waikanae church as an important construction produced by a capable and industrious work force.

Descriptions of the Waikanae church by other Europeans were generally favourable.[12] The comments on beauty and taste could be seen as the construction of categories, attempts to locate within a familiar architectural system. When the Rev. JF Lloyd visited the Waikanae church in 1849, he admired the church but not the siting of the building.[13]

The Waikanae church was located *within* a fortified pa,[14] an enclosed and palisaded settlement that would also have contained the homes of the people of that pa. On the coast, beside a source of food and means of transport, the pa staked claims to important land resources. Rangiatea, however, the later twin building that has been valorised by histories of New Zealand, was located in a missionary-instigated model village that removed the local people from the coast.

At Waikanae the location of the church within the pa could be seen as a move towards destruction of the pa as a settlement form. When occupied, and affiliated to the government, Waikanae was described as a vigorous church-going community. However when Te Atiawa left Waikanae in 1848, against the desires of the government, the descriptions of the pa changed in nature.

A number of reasons, not easily clarified, are given for the move of Te Atiawa to Taranaki.[15] Most significantly, the increasing value of the Taranaki land necessitated defence of Te Atiawa land from settlers and the government.[16] Te Atiawa left Waikanae in order to ensure continued claims on land at Waitara which Grey was intent on acquiring for new settlers.[17]

Grey, desiring the land in Taranaki and resenting opposition, suggested, as a method of control, that Te Atiawa could be resettled in a model village.[18] The pa as a settlement form that replaced or renewed itself,[19] a centre and site for cultural practice and strength, was to be replaced by English cultural forms, in particular the English village. In his endeavours to obtain land in Taranaki, Governor Grey, as well as destroying canoes to try to prevent migration,[20] was prepared to utilise architectural forms and ultimately force of arms to ensure acquisition.

Waikanae, following the departure of large numbers of Te Atiawa, came to be represented by visiting Europeans as a physical image of both decay and progress, an abandonment of Indigenous cultural patterns for the new.[21] In 1844 Taylor recorded in his journals the changing contours of the political and geological landscape that were reflected in the Waikanae pa:

> I felt sorry to see the sand drifting against this beautiful church and as I fear the natives are too lazy to remove it, it bids fair soon to be destroyed it is now forming a hill around one side three feet deep, and the natives seem determined to abandon Waikanae and sell it to the Europeans, through fear that if they do not Rauperaha [sic] will.[22]

Taylor imagined sand forming a moving hill that would engulf the church. Instead of an architecture that stood as a discipline to a landscape, enduring as a sign of propriety, he saw an architecture considered disposable, ephemeral and a sign of the disturbing effects of land negotiations. He eventually, in 1856, witnessed the ruined condition of the Waikanae church:

> At Waikanae I went to see the church, a solitary [remnant] ... of a once populous pa which is now partly fallen in, the floor rotting, the pulpit broken in pieces, the communion rail partly destroyed, a dead goat laid in the church. Perhaps it got in and the door closed and it miserably perished. The scene was most melancholy and presented a vivid picture of the transient nature of

> all earthly things. The last time I was in it I preached to a large congregation and admired its beauty. All have now left and before another year has passed it will have fallen. In the pa I noticed a few bits of carving and many burnt remains of houses with several skeletons nearly perfect lying mixed with the bones of pigs and dogs. Waikanae when I first visited it contained 6 or 7000 persons and I could scarcely reach Mr. Hadfield's house for the press. The buzz of man has given way to the solemn dash of the ocean waves.[23]

Taylor particularly noted the broken floor, pulpit and communion rail. The floor was a claiming of ground, above ground, on which to stand and preach and the communion rail ensured the maintenance of traditional ecclesiastical divisions. Taylor's reference to the loss of these illustrates the minimal architectural attachment with which missionaries operated; the building as shell just disappeared.

Outside the church the mixing of bones and carvings was 'noticed' as an undoing of confining categories and an illustration of the temporal limits of both bodies and buildings. Taylor, with melancholic tone, regretted the loss of beauty and the transience of the material side of life. His image of the 'solemn dash of the ocean waves' is, however, replete with movement, moment and insubstantiality.

An 1840s drawing by William Swainson, 'Outside the Old Waikanae Pa, in ruins',[24] suggests that the abandonment of Waikanae also presaged the disappearance or transformation of Maori.[25] As Carter puts it: 'the fantasy of ruination may, it seems, be critical in mobilising history, in bringing the seasonally self-adjusting land under the aegis of a linear temporality'.[26]

Near the centre of the drawing is a broken palisade post, a large carved figure having fallen against an earth bank. A solitary European male strolls by, staff in hand. In close proximity to and dwarfed by the carved figure, he nevertheless has a nonchalant air. Representing an English future he is contrasted with the carved figure, helpless on its back, no longer able to watch over the land.

Swainson, like Taylor, fabricated ruin as part of a linear progressive history, inevitable, then casting it as picturesque. The strolling figure mediates the horror of decay by turning the site into a tourist attraction. Swainson's rendition does not deny the power of the artefacts, but the energy and labour involved in the construction remain apparent but in abeyance.

Grey is said to have attempted to ship such carvings to the museums of Europe.[27] Building parts were transferred from pa to pa, and from New Zealand to Europe; architecture lodged in carved pieces was seen literally as mobile by both Maori and Pakeha. When the inhabitants of the Waikanae pa shifted to Taranaki and to other local pa and inland villages the architecture was dispersed rather than destroyed.[28] It was recorded that some of the carvings of the pa were incorporated in new settlements.[29]

Similarly, the Central Committee of the New Zealand Mission 'resolved [t]hat in the event of the removal of the Ngatiawa Tribe from Waikanae. The Mission House at Waikanae to be disposed of if a purchaser can be found or if not, that the materials be used in the erection of a New Mission House at Otaki'.[30]

The transferral of buildings from one place to another, the utilisation of impermanence, is also part of missionary conduct. There is an implicit acceptance that a building can be dismantled and re-erected to continue the missionary project. The underlying lack of commitment to foundations and the acceptance of a detached relationship to land is at odds with concurrent themes of gravitational security.

Transferral from building to building also occurred in discussions on the Waikanae church and Rangiatea, in that their descriptions tend to merge.[31] The Waikanae church tended to be located in the histories as a precedent for Rangiatea. It seems that there was some necessity for an antecedent state to be materialised. In missionary writing, a prior 'fallen' state was made explicit in order for notions of progress and advancement to be advocated. The Waikanae church foreshadowed the architectural future in that it shared some of the characteristics of the later 'model' but was itself represented as vestigial or flawed. Engulfed by the encroaching sand, unattended by any desire for maintenance, the Waikanae church, product of the pa, also disappeared in order to allow Rangiatea, the key of the new model village, to be constructed as a 'unique' architectural object signifying a reductive 'blending' of two cultures. This 'blending' that Rangiatea is said to signify – representing the victory of European maintenance culture against the decay of Maori – can be considered more accurately as, to quote a Maori proverb, what the shark does to the snapper.[32]

The Waikanae church is an architecture that streams across space and time, resistant to object status, multiple and repetitive like Taylor's passages across the island. The church was imagined, copied, built, used, repeated, dispersed and buried only to be re-found and memorialised during the course of the laying out of a subdivision in the 1960s. Taylor, operating over time and across cultures, watching the clouds and listening to the roar of the volcanoes, traced the multiple earthly architectures of the Waikanae church even as he himself looked to a more heavenly grounding.

Larrikins Abroad: International Account of the New Zealand Architects in the 1970s and 1980s

1999

ROBIN SKINNER

> We are beset with larrikins who lurk about in the darkness and deliver every sort of attack on the walls and roof with stones and sticks.
>
> HW HARPER, 1868[1]

Through the twentieth century, New Zealand architects were often represented or perceived in Britain as wild colonial boys. In the thirties their work was treated with condescension; however, by the mid-1970s and early 1980s 'kiwi' architecture had become fashionable. New Zealanders' work started to receive favourable and enthusiastic reviews in the international architectural press. The journals portrayed the buildings as the work of larrikin designers who were in conflict with the bureaucrats and who were tilting against the rules. They made the cover of the *Architectural Review*.

In the 1920s and 1930s, the British architectural profession valued New Zealand trained architects, and many established London practices employed colonials. William Gummer worked for Lutyens and Pascoe for Lubetkin, and practices such as Burnet, Tait and Lorne employed many New Zealanders. However, despite the respect that was held for this solid reliable office staff, work by some New Zealanders received poor review in the British press. Amyas Connell and Basil Ward were considered 'bad boys'. A 1936 item in Astragal's column in the *Architects' Journal* on their proposed designed for the house at 66 Frognal began, 'So Messrs. Connell, Ward and Lucas are in trouble again.'[2] In statements such as this, the architects were framed as childlike, and not only were they being disobedient and annoying, but they were doing it again.

Pevsner suggested that these architects set out to shock the bourgeoisie ('épater le bourgeois')[3] and it appears that it was a role that they enjoyed. While their work featured in the architectural press, the British institutions disregarded it.[4] Phillip Johnson may have included their design of 'High and Over' (1929) in the 1932 International Style exhibition at the Museum of Modern Art in New York, but in Britain they were marginalised. Michael Findlay notes that as late as 1959, John Summerson, who was unimpressed with colonial architects generally, described their progress thus: 'Amyas Connell and Basil Ward had *worked* their passage from New Zealand, *bashed* their way to academic honours and *descended* on us from the high eminence of Rome' (my emphasis).[5] Clearly these colonials were troublesome and were not to be encouraged.

Through much of the century when the British press reviewed New Zealand architectural work it gave, at best, reserved praise. In an extreme example from 1950, the editor of the *Architect and Building News* was very condescending towards an account of the first 'Group' house at Belmont, Auckland. Architectural commentators now value this building as a significant part of a revolutionary body of New Zealand work. However, the British editor in 1950 was unconvinced by the project. As well as belittling the students' scholarship and professionalism, he mocked the possibility that there could be contemporary design that would be indigenous to New Zealand. He negated the event. The item read:

> Six students from Auckland University College School of Architecture are designing, building, furnishing and selling houses on their own account. One of their number is qualified. I think that the New Zealand equivalent of the RIBA [Royal Institute of British Architects] Practice Committee will be after him, but that is by the way.
>
> The object of the exercise is to rehash the early New Zealand vernacular style of architecture. There has been much deep research. 'The Maoris lived here for hundreds of years so they ought to know what goes on', said one of

the group. 'They evolved a style of house suited to the climate and that is exactly what we are doing. Some of the people who come to see the houses remark on the modern designs and compare them with those seen in overseas magazines, but they are completely different. The basic design is peculiar to New Zealand'. You don't say.[6]

Typically, when lengthy articles on work undertaken in New Zealand were permitted in the authoritative arena, they were usually written by New Zealanders, although there were exceptions. Nikolaus Pevsner's writing in the late 1950s is the most obvious example. In the mid 1970s and early 1980s, however, there was a dramatic change in this pattern, and the work of New Zealand architects started to receive favourable and enthusiastic reviews, often written by foreign commentators. The work that received the most praise was by the Wellington architects, Roger Walker (b.1942) and Ian Athfield (b.1940). Their work was presented as lively, bold and rebellious, and it was featured in Britain, France, Italy, Germany, Japan, Australia and the United States. They were presented as attempting to develop a regional style distinct to the colonial past, environment and culture of New Zealand.

Roger Walker's international profile can be traced to an article entitled 'The Architecture of Ebullience' in the *Architects' Journal*,[7] which was written following his visit to Britain in 1978. While British architectural writer Alistair Best revealed some misunderstanding of New Zealand history,[8] and while he held a disparaging view of its culture, clearly Walker's work excited him. He wrote: 'In some respects kiwi culture may still be deep frozen somewhere around the year 1949, but architecturally it is bang up to date.' The New Zealand Institute of Architects (NZIA) was praised for permitting its members to form business liaisons with construction companies so long as it was in the interests of society as a whole and that it enhanced 'the stature of the profession'.[9] Walker was portrayed as a pioneer of this business relationship, who operated in a simple relationship with builders. In a country that was presented as being without architectural heritage, there was no crippling aesthetic control. New Zealand had space and there was 'a long tradition of doing one's own thing'. Best concluded wistfully to his British readership that '[the] Roger Walker phenomenon, more's the pity, couldn't happen here'.[10]

Response to the article was good. An architect from Petersfield subsequently wrote of the freedom that Walker could express 'down under'.[11] The writer of Astragal's column cited Walker's successful operation with developers, with the blessing of the NZIA, and cast a swipe at 'our own dear Portland Place'.[12] Whereas the entrepreneurial students of 1950 were cast as unprofessional, now Walker was appropriated as a model for RIBA practice. In Italy, text and photographs from Best's article were quoted and reprinted in an architectural magazine.[13]

Some months later, Russell Walden wrote from New Zealand taking exception to Best's claim that Walker had created a New Zealand style.[14] Rather, he placed it within international postmodernism and concluded with the challenge that Best 'bring himself up to date with the London–New York postmodern debate!' It seems that the writer at the margin was not happy with the latter-day colonisation. A British journalist was interpreting local work to an international audience. Walden extended his argument later, when he wrote an article entitled 'N.Z. Audacity' in the *Architectural Review* in 1981.[15] He now identified both Walker and Athfield as proto-postmodernists reacting to modernism ten years ahead of Charles Jencks's *The Language of Post-Modern Architecture* (1977). He wrote that, in his houses, Walker attempted to establish 'just *where* and *who* we are', stating, 'His first few [designs] helped define his sense of identity as a New Zealander, while exploring the local materials, topography, micro-climate and economic restraints under which all architects operate.' Walker's Britten house (1972–74) appeared on the cover. The publication was reported in New Zealand daily newspapers where the editor of the *Architectural Review*, Peter Davey, was quoted: 'We think this is some of the most interesting and lively architecture in the world at the moment ... We consider that, between them, Roger Walker and Ian Athfield have put New Zealand architecture on the map.'[16]

In 1981, Best again wrote on Walker's work describing the kitset house that was exhibited at the Homeworld 81 exhibition at Milton Keynes.[17] He declared the architect to be 'New Zealand's most valuable architectural asset' and he discussed the antipodean attitude to design, land and home ownership. '[T]he concept of the house as a freestanding idiosyncratic object in space says a great deal about the New Zealander's attitude to his [sic] home', wrote Best. He discussed Walker's Vintage Homes design/franchise operation in

New Zealand and his attempt to introduce his low-cost timber house designs into the United Kingdom. Unfortunately, the designs met with considerable market resistance in Britain and only one was erected.[18] Presumably, through exposure of the work in the British journals, Charles Jencks included Walker in his volume *Current Architecture* (1982).[19] Here he included the architect in his discussion of what he termed an *ad hoc* stream of postmodernism, and he later placed Walker on his postmodern flow diagram.

As early as 1974, Athfield's work was presented in Britain as an example of new wave New Zealand architecture. In his own house (1968–), it was claimed that he turned against Bauhaus austerity and instead revelled in the joys of romanticism. It was touted as a direct response to the unique New Zealand setting and lifestyle.[20] Understandably, this claim has been repeated through to the 1990s.

Following his 1976 success in winning the International Union of Architects competition to design a settlement scheme for people in the Tondo area of Manila,[21] Athfield received further international notice. He was portrayed as a rugby-loving, somewhat naive, untravelled architect who was passionate about his work. He attended the 1976 Habitat conference in Vancouver where his design was presented. At that time in the Tondo squatter settlement, there was a demonstration against the Marcos regime and the settlement clearance in which 2,000 people were arrested. Athfield, 'a sincere and handy bloke with a hammer',[22] found himself in the centre of a storm of controversy. He handled the situation adeptly, and with his 'down-to-earth, unpretentious and commonsense approach' he was reported to placate the various factions at Vancouver.[23] The long-haired architect who would 'go in there [to Tondo] virtually barefoot, to work with the people'[24] was reported around the world. In the end, the project was not carried out despite attempts by the organisers to persuade the Marcos regime to develop some of the competition ideas. Athfield later explained that to Imelda Marcos he was 'the most unpalatable form of Western decadence she could imagine. I lost the job because of my appearance.'[25]

Following the publication of his Walker article, Walden wrote on Athfield in the *Architectural Review* in 1982. Again the work of a New Zealander appeared on the cover. Athfield was introduced as a 'defiant rebel and genial extrovert, pragmatic builder and democratiser of architecture, caring revisionist and poet'. Walden discussed Athfield's conflict with bureaucrats, his personal anti-nuclear politics, his feel for the landscape, the use of Mediterranean metaphor, the houses, and construction by the client. The article included an image of the nuclear powered and armed USS *Truxton* passing behind the Athfield house as it entered Wellington Harbour in 1976. Neatly painted in lower case Helvetica type, on the prominent tower of the house, were the words, 'keep new zealand nuclear free'. This image had earlier appeared internationally as the single illustration to accompany the Athfield entry in the 1980 edition of *Contemporary Architects*.[26]

The appeal of these architects and their work can be placed within a larger context of 1970s culture. At this time there was an international trend, and an intellectual fashion, towards counter-culture. While a certain phantom rawness had long had appeal in Western thought, it had been institutionally suppressed. In the 1970s this rawness was sought.[27] In the 1960s and 70s in London, the rampant *ockerness* of the Australian had held a certain exotic charm, and by the late 1970s, it appears, New Zealanders began to be included amongst the fashionable antipodeans. Whereas Connell and Ward, or even the Group architects were perhaps feared and dealt with through condescension, now the New Zealanders and their work were fetishised.

The work of other New Zealand architects was also featured in Britain through these years, but none created the same excitement as Athfield and Walker. Reports of London work by Peter Beaven (b.1925) appeared in the early 1980s and included an article by Alistair Best.[28] According to Beaven, his designs were not readily associated with New Zealand, but were considered to be of a Knightsbridge or Chelsea character.[29] It seems that, while the work of the younger 'larrikins' was perceived to be a visitation of the Other, Beaven's designs were perceived to be a return of the *Same*.

As far back as 1901, British architectural journal articles that included antipodean work were reported in the daily press in New Zealand. It has been noted that, when Walker graced the cover of the *Architectural Review*, there was a report in the Wellington newspaper, *The Dominion*. The inclusion of examples of New Zealand architecture seemed to validate the work as being of international standard. In 1982, when he was back for a three-week holiday, Peter Beaven accurately listed the recent recognition of New Zealand work in British journals, and he suggested that the enthusiasm abroad was because the country was one of the first to shift from a 'functional stylism'.[30] A year later, he described his feelings when he saw Athfield's house on the cover of the May 1982 issue of *Architectural Review* at the same time as his own Highgate studio houses (1980–82) appeared on the cover of the *Architects' Journal*. He wrote in the *New Zealand Architect* that it was 'an entirely secret thrill to a New Zealander alone in the RIBA bookshop'.[31]

In subsequent years, Athfield's reported image became more professional and less raw. This is not surprising. Fashion had changed and the size of projects undertaken had increased so that more work took place in meetings. The editor of the *RIBA Journal*, Peter Murray, was surprised when he met Athfield in 1984. He wrote:

> The day I met him he was clean shaven and wearing a 'client suit'. Not what I had expected from the coverplate of the book of his work *Joyful Architecture* by Gerard Melling which shows Ath long haired and bearded as though he had just stepped out of the pages of *Whole Earth Catalogue*. I asked him why the image had changed. 'Partly because it's fashionable and partly because I am going to see BP this afternoon about a job.'[32]

Murray then wrote about the professional organisation of the Athfield practice. In the 1987 edition of *Contemporary Architects* the earlier image of the USS *Truxton* was replaced by the recently completed Buck house. While once he and Walker were described as *les enfants terribles*,[33] and their work termed a *cause célèbre*,[34] by 1992 they were given a new French epithet: writer, Eartha Post, coined the term '*École de Wellington*'.[35] They were portrayed as respectable.

Journals from other countries later picked up on the work of Walker and Athfield, and understandably do not project the image of larrikin to such an extent. The larrikin – the hooligan of the antipodes[36] – seems to operate in opposition to the imperial model gentleman. The figure is more readily understood by those who are party to the colonising process. Articles written for foreign readership were framed to each audience. To the Germans, their work was represented as young, raw and low-tech.[37] When trying to describe the work of Walker for the Americans, Gerard Melling described the Omaha beach house as highly comic, free form fantasy.[38] When describing Athfield to the same audience, Frances Fitzgerald labelled him a 'rebel and an innovator' and as a 'star' in a country that abhorred stardom.[39] She cited Maori legend and, possibly acknowledging the complexity of the colonising process, she suggested that a new winery being built in the Hawkes Bay would 'resemble the farms built by the first British settlers, who came to New Zealand by way of northern India'.

In conjunction with the Te Maori exhibition in Chicago in April 1986, Athfield joined Rewi Thompson, Roger Walker and John Blair on a speaking tour of America. They later reported back individually in the *New Zealand Architect*. In his fairly serious account of the trip, Athfield described the format that they developed for their lectures. It was 'to introduce New Zealand, its environment, qualities, its history, the Maori, the pakeha settlement, our work technology and dialogue, and why our voice should be heard beyond New Zealand'.[40] It appears that there was a mixed reception to the humour that was a significant feature of Walker's presentation to the college and professional audiences. The larrikin was incomprehensible to the North Americans. Humour was a major part of the tour generally. 'The security guard at Miles' [Warren] NZ Embassy were not amused by our description of ourselves as visitors from the Libyan embassy' wrote Walker.[41] The New Zealanders were unimpressed with much of the teaching and debate that they witnessed in America. Blair observed:

> We attended a seminar with [James] Wines at Cooper Union where Michael Sorking [sic.], James Polshek, Peter Frank and John Hejduk assisted by Chairman Bill Lacy, debated for an hour and a half on the essential nature of 'inventive detail', 'meaningful space' and the essential nature of something Hejduk described as 'OTHERNESS'. This latter quality of architecture unfortunately was as lost on the four New Zealand observers as it apparently was on most of the other 200 plus indigenous attendants.[42]

While Athfield continued to exhibit larrikin behaviour – as was evidenced in his bawdily humorous speech at the RIBA[43] – architectural writing suppressed this aspect of his personality. In 1993, an issue of the Japanese journal *World Architecture Review* was devoted to the work of Athfield Architects and Aasen • Athfield + Co.[44] Here, practitioner and academic Clarence Aasen discussed the work of the practices. He presented Athfield as 'one of the most influential, versatile and compelling architects in

Australasia and the South Pacific'.[45] The writer clearly placed the work in the context of a settler colony on the periphery of the world – a country that was 'built on the mythology of a fearless indigenous population, and still carrying the ponderous burden of an exploitive colonialism'.[46] Athfield's 'long standing commitment' to the Indigenous Maori and South Pacific peoples was now acknowledged.[47] While Aasen noted Athfield's conflicts with local bodies and 'self-serving neighbours', and his impatience with societal hierarchies, these issues did not feature as much as they did in the commentary of the early 1980s. Instead, the commentary focused on the design process. Over 150 photographs of Athfield's work were included, yet the once often reproduced images of the USS *Truxton* and of the shirtless Athfield were nowhere to be seen. By 1993, it seems, the larrikin had simply lost its currency. New Zealand was no longer a land of pioneering builders; rather, it had become a slick corporate state, newly fashioned by neo-rightist economic reform.

However, for some writers in the 1990s, the British perception of the New Zealander has never advanced beyond that of the unpredictable colonial. For some, the New Zealander may still be no better than the interpretation of Connell and Ward in the first half of the century. In the mid-1990s, British heritage writer Hugh Meller pondered how seven drawings of Castle Drogo, which were possibly drawn by Lutyens himself, came to be held in a New Zealand university collection.[48] He asked, 'How had these drawings escaped? The staffing of Lutyens' office provided the answer.' He noted that a New Zealander, WH Gummer, was working in the office at that time and added, 'One can reasonably assume therefore that Gummer was caught up in the excitement and managed to retain seven of his employer's drawings.' This interpretation seems rash.[49] The drawings may be by Gummer, or may have been given to the New Zealander by his employer. Meller's assumption of theft clearly judges the antipodean to still be untrustworthy. Clearly for some, the larrikin would remain beyond the possibility of reform.

Post-European and Indigenous Architectural Histories in Aotearoa New Zealand

2000

DEIDRE BROWN

This is not a paper about architecture, but about architectural history, specifically the directions that history may take in the near future. Within these new fields, Indigenous Maori architectural histories will continue to be written, and locally derived philosophies about Pakeha architecture – called 'post-European' in this context for want of a better term – will evolve.

Architectural historians have published a number of books detailing the history of buildings made by Pakeha. Yet it is ironic, when looking beyond the recent past, that over the last 100 years none of the published books on Maori architecture have been written by architectural historians. Instead, the authors of these books fall into three general categories. First, there are the tribal and institutional historians, such as Pei Te Hurinui Jones and Leo Fowler, amongst others, who have written about specific buildings within their domain.[1] Second, there are the ethnologists who search for connections between regional and genre styles, including Elsdon Best, Hirini (Sidney) Moko Mead, Roger Neich, WJ Phillipps and David Simmons.[2] Third, people with a direct involvement in Maori politics and education who are interested in the politicisation of architecture; this group includes luminaries such as Sir Apirana Ngata and Ranginui Walker.[3] Maori architecture was perhaps not legitimised as a field for architectural academics until Michael Austin's

PhD thesis, 'Polynesian Architecture in New Zealand', was accepted for examination in 1976.[4]

The studies of Maori architecture by architectural historians made since 1976, and Pakeha architectural histories, tend to use philosophies and techniques that are appropriated from other cultural disciplines, most notably art history, history, philosophy, ethnology, archaeology, anthropology and, more recently, cultural studies. In order to identify the future directions of our architectural histories, we can capitalise on the time delay between origination and appropriation, and examine the contemporary cultural theories in other disciplines that may influence architectural writing. There are at least three distinct strands of culturally based theory being used by New Zealand and Australian academics at the moment, namely a reinvigorated 'invention of culture', revisionism and foundational narratives. While Maori architectural history has already been a subject of interest for scholars working in the first two strands, the theories and philosophies of the last strand will inevitably be extended to Maori and Pakeha architecture in the near future. Notably, in all three strands, the development of Maori culture before Pakeha arrival, including architecture, is largely ignored.

Invention of tradition

Some contemporary social anthropologists have described developments in twentieth-century Maori art and architecture according to the 'invention of tradition' model. Their work has generally focused on the buildings of the School of Maori Arts and Crafts, constructed during the 'first Maori renaissance' of the 1930s and 1940s, and the artistic developments that have occurred during the 'second Maori renaissance', which began in the 1970s and has continued to this day. The arguments presented as part of the latter focus have yet to be fully extended to architecture.

Allan Hanson was the first academic to apply the 'invention of tradition' theory to Maori culture in his 1989 essay 'The Making of Maori: Culture Invention and its Logic' published in *American Anthropologist*.[5] Hanson argued that, while nineteenth-century Maori culture had been presented in a way that stressed its similarities with Pakeha culture, in the following century it was the differences between the two cultures that were being emphasised by revisionist scholars. There was an immediate backlash response from a number of leading New Zealand academics, both Maori and Pakeha, who questioned the sensitivity and wisdom of an approach that attempted to reveal the 'inauthenticity' of twentieth-century Maori architecture, amongst other *taonga Maori* (Maori treasures).[6] Nevertheless, scholars such as Jolly, Keesing, Linnekin and Trask have followed Hanson's lead and analysed Maori culture in order to find its artful 'inventions' and 'constructions'.[7]

Jeffrey Sissons sought to offer a more moderate interpretation of the 'invention of tradition' philosophy in his essay 'The Traditionalisation of the Maori Meeting House', published in a 1989 edition of *Oceania*.[8] He explains: 'by traditionalisation I mean a process or set of processes through which aspects of contemporary culture come to be regarded as valued survivals from an earlier time', assuming that 'there was a time when they were not so regarded.'[9] Sissons created some distance between his own work and that of Hanson and colleagues by suggesting that he was not attempting to demystify 'tradition' by raising the issues of inauthenticity and concealment. Traditionalisation approaches, he stated, were based on the premise that there were certain circumstances that required the contemporary to be placed 'out of time'. This statement is not so much a dismissal of Hanson's original argument as a variation on its theme.

For Sissons, the 'year zero' of the carved Maori meeting house, or the time when such structures were not regarded 'as survivals', begins around 1850 and lasts until 1890. These were the buildings that were developed in the central and eastern North Island in response to the teachings of Te Kooti Arikirangi Te Turuki and his Ringatu church.[10] Sissons uses the highly problematic word 'hybrid' to describe the buildings' stylistic and formal amalgamation of mission church, pioneer hall and chief's house. Ringatu architecture cannot be the essentialised yardstick against which all subsequent revivals are measured, as Sissons suggests, when the term 'hybrid' raises so many Hanson-style questions about 'authenticity'.

Sissons continues by presenting the carved Maori meeting houses made by Ngati Tarawhai for the New Zealand International Exhibition, held in Christchurch over 1905–06, as being a subsequent traditionalisation.[11] Using

Roger Neich's masters thesis on Ngati Tarawhai carving as source material, he notes that the exhibition's Maori village, built and decorated by the tribe's *tohunga whakairo* (master carvers), was a manifestation of tourist art which also illustrated the aesthetic philosophy of their Pakeha supervisor, Augustus Hamilton.[12] 'The meeting house,' Sissons writes, 'previously a threatening political symbol to colonial administrators, became neutralised, commodified and aestheticised' in this context.[13] The traditionalisation of the International Exhibition's Maori architecture assumes that Maori-made tourist buildings do not qualify as either a 'hybrid' or an 'authentic' continuity of building between 1890 and 1905, and that Ringatu architecture was somehow 'oppositional' when compared to Pakeha architecture. Once again there is an implicit essentialisation in Sissons's argument. No commentator has ever said that architecture made by Maori for Pakeha patrons rather than for Maori patrons is not Maori architecture. Furthermore, Ringatu architecture was generally built to celebrate Maori spirituality, and not to threaten colonial administrators. In many ways these buildings illustrated a Maori desire for peace rather than opposition between cultures and tribes.

Sissons views Apirana Ngata, the founder and unofficial head of the School of Maori Arts and Crafts, as continuing this traditionalisation process begun in 1905. However, there is nothing in Ngata's writings to suggest that he was especially aesthetically influenced by the buildings that he saw at the International Exhibition. Indeed, in 1927, carvers from the Ngati Whakaue tribe were hired to be the School's first instructors, with the only Ngati Tarawhai carver, Eramiha Kapua, being employed much later in 1930 as an adze expert.[14] Sissons noted that, during the most recent traditionalisation process, the current Maori renaissance, the meeting house has been repoliticised and systematised as a symbol of 'ethnic and indigenous distinctiveness' rather than political neutrality. He continues, 'it is conceivable that the Maori cultural renaissance of the 1970s and 1980s would not have gained the wide public support that it did without the "traditional" meeting house.'[15]

Toon van Meijl has recently extended this argument by claiming that Maori oppositional narratives have been formulated by an educated Maori elite, who have benefited from the economic and social opportunities that essentialism presents in state-run and corporate institutions. He claims that

Morehu, who are Maori who do not belong to this elite, can 'barely identify in terms of the tradition-oriented model for a Maori identity, since their identity is chiefly shaped by their position in the gutter of European society'.[16] Van Meijl's claims seem to be an overstatement of the actual situation, not just because he is unable to identify who the elite are, but also since he is ghettoising the histories of the so-called Maori underclass. Over the last ten years, Maori architectural history has recorded the constructional achievements of both traditionalised and Morehu builders.[17]

The invention of tradition theory, even in its revised form, raises important issues not only about the interpretation of the past, but also about the interpretation process. On the one hand, it allows the architectural historian the freedom to examine the processes that connect particular building types to nationalist movements; on the other hand, it constructs an invented identity for the architectural historian, one that claims 'access to a true or superior understanding of history and identity'.[18]

Revisionist histories

Revisionist histories attempt to correct earlier 'biased' histories. The two most prominent New Zealand revisionist historians are Anne Salmond and James Belich, who both work in the field of Maori and Pakeha 'interaction'.[19] The two main criticisms of revisionist histories in New Zealand are that they tend to recast Pakeha pioneers as invaders, and do not apply the same rigorous process of analysis to their Maori sources as that given to their Pakeha sources.[20]

Salmond's 1975 book *Hui* examined meeting house architecture in terms of its semiological meanings. Her most significant contribution to architectural discourse is her presentation of the meeting house as a set of structuralist binary oppositions (*tapu/noa*, male/female, front/back, *marae*/house, visitors/guests etc.), using Maori oral histories and many Pakeha text histories as source material.[21] From an invention of culture perspective, her observations are now part of our traditionalised understanding of the meeting house, influencing the writings of subsequent scholars, most notably Roger Neich and Ranginui Walker.[22] One future revisionist project will surely be the re-analysis of this source material to discover whether these binary oppositions are still apparent in a post-structuralist age.

Some historians, such as Miles Fairburn, have suggested that revisionist histories that use Maori and Pakeha source material are mixing the incompatible since Maori narratives are never scrutinised, as they are designed to unite communities, whereas Pakeha scholarship is founded on the criticism of knowledge.[23] The observation by historians that, for better or worse, Maori history and ancestral narratives are accepted unquestioningly by Maori, has been challenged by Michael King. He writes: 'having witnessed many times the intensity of [Maori] debate over aspects of *whanau* [family] or *iwi* [tribal] history, and the vigorous Maori examination of competing tribal resource claims, I think ... [Fairburn and others] underestimate the rigour of the process of internal critiquing involved in matauranga Maori [Maori knowledge].'[24] Indeed, in *Painted Histories*, Roger Neich has shown that Maori architecture, built after the arrival of Pakeha, successfully joins the two types of histories (narrative and chronological) for a common purpose.

A type of revisionist architectural pre-history has been written by at least one post-processual archaeologist. Doug Sutton, a lecturer in archaeology at the University of Auckland, has controversially used mythology as an interpretative tool when analysing the structures found at the Pouerua site in central Northland.[25] The 500-year-old 'Type 1' dwelling at this site, in Sutton's words, 'restated the myth of Rangi [the mythological sky father] and Papa [the mythological earth mother]'. In his view Type 1 was a prototype for the modern whare *whakairo* (decorated meeting house) because of its arrangement of posts, walls and fireplaces. He identified the front, central post as representing *mauri* (life force) and the *mana*, or 'prestige and stability', of the tribal group. Likening the post to a *tuahu* (shrine), he notes that it was not just a structural support but 'a symbolic representation of the earth/floor sky/roof separation' as outlined in the Maori origin myth. Type 1's greater length, when compared to other houses excavated at Pouerua, was explained as a reflection of the original occupants' 'relationship to death and passage after death', with the entry doorway representing Hine-nui-te-Po's (the goddess of death) vagina and the divergent side walls her parted legs. Sutton calls this interpretative technique 'Maori archaeology'.

Steven Webster describes Sutton's Maori archaeology as an 'ardently humanist reaction against several decades of restraint in deducing social organisation from the reticent data of archaeology ... drawing moral and theoretical inspiration from ethnic politics, the legitimating expedience of ethnographic fieldwork, and the meanings-based theory which has become so successful in social and cultural anthropology'.[26] Webster likens Sutton's approach to that of Salmond and Mead, and points out that Sutton's prototype whare is as much the product of colonial period development as it is the embodiment of mythology. Interestingly, the divergent side walls of the Pouerua Type 1 house became the prototype for the divergent side walls of the Tane-nui-a-Rangi meeting house at Auckland University's Waipapa marae.[27]

Foundational histories

'Foundational' historians purposefully locate themselves between the extreme positions of the 'invention of tradition' anthropologists and revisionist historians. As the editors of *Quicksands* note in their introduction, 'for us [the foundational historians] the problem is not "identity", contrived or not, but the rhetoric of identity in history, with the ways national identities and national histories are caught up in each other and argued through each other'.[28] In other words, the myths of the founding narratives are analysed with a view to creating alternative histories which one assumes either avoid or acknowledge the presence of these myths.

The 'foundations' referred to in foundational histories are not Aboriginal or Maori, but those of the Western coloniser. Thus the 'year zero' that Deborah Bird Rose refers to in her essay 'Hard Times – An Australian Study' is the year of European arrival, which marks the end of an assumed indigenous 'timelessness' and the beginning of historical chronology in time-based narratives.[29] Nicholas Thomas has identified two distinct Maori artistic philosophies of time, founded on pre- and post-colonial interpretations of art history, which could provide a framework for interpreting contemporary Maori architecture. He characterises the first philosophy as that which developed from the *Te Maori* exhibition, where 'the past is ... a source of techniques, forms, styles, motifs and generalised cultural principles such as tapu – but not of events'.[30] Mythological narrative, from the very distant past, rather than more recent *whakapapa* (Maori genealogy), is what is portrayed. He resists the temptation to call 'generalised cultural principles' 'tradition' or 'traditionalised', and makes no attempt to analyse their foundation to discover their 'inventiveness' or otherwise. In an architectural context, this philosophy of time is expressed by the contemporary carved meeting house which, due to the standardisation promoted by the School of Maori Arts and Crafts and its successor the Rotorua Crafts Institute, exudes a timelessness associated with style, form and ritual but not necessarily events.

According to Thomas, contemporary Maori artists, who are Indigenous artists working in the Westernised genre, 'resist this dehistoricising aesthetic ... and refer extensively to colonial relations in terms that frequently unite mythological references and recent developments'.[31] Since architecture never had a 'Tovey' generation, in which Maori practitioners were actively encouraged to combine mythological concepts with the Western aesthetic (modernism in the case of Tovey), the powerful combination of distant and recent past has not yet been fully achieved.[32] Thomas is referring to the art of Robert Jahnke and his peers and successors, the closest architectural equivalents being the work of Royal Associates and Rewi Thompson. The Royals and Thompson use plans and spatial arrangements that derive from myth, with the colonial referents mainly being materials and their respective modernist and postmodernist styles.[33] Contemporary Maori art has much stronger political content and a more highly developed aesthetic that often samples the Morehu art and architecture of the Pai Marire, Ringatu, Parihaka, Iharaira and Ratana movements. As Thomas notes, Morehu arts 'were not generalised expressions of tribal and ethnic identity, but biographical and legendary movements ... [the works] were elements in the architectural environments within which genealogical narratives concerning those figures were normally recounted'.[34] Rewi Thompson's City to Sea Bridge in Wellington, which he completed with the sculptor Paratene Matchitt (a Tovey-generation artist), approaches this philosophy, although the Morehu-derived forms on the bridge are Matchitt's innovations. It is only a matter of time before the historicised forms of Morehu architecture will begin to be a more prominent feature in contemporary Maori architecture.

The foundational history philosophy could also be applied to Pakeha architectural histories. If previous foundational histories of Pakeha culture are any guide, then the earliest pioneer architecture becomes the year zero of these narratives. The pioneer architect faces a dilemma. By wanting to establish a building in the new country, they must forget the old country. But in order to 'resist the indigenous presence', they must draw on their memory of the old country to have a distinct identity.[35] There is a danger in foundational architectural narratives that the pioneers and their buildings become 'over-romanticised'. It should be remembered that most Pakeha are urban dwellers, descended from twentieth-century migrants and not pioneers. More recent foundational narratives need to be established for these twentieth-century migrant ancestors – for example, stories about the movement of modernism from Europe to New Zealand as a consequence of the Second World War – to address any potential origin imbalance.

When Pakeha forget or abandon Europe, Pakeha architecture will enter a post-European state. Some foundational histories discuss the 'forgetting of Europe in socioeconomic terms, with important steps in the abandonment process being migration, the colonial experience of the World Wars, and Britain's 1973 admittance to the European Economic Community'.[36] The movement to a republic and the angst-free settlement of Treaty of Waitangi claims are, perhaps, the final steps in the process of forgetting Europe. As it stands, the beach and the bach (holiday home) remain romanticised places of Pakeha identity because of their pioneering connotations. Stephen Turner writes in his 'Settlement as Forgetting' essay, '... going to the beach has become an important form of acculturation for Pakeha – not just an enjoyable activity, but one that acknowledges a common culture. While the interior landscape still breathes the dissension of history that threatens settlement, the beach is a comfort zone for Pakeha, a settled perimeter, seemingly a place without history.'[37] Thus the bach is an important feature of Pakeha middle-class identity for the time being.

The place at which Maori and Pakeha foundational histories overlap is still to be defined, and therefore the architectural implications are not clear. Jonathan Lamb has identified the two types of pioneer histories that have been written in the past fifteen years as being either histories of pioneer utopia and romanticism, or histories of the pioneer seizure of Maori land.[38] Architectural histories will also need to work through these issues in order to find some common ground.

Conclusion

There is often a disjunction between theoretical culture and actual culture in postmodern writing. Few Maori people reading Nicholas Thomas and Jeffrey Sissons, for example, would even recognise that it was their culture that was under discussion. As Webster writes, 'the ways in which manifold appearances of contemporary Maori culture are ideologically separated from the everyday realities of Maori life suggest, indeed, that images of the culture refer only to other such images and "bear no relation to any reality whatever".'[39] The argument could easily be translated for the Pakeha experience of such writing. Nevertheless, the vocabulary of theoretical culture has been changed to suit local conditions. Terms such as 'pre-contact' and 'post-contact' have slowly dropped out of New Zealand academic language because they define the Maori past solely in terms of Pakeha arrival. The term 'post-colonial' has almost dropped out of the New Zealand art history vocabulary since many academics working in the field believe that our country still remains in a colonised state. Foreign 'post-colonial' theory remains in use under the broader title of 'post-structuralism'.

The ethnic bias of terminology raises another critical question about architectural history writing in the future: exactly who should write about whom? While Toon van Meijl's comments about a Maori academic elite setting a cultural agenda may seem a little far-fetched, his words do hint at a problem in Maori scholarship. The essentialisation of Maori culture, which has taken place from the mid-1980s, has put a significant amount of pressure on Maori academics, who are sometimes expected by their institutions to assume the type of 'traditionalised' role which is either unknown to them, or had to be suppressed during their time as students. As Margo Neale, Curator of Indigenous Australian Art, noted in an often quoted remark, 'once we were punished for being too black: now we are punished for not being black enough!'[40] The essentialisation of Maori culture has also seen many Pakeha scholars specialising in Maori studies sidelined. Oddly, foundational and revisionist histories, and their northern hemisphere predecessor 'Whiteness Studies', encourage writers of non-European descent to write about 'white' or Pakeha culture.[41] There is, perhaps, an assumption that people of European descent are the 'dominant' culture which can be safely critiqued; however, this opinion is based on the less-than-enlightened presumption that Indigenous peoples are 'subordinate' or 'marginal'.

The near future presents many exciting possibilities to architectural historians in Aotearoa New Zealand. Now that the inventiveness or traditionalisation of Maori architecture has been 'exposed', will the traditionalisation of Pakeha architecture be similarly demystified? In order to accomplish such a project 'Pakeha architecture' will need to be defined, and the nationalist middle-class icons of the bach and the boat shed will almost certainly feature. A revisionist history of Maori and Pakeha culture may expose working-class buildings like the state house, saw-mill, sheep shed, shopping mall and public bar, which can be added to this list. In any event, it seems highly likely that architectural history will become more widely debated, more theoretically-based, more nationalistic and much more interesting in the early part of this century.

Polynesian Influences in New Zealand Architecture

2000

MIKE AUSTIN

The influence of Polynesian architecture on that of Aotearoa/New Zealand has always been taken to be restricted to decorative motifs, but with changing views of the role of ornament in architecture this influence needs to be re-evaluated. With the Maori renaissance over the last few decades, an awareness of the significance of Polynesian architecture has become increasingly apparent. Recent buildings prompt some questions about the relation of Maori and Pakeha architecture. As Walden has said: 'It seems incredible that a creative profession such as architecture has denied the value of a Polynesian heritage. In my own judgement, New Zealand architects could have sympathetically considered the European/Polynesian synthesis as a fundamentally enriching objective.'[1]

The influence of Polynesian architecture on that of Aotearoa/New Zealand is, we have been regularly reminded, very small. Hurst Seager, writing at the turn of the century, is usually taken to be the first commentator on New Zealand architecture. 'Here in New Zealand the only historical examples of art we have are the works of the Maoris; and these, though excellent examples of savage art are scarcely suitable as standards on which to found our national taste.'[2]

This relies on a clear and comfortable differentiation of the savage that was the focus of Loos's proposition that the tattoo was acceptable on the savage but not on the civilised.[3] This distinction continues with Knight's professorial pronouncement half a century later, where civilisation is further defined as British. 'The Maori race, dominant in some other fields, had little architectural influence. They have it is true a native architecture interesting and valuable from a historical point of view, but it served a way of living entirely opposed to the British civilisation. Apart from some influence in detailed ornament it could have little effect upon contemporary design.'[4]

Maori architectural influence is confined to the ornamental in much the same way that the role of Maori in New Zealand public life used to be restricted to the entertainer. This consignment to the history and ornament categories has meant to the margins, but there is now an increasing interest in both history and ornament – and the marginal. According to Knight, Maori architecture as well as being ornamental is concerned with detail, and a few years later Pascoe and Hall say: 'Except for the typical carving on early Maori buildings, there is little in New Zealand architecture that can be said to be distinctive or indigenous.'[5] The word 'indigenous' raises the issue of identity – just who is indigenous?[6] In the nineteenth century a New Zealander was a Maori.[7] The twentieth century saw the term refer to Pakeha as well. 'Indigenous', however, has now returned to referring to Maori only. On most international arenas and occasions New Zealand appeals to Maori identity which, like the haka, is then cheerfully ignored or neglected at other times.[8]

Pevsner on his 1958 visit to New Zealand declined to comment on Maori art and architecture because he said he was 'not an expert'. This lack of expertise did not however prevent him from pointing out that: 'the crafts of the Maoris are gone'.[9] Shaw continues this nostalgia of loss when he says in a note at the beginning of *New Zealand Architecture*: 'Very little of the old Maori architecture survives today.' This book commences with: 'A history of the architecture of New Zealand must begin with the buildings of the *tangata whenua*, the people of the land.'[10] Shaw gives Maori architecture, including these beginnings, half a dozen or so pages out of the 200 in the book. Stacpoole and Beaven do not discuss pre-European architecture at all (for which they were criticised at the time) but they illustrate two Maori buildings.[11]

Stacpoole in *Colonial Architecture* summed up the conventional wisdom that there was 'no significant architecture to be digested'.[12] This is a peculiar expression (as is Hurst Seager's 'national taste'), given the association of New Zealand with anthropophagy and the tendency to cannibalise Maori architecture and museums. Recent work on cannibalism focuses precisely on the question of just who the cannibals were at the moment of intercultural exchange.[13] Cannibalism, as the sign of the other, has become a sign of undecideability. Consumption and (mis)appropriation of Maori aesthetic production is at stake and, as Steiner has argued, architectural discourse and practice have not been prepared to engage and grapple with the issue in the way that artists have done.[14]

Mitchell and Chaplin's *Elegant Shed* mentions that Rewi Thompson has Maori ancestors, while two books on New Zealand architects by Melling make no mention of Maori.[15] The most recent publication, *Looking at the Local*, refers to the *whare* in association with the hut and the bach in the context of a paper by McKay.[16] The general dismissal of Maori influence, however, continues up to the present where just last year Stewart writes: 'There must also be a question over claims of Maori influence in an art form which has a very limited resource in Maori tradition.'[17]

This is in the context of a discussion about John Scott, the architect of Futuna Chapel, which is the subject of a book by Walden, who implies that Scott's Maori ancestry is no more important than his Scottish and Irish origins, and possibly less significant than his Catholic upbringing, in the design of the chapel.[18] The building, which commemorates a martyrdom on the Polynesian Island of Futuna, is claimed by Walden to be an 'architectural watershed in our indigenous struggle to be ourselves as Pacific people'.[19] 'Indigenous' here includes Pakeha, but Beaven and Stacpoole evoke colonial descriptions of Maori when they say about Futuna: 'Integrity, decoration, and mysterious moods come together in this building to create one of the finest architectural experiences in New Zealand, and place the chapel in world class.'[20]

The intensely local, it seems, evokes the international. However, it is not clear why the building is considered to be decorated. Presumably it refers to the artwork and the coloured perspex glazing, which happens to be the work of a Pakeha artist – Jim Allen. Walden says that Futuna is a 'faithful celebration of Maori and Pakeha' and that 'the marriage of Maori and Pakeha is legitimate'.[21] There is maybe a certain anxiety about propriety and ownership here and, while the issue of paternity is raised, there is no clue as to how this marriage was consummated other than 'a new synthesis of Maori and Pakeha values'.[22] Nor were there any offspring. Walden makes references to European precedents, with illustrations, but while the *marae* and meeting house are mentioned in terms of pedestrian approach and the crossing of the threshold, there are no illustrations of Maori precedents.

And there was a Maori precedent. Almost exactly a century earlier there was a building with an uncanny resonance with Futuna. This is the so-called 'Maori Church' Rangiatea which, like Futuna, was named after a Polynesian island and was remarkably similar to the later building with its timber posts, exposed rafters and branches of freestanding diagonal struts. This building was also described as 'decorated' although it was explicitly not carved, the decoration being confined to *kowhaiwhai* rafter patterns and *tukutuku* wall panelling. Walden doesn't mention Rangiatea as an influence on John Scott but it is very unlikely that Scott didn't know the building – or rather representations of it.

The many representations of Rangiatea (which is the subject of Treadwell's doctoral thesis) are diverse, sometimes implying that the building was no longer in existence and perpetuating the nostalgia of loss – prophetically as it happened, as the building was burnt down in 1995.[23] Shaw begins Chapter One with an interior photograph of Rangiatea (and Chapter Nine with Futuna), claiming that this building was 'the first to blend Maori and European building traditions'.[24] He does not say how this occurred and Treadwell has articulated in detail the ingredients and complexity of this 'blending'. Stacpoole and Beaven insist that the initiation and the supervision of the structure was by Europeans, which is again to simplify a matter of some complexity.[25]

There is then not a lot of material on Maori architecture in these publications. On the other hand academic endeavour in general in New Zealand has tended to focus on Maori issues, and this is arguably true in architecture, where there are theses and a number of papers dealing with Maori architecture. Recently McCarthy has drawn attention to the complex architectural exchange in Dunedin's 'Maori House'.[26] There is a scholarly and thorough history of nineteenth-century meeting houses by Roger Neich, while Alfred Gell uses the meeting house as his exemplar for a comprehensive theory of art.[27] There is a possibility that the influence of Maori architecture has been more significant than is acknowledged, in the same way as the Pacific has been influential in Western thinking.[28]

Up until the 1950s, Maori motifs were incorporated in building ornament and often Maori motifs were used as part of the orders that are the very authorisation of the building as architecture.[29] According to this view, Maori provide the architecture, reflecting the comment of the New York art critic who said that the Maori had produced the only architecture in New Zealand. There are well-known examples incorporating Maori motifs in the Art Deco decoration in Napier and here the local is somehow legitimised by the international.[30] The ornamental is the repressed side of modern architecture so that, by being restricted to the decorative, Maori architecture became doubly dismissed.

McKay argues that fifties modernist architects, with nationalist concerns, attempted to incorporate Maori forms in the architecture of timber and pitched roofs against the white planes and flat roofs of international modernism. He admits nevertheless that 'the *whare* form does not appear frequently in the buildings of New Zealand modern architects'.[31] Shaw proposes that 'the appropriation of Maori forms were symptomatic of the desire of many architects and artists to find a means of expression which could possibly be called a New Zealand vernacular style'.[32] He goes on to suggest that it was a motivating factor behind the work of the Group – especially the Second House, which was called the 'pakeha house'. Paradoxically, the Group's reverse reference to Maori was commented on in two English architectural journals.[33]

Toy referred to the *marae*/meeting house complex in two of his churches – implicitly at All Saints in Ponsonby and explicitly at the Auckland Cathedral. But it was the form and not the decoration (or for that matter the structure) of the *whare* that was taken seriously. This of course was consistent with modernist views, but it meant that Maori architecture continued to be seen as different from mainstream New Zealand architecture. One way of ignoring Maori architecture is to consign it to the traditional so that, as the other, Maori might have produced a certain Englishness in New Zealand architecture in the way that the Waitangi Treaty relies on the differences between English and Maori for its very existence. In any case, at the time of the Treaty there was not any question that what the Maori built was architecture: 'With a view to perpetuate the singular and beautiful architectural remains of these people, I made carefully finished drawings on the spot of all those most worthy of record, and thus rescued from certain and speedy oblivion the works of art of a race of men who are undergoing a most rapid and extraordinary change.'[34] This comment initiates the nostalgia of loss that characterised the subsequent discourse, which assumes that the influence flows one way from European to Maori. However, it has often been suggested that in early contacts between Maori and Pakeha 'the qualities of the indigenes are the most profound influence on kind of settler society which is imposed upon them'.[35] This was certainly true architecturally. From the beginning of European settlement the immigrant was dependent upon Maori goodwill and construction when Maori controlled coastal shipping and much of the food production.[36] This was also the time of the flowering of the store house (*pataka*) – when carving appeared on the surface of the building instead of being confined to the interior. These buildings, along with war canoes, died and were buried in museums.

In the 1860s Maori won the battles but lost the wars, leading to a drastic decline in Maori population for the next 30 years.[37] This period, however, produced a most extraordinary architectural response, which was to develop the architecture of the meeting house. Deriving from the *whare*, this building owes much to the church to which it is spatially similar but theoretically and conceptually quite opposed. European elements such as doors, windows, fretwork, roofing iron and weatherboards were appropriated and experimented with in the development of the house. This was an assemblage rather than a 'synthesis' by Maori, where European elements were collaged onto the *whare* form. Te Kooti was the definer of the classic form of the house which has been the model ever since.[38] However, as Linzey points out, it is also necessary to recall that Te Kooti built these significant houses while a fugitive from the British; he was reviled until relatively recently in Pakeha imagination, and the religion that he founded (Ringatu) was suppressed for over half a century.

McKay argues that there has been a suppression of other architectural forms than the standard meeting house and points out that there were many other pre-European and post-European architectural forms. He argues that this stereotyping serves to limit understanding of Maori architecture and its substantial regional variations. On the other hand the meeting house is an extraordinary achievement, and to repeat its most remarkable aspect was that it achieved its classic form in the 1870s and 1880s – at the very moment Maori population was in crisis from wars and disease and the European role was seen to 'soothe the pillow of the dying race.' The house looked to the past where, alongside the well-known symbolism of the ancestor's body, there is also the multi-layered self similarity of the numerous other figures. However, it also looked to the future providing hope for a possibility that no European believed existed.[39]

The Maori meeting house confuses the easy opposition between structure and decoration that is now a commonplace. In the house it is the structure that is decorated with carving, while the infill (*tukutuku*) panelling has its patterns created by the process of constructing a structurally stable flat panel out of reeds and fibre. These patterns are named, but can be shown to be limited to the fabrication process. With carving (as with the tattoo) the decoration is not applied, but rather cut into, the surface of the material and this might be seen to open up and structurally weaken the members. It was a destruction of the surface, which Loos would argue was a disfiguring. But the intention was quite the opposite. The carvings were all human figures and prior to Loos they would be seen to strengthen rather than weaken the structure. Owen Jones (half a century before Loos and his Papuan paddle) spoke about the Maori paddle, which he claimed 'would rival the works of the highest civilisation' and he noted: 'He (the New Zealander) desired not only that the paddle should be strong, but should appear so, and his ornament is so disposed as to give an appearance of additional strength to what it would have had if the surface had remained undecorated.'[40]

Today no visitor to a meeting house is in any doubt that the architecture of such a building is constituted by its decoration. John Scott himself said: 'The Maori will not worry about buildings but he will worry about those particular kinds of things he has around – the carvings and *tukutuku* work.'[41] Those committed to the nostalgia of loss mourn the present-day absence of a structural role for the carvings, but the Maori view (that the ornament is the architecture) has given architects the secondary role of supporting and holding up the ornament. For example, in the Auckland University meeting house the structure is a steel frame with timber infill to which the carvings are attached. The steel frame can be seen as subservient to the carvings, producing the typical Semperian and de Stijl reversals that seem to occur around this topic.[42] Carving is allowed (necessary even) on meeting houses but not on European buildings – reinforcing the difference.

The meeting house is always associated with a *marae* and it is now difficult to believe that it was assumed 30 years ago that this institution (along with Maori language) would be restricted to occasional and ritual use.[43] Some claimed that only traditional sites and structures were allowable for the building.[44] However, *marae* have now replaced churches as community buildings, being built at almost every educational and community institution in the country. The *marae* was central to the design of the National Museum Te Papa where, instead of just being enclosed as in other museums, the *marae* and meeting house gets lifted off the ground and interiorised. The Te Papa meeting house seems to respond to this isolation where the decoration is wonderfully innovative and excessive, crawling out over the *maihi* (bargeboard) as if it has been held inside for far too long. However, the decoration and indeed the marae never makes it to the outside of the building.

Kawiti has pointed out that Te Papa is located on the beach – the site of arrival, departure and pleasure for the European.[45] Certainly, with its axes and cleavages, the building owes more to Europe than to Polynesia. The device of the wall around which the building is organised is not a Pacific form and, although the building is ostensibly Maori, it is so only in name. Giving European buildings Maori names is well established as an attempt to belong and to possess. 'Our Place', however, lost the opportunity to use the *marae* as approach and to use ornament on the exterior. Yet interestingly, this is at the very moment when there is international interest in exterior ornament and the specifically Polynesian decorative device of the tattoo.

There is another building by John Scott, not mentioned by Walden, where carving did make it to the exterior as 'decorative' panels on the facade.[46] This is the Maori Battalion building in Palmerston North: 'It initially seems strange that this building is so unrecognised by the architectural profession. In the many retrospective articles in *Architecture New Zealand* dedicated to Scott's work then is no mention of this building. In comparison *Te Ao Hou: The Maori Magazine* dedicated a front cover and article to this work, showering the building with praise.'[47] Steiner has written extensively about this project where Scott appropriated English New Brutalism and combined it with Maori carving around the tradition of the canoes. In this building the carvings weave their way across the glass façade so that the 'equivalent sized windows and carvings become, in many ways, a reversal or negative of each other'.[48] Steiner gives several readings of the impropriety of this façade arguing that this is no easy harmonious mixing. On the other hand Maori commentary said: 'Here at last is a building incorporating both Maori and European elements of architecture which are not only happily and harmoniously wedded, but which show conclusively that it is possible for New Zealand to develop unique architectural forms.'[49]

Again the marriage metaphor and again, it seems, a union without issue. No one else has dared to do this – not even (or maybe especially) Maori architects. Interestingly, Scott and some other Maori architects (like the Maori prophets Te Whiti, Rua and Ratana) have never felt entirely comfortable with the meeting house. Some have worked hard to change the wooden aspects of Maori architecture. Other Maori architects have resisted a racial identification, but these days it leads to commissions.

Pakeha architects, it seems, have difficulties with Maori influences and associations, but this does not prevent them making claims on the Pacific. Perhaps it is because the Pacific Islands voice lacks local power. For example Kermadec restaurant in Auckland uses suspended Pacific Island mats and paintings as a ceiling lining, a notion that would no doubt produce an outcry from Maori. Perhaps it is because Pacific buildings do not have the decorative dilemmas of the caned house. The recent book *Pacific Island Style* has no examples from New Zealand, while *Pacific Island* on the other hand includes New Zealand and explicitly claims Polynesian influence.[50] In it Andrew Patterson claims an inner-city courtyard house is based on the *marae* but once again it is a closed courtyard as against the openness of the *marae*.

This mention of the Pacific returns us to the title which continues to be problematic. 'Polynesian' does not distinguish between the various and different Pacific Island groups and between them and Maori. Talk of influence is to perpetuate the New Zealand obsession with origins and sources and anxieties about ownership. Influence is in the end about power and it is not sufficient explanation of the complex interrelated formations and decisions that constitute a piece of architecture.

A Myth in its Making: Federation Style and Australian Architectural History

2000

JULIE WILLIS AND PHILIP GOAD

This paper is about the problems of defining and coining stylistic terms. It might appear to some to be a pedantic task that falls within the dusty realms of taxonomic history and deserves little discussion. The fear in tackling such an issue is that one will succumb to the documentation of architecture as a progression from one hotly-argued stylistic label to another; that history will be seen as the rise and fall of its labels, and its documents as representing little more than gazetteers of dictionary definitions. But it is at times a necessary and difficult task to test the discipline's own language and its own terms of reference; to actually see whether the basis for the discussion of an historical period has itself been subjected to a previous construction of language from which there have been conclusions too swiftly drawn or assumptions unwisely made. This is one such occasion.[1]

It is especially important to examine the use of style names in Australia, as the point at which Australian characteristics began to assert themselves was a time of great stylistic eclecticism. Three things complicate the discussion. Firstly, not until the nineteenth century was there a firm understanding that there could be a number of architectural styles; that is, that architects and clients could choose between quite different architectural expressions. That century saw a protracted battle amongst a number of revival styles, principally classical and gothic derivatives. AWN Pugin and others had advocated a scholarly revivalism, but towards the end of the century architects sought to use architectural languages of the past within their own compositional sensibilities, prompted in no small part by the Arts and Crafts movement. Thus, secondly, architects were not only experimenting with different architectural languages, but were also using them to forge new languages. Thirdly, there has been no clear or definitive statement elsewhere in regard to naming styles of this period – the elastic descriptions that are still in use in Britain and America only serve to make the task of defining the Australian end of such architectural development all the more difficult.

To closely examine the coining of stylistic terms in architecture is to call into question how and why such terms were adopted. Far from being a simple task, where a single style has been developed (and even named) hundreds, if not thousands, of years ago, terminology for more recent developments must reflect a common understanding of both the sensibility being employed and the period of time in which it was created.

As Australia approaches the centenary of its Federation, the amalgamation of the various British colonies occupying the Australian mainland and some surrounding islands (New Zealand declined the invitation to join the new nation), the years around 1901 are the subject of renewed interest. There is a prevalent assumption that the move towards and the success of gaining Federation were fundamental to an idea of an apparently separate Australian nation. Now the term 'Federation' is seen to embody independence from the 'mother country', Britain, and a sense of individual identity amongst English-speaking nations.

Australia's architectural history of the period has not yet been put under full critical scrutiny. As with much of the architecture of the twentieth century, discussions of architectural matter at the turn of the last century have been primarily concerned with domestic architecture.[2] And it is with domestic architecture that the so-called 'Federation style' is almost exclusively associated. This paper will examine the creation and definition of the term 'Federation style', the motivations behind the coining of the term and the complexities now inherent in its use. One may well ask why Federation architecture is seen as appropriate only for domestic architecture and has not, thus far, been associated with any of the architectural projects created for, or as a result of, the act of Federation.

In examining the architecture of the period 1890–1915 in Australia, it is not difficult to become ensnared in the conflicting use of style names (Federation, Edwardian, Queen Anne, Arts and Crafts, etc.) and the competing philosophies of the architects themselves. It was a time of vibrant and eclectic appropriation of architectural languages of the past, combined with novel and inventive compositional techniques. In Australia the influence of Britain was still strongly evident, with many architects having either trained there or received their training from an emigrant architect in the 1870s and 1880s. But America, too, was starting to exert influence, particularly through the work of HH Richardson. Some of this American influence was direct and some filtered through Britain, where Richardsonian Romanesque was being well received and even copied.[3] As in Britain, there was a distinct split between the type of architectural language used for domestic architecture and that used for institutional and commercial building (that is, medium- to large-scale urban architecture). This split has been one of the continuing difficulties in the use of the term 'Federation' and in its exclusive application to domestic architecture.

Coining the term

The adoption of the term 'Federation' to describe architecture in Australia between 1890 and 1915 came about through an extended dialogue between the eminent art and architectural historians Bernard Smith and David Saunders between 1969 and 1973. Both were at the time teaching at the University of Sydney's Power Institute, Foundation for Art and Visual Culture. Smith was its inaugural Professor, Saunders a Senior Lecturer. Although it was seemingly speculative at first, there was a growing confidence in the use of the term as each historian quoted the other's use of it as evidence of its appropriateness. The use of the term also had fortuitous political overtones in the late 1960s and early 1970s. At a time of student unrest and intellectual cultural upheaval, the term 'Federation' would arguably, in academic circles, have had connotations of independence and release from Empire, and coincided with the early 1970s shift to and rise of the intellectual Left in Australia. In addition, the recovery of the so-called Queen Anne was a recovery of a style from its modernist outcasting; here was an apparently local idiom that could be resuscitated and reinvigorated and was healthy and original.

In 1969, David Saunders published an important article examining domestic architecture in Melbourne and Sydney, 'Domestic Styles of Australia's Federation Period: Queen Anne and the Balcony Style'.[4] The article was the culmination of research undertaken over the previous three years, both in Melbourne and Sydney, and was the first real attempt to formulate stylistic definitions for domestic architecture of the period. It is important to note that Saunders did not refer to a single 'Federation style', but rather the plural, 'styles', which he included a number of subsidiary styles, including Queen Anne and the 'Balcony' style. Saunders acknowledged that it was Bernard Smith who proposed the term 'Federation', seeing the 'usefulness of the title' and noting its 'hint of nationalism'.[5] It is important to understand that, at the time Saunders was researching and writing about turn-of-the-century Australian architecture, little substantive research on the period in Britain or elsewhere had yet been undertaken, or published. It was not until 1975, when the edited collection *Edwardian Architecture and its Origins* was published, and 1977 when Alastair Service's *Edwardian Architecture: A Handbook to Building Design in Britain, 1890–1914* and Mark Girouard's *Sweetness and Light: The Queen Anne Movement, 1860–1900* were released that substantial architectural scholarship on the period in Britain became available. Saunders, therefore, was writing about a period about which much derogatory comment had been made in relation to the architectural styles, especially the so-called Queen Anne.[6] Saunders, however, was careful to note the confusion and difficulties of using the title 'Queen Anne', yet found it to have continuing usefulness: 'That name [Queen Anne] tends to rub off on all that happened in the period. It is a name that had international currency, but meant different things in different places. The style it refers to in this country is uniquely Australian. In the leading examples it represented a fundamentally new architecture.'[7]

Saunders used the term 'Federation' to refer to a period of time, taking in spirit the custom of naming an architectural style after the incumbent monarch but substituting the more democratically appropriate reference to Federation. Saunders allowed the possibility of numerous styles falling under the broad banner of Federation, although he concentrated upon domestic architecture in his article. This was not a wholesale adoption of Smith's term, but a cautious acknowledgment that the term might have use in denoting an emerging Australian strain of architecture.

Bernard Smith, both in his review article of JM Freeland's *Architecture in Australia* (1969) and (with Kate Smith) in *The Architectural Character of Glebe Sydney* (1973), did not offer such delicate distinctions. Smith proposed the singular, a Federation style, to describe domestic architecture at the turn of the century. Scathing of the use of 'Queen Anne' to describe this architecture, and calling the term inadequate, Smith wrote:

> The style in question is an Australian style if ever there was one, and deserves its own name. My own nomination would be Federation style. For it was born within the context of a discussion about the nature of an Australian style which parallels the political discussion that led to the foundation of the Commonwealth, and its decline parallels that loss of national energy consequent upon ... Australia's human losses in the First World War. During the last decades of the century architects ... seriously discussed the possibility of creating an Australian style of Architecture. Perhaps it is time that we began to take that debate more seriously; because it is just possible that they succeeded in producing what they had set their minds to; a style, that is to say, with characteristics as marked and definable as any domestic style within the tradition of western architecture.[8]

Smith's sentiments in this article are very much a reaction against Freeland's *Architecture in Australia*. The discussions between Smith and Saunders (mentioned in Saunders's article) suggest that Smith was not making a flippant or passing suggestion, but rather attempting to demonstrate an ethereal, but emerging, Australian development in architecture (Smith wrote of its 'originality').[9] Smith's mistake, in reacting to Freeland, was to propose the term for domestic work only. In fact Smith made no attempt to define Federation style – perhaps not seeing it as appropriate in the review of another's book – and only alluded to its possible definition in a description of the so-called Queen Anne style and naming a number of architects with whom the style could be associated.

By 1973, Smith was sufficiently confident of the term to use it in the book *The Architectural Character of Glebe Sydney*, authored with Kate Smith. The last chapter of the book was devoted to and titled 'The Federation Style'.[10]

The Smiths began with the question '"Queen Anne" or "Federation"?', going on to label Queen Anne as both 'unsatisfactory' and 'misleading':

> It seems ... unwise to persist with the label 'Queen Anne' in order to describe the style.
>
> Here we shall call it instead, Federation style. Firstly, because it was a style that flourished throughout Australia from Fremantle to Bondi during the years immediately before the federation of the Australian colonies into the Australian Commonwealth in 1901. Secondly, because it developed a character that is unique to Australia and deserves therefore an Australian name.[11]

Yet they went on to say 'It is not possible here to provide a full account of the style.' The Smiths did, however, briefly discuss the main characteristics of the style, concentrating almost entirely on the types of materials used. The style, therefore, was defined by example and those examples appear to have been chosen by virtue of their date of construction, rather than being exemplars of an identifiable style. Some of the housing shown owed far more to the Victorian era in their composition – their 'Federation' era dressing merely icing (or in these cases barge boards) on the cake.

Some attempt was made to include architecture that was not housing: two paragraphs were devoted to the discussion of 'civic architecture', considering just two buildings. The first, St John's Parish Hall (1897) had an awkward, blockish style that showed none of the 'irregularity in massing and planning'[12] that the Smiths ascribed to it. The second, the Glebe Fire Station (Walter Vernon, 1906), was supposed to show 'the then current interest in the work of Charles Annesley Voysey in England and Henry Hobson Richardson in America'.[13] Voysey perhaps, at a pinch; but there are no apparent effects or influences of Richardson in the building at all. It seems as though Smith was too eager to coin the term and failed to clearly and carefully define the style in scholarly terms. Intuition seemed to precede analysis.

Yet the die was cast. The term was quickly adopted, with authors again and again referring back to Smith's and Saunders's definitions, but almost always as the single Federation style, rather than the plural styles. This culminated in 1989 with the publications of Howells and Nicholson's *Towards the Dawn: Federation Architecture in Australia 1890–1915*. The work contained therein was overwhelmingly domestic architecture and small-scale (less than three storeys). The editors in their preface wrote of the difficulties and, within the book, their own distinctions (without necessarily defining them) of the terms 'Federation' and 'Queen Anne'.[14] The first chapter, by Trevor Howells, discussed the event of Federation, including illustrations of some of the temporary structures associated with the event itself. The second, likewise by Howells and titled 'In Search of a Grand National Style', defined Federation architecture as 'in essence ... largely domestic in scale and in building type'.[15] In a footnote, 'Federation' and 'Queen Anne' were explained as the then-used style names for domestic architecture of the period in both New South Wales and Victoria. This is borne out by George Tibbits, in his chapter 'An Emanation of Lunacy', where he steadfastly avoids 'Federation' as a stylistic term.[16] Indeed Tibbits does not restrict himself to a discussion of domestic architecture – it appears that his use of numbers of stylistic terms allowed a greater appreciation of architecture of the period. What is extraordinary about Howells's idea of a 'Grand National Style' was that it appeared to be an attempt to correlate Australian domestic architecture of the time with the British notion of the 'Grand Manner', although the 'Grand Manner' was only ever applied to large-scale buildings that owed much to the Edwardian Baroque, not domestic villas.

Why would a term such as 'Federation' be contentious? The adoption of it by some sectors of Australia's writers of architectural history has gone without question. The difficulty lies in the level and type of nationalism now being associated with the term and, as we approach the centenary of the event itself, the fact that the architectural expression of the event, albeit mostly temporary, had little to do with so-called Federation architecture. For example, the arches and pavilions built to celebrate Federation had nothing whatsoever to do with Smith's definition of the Federation style, yet these are the very structures that deserve the title, if there is to be only one, of Federation architecture. The plethora of styles in use at the time means that one cannot easily define the Federation style, but rather only one of a number of Federation styles.

The context of nationalism

In discussions with the authors, Tibbits has spoken of the understanding (or context) of nationalism in which he believed architecture and writings were conceived within in the 1890s.[17] Rather than an idea of national pride focused primarily upon Australia, Tibbits believes that nationalism was more to do with an identification with Anglo-Saxon, English-speaking people across the world: a sort of 'global cultural brotherhood'. Thus, the architecture of Britain was equally as appropriate as the architecture of America, or indeed the British Raj in India. This understanding of nationalism fits more clearly with parallel searches of national styles elsewhere in the English-speaking world. Tibbits likens the search for an appropriate architecture for Australia at that time as being the equivalent of a search for appropriate architecture in Surrey: the details may be local, but the spirit of the architecture was evident worldwide. This understanding also suggests that architecture was not necessarily about the expression of Empire, but more a manifestation of race. This conception of race was fundamental for the move towards and the gaining of Federation at a time when Australia wished to define itself not as part of Asia or the Pacific, but as white.[18]

Diversity of idioms

With such a qualification in mind, there needs to be acknowledgment of the range of architectural idioms employed at the time; not an idea of a singular style but a diverse set of regional derivations for a series of approaches to architectural design. Richard Apperly, Robert Irving and Peter Reynolds in *A Pictorial Guide to Identifying Australian Architecture* go to the other extreme from Smith's single style, providing a series of twelve style names, from 'Federation Academic Classical' to 'Federation Filigree'.[19] Their intentions are admirable but the divisions are too numerous and too prescriptive, clouding the important and significant hybrid nature of the design tradition. To talk about Federation Anglo-Dutch reaches the point of arcane label creation. It also ignores the inventive borrowing and assimilation underpinning the tradition that a rich mixture of styles is an intrinsic component of the design method. Apperly, Irving and others ignore the potential for such a series of buildings to eschew referent models. While such a proposition cannot be said of the so-called Edwardian Baroque (which they for some reason omit), there appears a reluctance to admit the modernity of the compositional techniques employed at the time.

What is surprising about these publications that either call for, concentrate upon, or include notions of a Federation architecture is that they do not consider that there was an identifiable design or compositional tradition of the time. The scholars seem to be caught within an understanding that style can be only be determined by a recognisable and elementary language of architecture or must include all that was built within a period of time. Yet the end of the nineteenth century was an important period of extensive experimentation and consideration of design philosophy. In this way, the period 1890–1915 laid the foundation for the emerging modern movement. To consider architecture emerging from this period in terms of a design or compositional theory, rather than an elemental language, is more appropriate to the context of its creation.

Service's notion of a free style

It is worth briefly turning to consider Alastair Service's treatment of the same period in Britain.[20] Faced with very similar problems of multiple definitions, Service makes some neat distinctions. In particular he uses the notion of a 'Free style' which is an inventive compositional tradition partially born of the Arts and Crafts movement. By concentrating upon the compositional sensibility, Service steps around the split between scale and language evident at the time. Hence, buildings can still be identified in terms of architectural language (Edwardian Baroque, Neo-Georgian, Arts and Crafts), but can still be bound together by a similar approach to architecture. While the domestic architecture featured by Service is not identical to that identified with Federation style in Australia, it is reminiscent of some of the work of Harold Desbrowe Annear and Robert Haddon. The large-scale and urban work considered by Service under the banner of 'Free style' does, however, seem closely related to much similarly-sized work in Australia. In Australia, it would appear then that more generic terms are useful; hence, Service's 'Free style' is more embracing (but bears an unfortunate closeness to a swimming stroke). Conrad Hamann's notion of a 'virtual "Federation Agreement"'[21] amongst designers might offer a more realistic picture of the complexities of an assimilative design ethos. Yet even Hamann talks in nationalist terms, speaking of 'an imaging of Australia in architecture', and he perhaps unwisely highlights what he describes as 'the synthesis of new, often conspicuously non-British approaches to architectural form'.[22] This is not entirely accurate, but Hamann's recognition of an implicit design agreement or sensibility has merit.

A Federation Agreement

Hamann's idea of a Federation Agreement is perhaps the closest understanding of a compositional sensibility in architecture at that time in Australia. It is in this way that any association of the term 'Federation' with architecture should be understood. It means that the term does not simply refer uncritically to a period of time, but imparts an understanding of the political and architectural context. It also harks back to a statement made by Bernard and Kate Smith, which in their publication was not elaborated upon, that has surfaced as an understanding of Federation style in subsequent publications – the notion of the 'irregularity in massing and planning'[23] as being a truer test of a Federation architecture than materials or date of construction alone. It is therefore possible to divide Federation architecture into a number of types or styles, such as Federation Domestic Architecture and Federation Urbanism. A consideration of smaller divisions of style can fit beneath and as part of this broader understanding of the period. But at the same time, concentrating on the compositional method evident at the time does not necessarily engender a consideration of scale in the first instance. The implicit theoretical understanding within a Federation Agreement, with its use of traditional elements, links the period both to the twentieth century and the nineteenth: appropriate for its *fin de siècle* position.

The argument for using the term 'Federation' is that it marks a point in time in building production. The value in doing so is to point to the especially

Australian aspects of the design in question. However, two important aspects of our use of the term 'Federation' must be recognised. First, the idiom should not be regarded as being exclusively Australian. The compositional methods inherent in the then-current fashion for stylistic variety and formal variation were not unique to Australia. Second, there is an undeniable attraction in adopting the term, which implies cultural and political independence from Empire. However, the ease with which historians, and some of our best, have adopted the term without clear definition or critical analysis is of concern. The term was one created by historians; it was never used at the time to describe buildings or the period. In adopting the term 'Federation', historians also need to see that, like its political reality, it is a matter of convenience. For like the six states (colonies) of Australia in a time of Imperial anxiety, Federation enabled the appearance of a unified conversation to occur. The same can also be said of architectural history. We desire such (potentially troubled) terms to simply talk and write about our buildings and structure our analysis of production. Federation was an act of necessary dependence. Our adoption of such terms needs to be understood in the same way.

Between the Georgina and the Great Western Railway: The Transformation and Maintenance of Aboriginal Architecture in North-West Queensland

2002

STEPHEN LONG

In a paper concerned with the evolution of Australian Indigenous architecture the researchers Memmott and Go-Sam challenged non-Aboriginal concepts of architecture with examples of the minimalist and dynamic architectural properties of temporary Aboriginal camps. Yet the same paper limited Aboriginal 'ethno-architecture' by defining it as buildings produced by their users and by placing it 'out bush' and on the fringes of towns and settlements.[1] In doing so, a significant component of Aboriginal architectural history was overlooked – the maintenance and transformation of architectural traditions by Aboriginal groups interacting with non-Aboriginal buildings and environments. The current paper demonstrates these architectural traditions through a case study of the transformation and maintenance of the architecture of the Dajarra Aboriginal community.[2]

Between the Georgina and the Great Western Railway

Dajarra is a small town located on Carbine Creek, 150 kilometres south of the North-West Queensland regional centre of Mt Isa and approximately 120 kilometres east of the Georgina River. A majority of the Dajarra Aboriginal population, of approximately 250, originally came from the Georgina River and identify as Waluwarra people.[3] The population also comprises East Arrernte, Wakaya, Garawa, Waanyi and Kalkadoon.[4]

The Georgina River system is part of the extensive and internal Lake Eyre drainage system. The perennial waterholes on the Georgina are the only reliable source of surface water in this region, which is characterised by a hot-dry climate with high evaporation rates.[5] These waterholes are important Waluwarra places of ceremonial, economic and residential activity. The Georgina and its tributaries are travel corridors utilised by the Waluwarra and other Aboriginal groups and they were part of the trunk trade route of Aboriginal Australia.[6]

The European invasion of the Georgina, which commenced in the 1860s, was characterised by attempts to usurp the waterholes from traditional owners.[7] Aboriginal people were 'hunted' from the waterholes and they were massacred on the banks of the Georgina. Cattle stations occupied many of the significant waterholes and the Georgina became a key stock-droving route. Aboriginal groups resisted these incursions with acts of economic warfare such as killing and wounding cattle, and they performed special ceremonies to summon powerful and destructive forces on the invaders.[8] Conflict over the waterholes was exacerbated by lengthy droughts in the late 1800s and early 1900s and the devastation amongst the Georgina River groups by introduced diseases.[9]

During these droughts the Waluwarra and other groups formed camps on the Georgina River cattle stations and at the fledgling township of Urandangie where they were able to obtain food supplies and medicines.[10] Aboriginal people were then forced to work the North-West Queensland stations under various government acts that were enforced by the police officer at Urandangie (the local 'Protector of Aborigines') until the 1960s. On the stations and at Urandangie, Aboriginal people built their own dwellings and they experienced new architectural types such as the 'big house' (the manag-er's quarters), large timber and tin structures such as the Coona and Rochedale woolsheds and limestone dam walls constructed by Chinese labourers.[11] In addition to working sheep and cattle, Aboriginal people were involved in the construction and maintenance of the 'industrial architecture' of the cattle stations, which included bores, wells, fences, yards, tanks and sheds.

In 1917 drovers travelling down the Georgina began to branch off at Urandangie and walk their mobs east to a new destination – the Great Western Railway, which had reached the east bank of Carbine Creek.[12] The railhead was named Dajarra after a nearby Aboriginal story place.[13] Work on the planned extension of the line to Darwin was suspended in 1920, making Dajarra the westernmost point of the Queensland rail network.[14] As a critical link to east coast ports it quickly became a bustling cattle trucking centre for most of northern Australia.[15]

A series of migrations of Waluwarra, from the Georgina and cattle station camps to Dajarra, commenced in the 1930s and culminated in the early 1970s with the forced movement of a group of mostly Arrerntic people to Dajarra from Urandangie by the Department of Aboriginal and Islanders' Advancement (DAIA).[16] At Dajarra, the Waluwarra and later East Arrernte immigrants camped in clusters of extended family groups 'across the creek' at the West End where they built 'tin sheds' or humpies.[17] In the late 1960s some of the Waluwarra moved into the first Aboriginal housing built in town.[18]

In the early 1980s, architect-designed houses were built to replace the remaining self-built camps at the West End. Meanwhile, the railway had been made redundant by the success of articulated road trains and the line was closed in 1988. Dajarra had developed quickly from a large railway camp of predominantly non-Aboriginal people to a town with a majority Aboriginal population. For Aboriginal people, Dajarra has developed over 70 years from being a destination for a series of forced migrations from the west to being a residential base, and a 'home'. Whilst people maintain identification with their respective countries they have a shared identity as 'Dajarra people', which is expressed in terms such as 'DJ mob' and 'DJ Rockers'. More broadly, the town has become one of the centres of Aboriginal lifestyles in North-West Queensland. Throughout the 1900s Dajarra people regularly returned to the Georgina and Urandangie where they constructed temporary camps for periods of fishing, recreation and social interaction and they continue to do so.

Architecture of the Georgina River people in the 1890s

The architecture of the Georgina River area of North-West Queensland was first documented by the English ethnographer Walter Roth amidst the violence and displacements of the late 1890s.[19] Roth observed four types of domiciliary architecture: (i) wet weather domes, (ii) cold weather domes, (iii) shade structures (bough-shed) and (iv) windbreaks.[20]

The wet weather domes were constructed of layers of bushes, grasses and dirt or mud over a timber frame. The primary structural element of this frame was a central 'arch' constructed of two interlocking forked sticks. The cold weather shelter consisted of a similar domed structure constructed over a flat-bottomed hole dug to a depth of approximately half a metre.[21] Shade structures, or bough-sheds, were lighter timber structures with grass and bushes placed over the top. According to Roth this structure was commonly attached to the entrances of wet and cold weather domes to protect fires positioned there.[22] It is likely to have also been employed as a shade structure during hot weather, as found elsewhere in the hot-dry areas of Australia.[23] Windbreaks were constructed of interwoven saplings and grasses to a height of 750–900 millimetres. Windbreaks were added to the sides of the leeward entrances to cold weather shelters, protecting fires and people occupying this space from prevailing southerlies.[24]

A number of modifications to the structures of North-West Queensland occurred with the introduction of new materials: (i) the interlocking forked structure of the domes was occasionally replicated by spliced timbers that were bound by ropes; (ii) cattle hides were placed over the domed structures in lieu of the mud and grass composite; and (iii) the depth of the holes of the cold weather shelters decreased whilst the height of the timber structure of these shelters increased, to the extent that the cold weather domes seemed to 'disappear'. According to Roth, these changes were influenced by the introduction of clothes and blankets that had reduced the need for the warmth provided by this shelter type.[25]

Roth observed that when people arrived at a camp 'they take up their quarters or build temporary huts around the visited, their hosts, camp upon that side of it in the direction whence they came'.[26] This description contains two principles of socio-spatial patterns that have been documented amongst other Aboriginal camps: (i) camps are transformed by a process of 'social accretion' where new arrivals attach themselves to others on the basis of social links, and (ii) people orientate themselves in relation to others according to 'locational principles' such as the direction of travel, or country.[27]

This short excerpt from Roth implies that camps are not necessarily composed of built enclosures; it therefore alludes to a fifth architectural type, the 'open camp' – an external living environment that is characterised by minimal transformations in the physical environment or minimal built elements.

The West End town camps in the 1970s

In 1973 and 1974, just a few years after the last forced migration from Urandangie, an architectural researcher, Paul Memmott, observed the architectural environment of the West End town camps of the East Arrernte and Waluwarra. A dichotomy existed between the town campers and Aboriginal people living in the town which reflected different social groupings and different architectural environments. While the town campers occupied self-constructed camps dominated by the architecture of external living environments and small built forms, the earlier immigrants were occupying masonry DAIA houses and old timber and tin cottages of European tradition in town.[28]

The lifestyle of the town campers was predominantly externally orientated. One of the defining physical characteristics of these external living environments was the ground, which was maintained by the regular raking away of debris, the regular wetting down of dust and consistent occupation. These actions produced a compact and clean floor surface that was marked by a line of debris at the edge of the space. These external living environments were also shaped through the use of windbreaks, shade structures, fires and enclosures.

The enclosed forms included humpies that were mostly small rectilinear buildings of corrugated sheet metal over bush-timber frames, caravans and cars. These enclosed structures were utilised as much for the attributes they contributed to the external living environment, such as shade and screening, as for the internal environment they provided. During gusts of cold southerly winds, fires were maintained in the external living environment to the north of these structures and some people heated the internal environment at night with gidgee coals placed on a sheet of corrugated metal.[29] The physical environment of these camps was regularly transformed in relation to changing social and climatic conditions. All of the architectural types described by Roth were present in these camps: (i) wet weather and cold weather enclosures (the domes being replaced by rectilinear structures), (ii) shade roofs, (iii) windbreaks and (iv) open camps or external living environments.[30]

In 1974 Memmott was concerned that a threat by authorities to destroy the town camp would present a loss of freedom to create and maintain preferred socio-spatial patterns, preferred domiciliary environments and preferred domiciliary behaviour.[31] However, self-constructed camps remained at the West End until the early 1980s and a small camp was constructed there as recently as 1997.

Transformations and maintenance in the contemporary architecture of the 'DJ mob'

In 1996, when I first visited Dajarra, there were no obvious signs of the camps at the West End; instead Dajarra people occupied a variety of houses built by government agencies and the community housing cooperative called Jimberella. However, the move from 'camp' to 'house' had not resulted in a total loss of freedom to define architectural environments. In the 1990s Dajarra people were regularly transforming and maintaining architectural environments 'in town' and 'out bush'. A selection of these environments are now examined.

The first example of contemporary architecture under consideration is the temporary articulation of a place with architectural properties – the architecture of temporary camps or 'travellers' camps'.[32] During 'bush trips' Dajarra people regularly transform places in the broader Aboriginal environment into 'architectural environments'. Such transformations are often made quickly and temporarily; they involve minimal or negligible transformations of the physical environment, and they may simply involve carrying out patterns of behaviour within the existing and naturally occurring physical properties of a place. A common example of this type of transformation is the selection of a shade tree in the environment to occupy for a period of time, perhaps as little as a few minutes.

An example of this type of transformation is provided by the 'dinner camp' (lunch camp) of a group of men and boys on a hot day:

> The men spent time selecting an appropriate place for the 'dinner camp', eventually turning back on their tracks to a stand of low gidgee. As soon as the vehicle pulled up the group collected firewood from the base of the trees and a fire was lit at the fringe of shade they provided. While some of the men stood in the shade at the edge of the gidgee and tended the meat cooking on the hot plate, others pushed inside the gidgee to occupy the low, shaded space created by the intersecting foliage of a number of trees (the space was approximately 1.5 metres high to the lowest branches). An esky was taken into this space and used as a food table. The men left the shade in turn to take a piece of meat from the hot plate and to pour a pint of tea from the billy. Once all of the meat was cooked the remaining pieces were placed on a bed of gidgee leaves on top of the wood heap. On returning to the shade some of the group brushed the ground surface with their feet before sitting down to eat their meal. Once everyone had 'a feed' and 'a drink of tea' the esky and hot plate were loaded into the vehicle, the fire doused, and the group continued on their journey.[33]

A further example is the transformations of a place with the behavioural and physical properties of a camp of longer duration (overnight or longer). While visiting popular camping places on the Georgina, including Urandangie, Dajarra people generate camps that are characterised by minimal transformations of the physical environment. These are 'open camps' or external living environments, which involve changes in the physical environment such as: (i) raking or clearing the surface of the camp of debris, (ii) the placement of gidgee wood heaps, (iii) the placement and maintenance of gidgee fires, (iv) the positioning of swags, (v) the positioning of vehicles to be used as screens, shade walls or furniture and (vi) the construction of minimal built forms such as windbreaks and occasionally roof structures and the use of existing elements such as shade trees. 'Out on the flat' these camps are exposed to cooling breezes and are a focus of nocturnal activities during hot weather with other environments such as shade trees used during the day.

Some environments (or places), including these camping places on the Georgina, are transformed at regular intervals by groups of people enacting consistent patterns of behaviour. Outside of these times of occupation it is often the case that very little evidence remains of these architectural transformations. Thus, there are environments that do not possess permanent architectural forms but are places of regular and consistent architectural transformations. There are also places, such as the dinner camp, where patterns of behaviour are used to generate a unique architectural transformation that is unlikely to be repeated at that place (although similar transformations may occur elsewhere).

These examples support Memmott's notion of a 'minimalist camp architecture'. From his observations of Aboriginal travellers' camps, including that of an Alyawarre camp in Mulga scrub, Memmott produced the following definition of architecture 'as a selected, arranged and constructed configuration of environmental properties, both natural and artificial, in and around one or more activity spaces, combined with patterns of behavioural rules, to result in human comfort and quality of lifestyle'.[34]

Memmott observed that these 'travellers' camps' challenge prevailing concepts of architecture.[35] Certainly, some architectural academics have found it challenging to recognise these camps as 'architecture'. Yet it is interesting to note that a popular aspiration in Australian architecture, particularly amongst Queensland's non-Aboriginal architects, is to design buildings that transcend the divide between 'inside and outside'.[36] 'Travellers' camps' and other types of Aboriginal architecture are excellent examples of environments that possess this 'inside/outside' quality. These temporary camps or 'travellers' camps' have the potential to inform non-Aboriginal architects and to challenge them to journey outside Western architectural models – to journey beyond enclosures comprising hardwood screens and polycarbonate sheets and into the Australian environment.

The maintenance of architecture

In the camps 'out bush' and within domiciliary environments 'in town' there are many examples of the contemporary maintenance of architectural elements described by Roth. One of the most common and readily identifiable architectural elements is the windbreak. 'Out bush' these are occasionally constructed of bush-timber frames and foliage. Sometimes windbreaks are free-standing structures supported by metal star pickets (fence pickets). They are also constructed by using trees as vertical supports to timber rails. A common free-standing windbreak is a sheet of corrugated metal tied to star pickets with a 'cobb and co' – a common and multi-purpose wire joint. Single corrugated sheets produce a windbreak 760 millimetres high, which is the height of the windbreaks described by Roth.

Windbreaks are added to a variety of enclosures to produce warm, north-orientated cold weather environments such as the camp of a Dajarra man at the West End in the 1990s. The main space of this camp was an external living environment constructed around a bloodwood tree (*Corymbia terminalis*). This rectilinear space was screened by caravans placed to the south and west of the tree in combination with windbreak walls to the south and east made of corrugated metal fixed to a structure of timber rails and star pickets. The western caravan was used for sleeping and cooking during wet or very cold conditions and the southern caravan was used for storage. The external space was filled with imported, coarse-grained creek sand, which created a soft floor surface that was easily maintained. This space was the focus of social interaction and diurnal and nocturnal activities including sleeping. Despite obvious differences such as the use of caravans instead of domes and the use of imported materials instead of bush materials, this camp works in the same way as the cold weather dome and windbreak environment described by Roth. Thus camps such as this not only display the maintenance of architectural elements such as windbreaks, but also display the maintenance of architectural environments, in this case a cold weather environment.

Transforming architecture

Most of the old timber and tin cottages of Dajarra have been replaced by standard house designs produced by the Queensland Government and prefabricated houses selected by the community from a range of houses produced by east coast manufacturers. These are generic houses that have not been designed to meet the preferred lifestyle or spatial requirements of the occupants nor the climatic conditions they encounter. Since the 1970s a number of researchers have been concerned with the negative impacts of such generic, non-Aboriginal designs on Aboriginal societies.[37] Yet there is an equally important investigation concerning these houses and other non-Aboriginal designed buildings used by Aboriginal people: how have Aboriginal people (in this case Dajarra people) creatively transformed such bland buildings into Aboriginal environments and Aboriginal architecture with particular reference to place and culture?

Dajarra people have transformed non-Aboriginal architecture into Aboriginal architecture in one or a combination of the following three ways. Firstly, Dajarra people regularly transform houses in response to preferred patterns of domiciliary behaviour and climatic conditions by adjusting the physical properties of the house. This is most evident in the external living environments of yard spaces. One example of this type of transformation is the creation of warm windbreak spaces against the northern elevation of four identical low-set houses. In each case the residents have blocked the space between the floor and the ground with sheet metal, which transforms the whole house into a large windbreak. With a gidgee fire these leeward spaces are the warmest environments in Dajarra on a cold winter's day, at which time the households swell with visitors, and they are the focus of social interaction and domiciliary activities. In two cases people have added roof structures to these windbreak spaces, one constructed of recycled material and the other a recycled bus shelter. These flat-roofed structures shelter warming and cooking fires in much the same way as the bough-sheds attached to cold weather domes described by Roth. Other transformations include the construction of shade/shed structures,[38] the movement of furniture (including beds), the maintenance of earth floors by raking and wetting the ground, the maintenance of grassed areas, the planting of shade and fruit trees, and the construction and alteration of fences and gates. Internal spaces are personalised with items of individual and community identification such as trophies from regional sporting events, photographs, artworks and furniture.[39]

Another way in which Dajarra people transform non-Aboriginal environments is through the occupation of these environments and enacting culturally distinct patterns of behaviour in them. For example, it is common for extended family groups to occupy three-bedroom houses in alternative ways, such as sub-groups (nuclear families or gender-specific groups) 'camping' in 'lounge rooms' and external living environments as much as in 'bedrooms'. Patterns of behaviour include preparing and cooking bush foods, the maintenance of gidgee warming fires and cooking fires (including ground ovens), and social interaction in gender-specific groups.

The third way in which Dajarra people transform non-Aboriginal environments into Aboriginal environments or Aboriginal architecture is through the association of knowledge properties with those environments. The Dajarra community has named a number of architectural environments after an important place on the Georgina River called Jimberella. When the community formed a housing cooperative in 1974 they named it Jimberella. The houses of the cooperative are known as the 'Jimberella houses' in contrast to government and privately owned houses. Buildings purchased and built by the community have also been named after Jimberella: 'the Jimberella store', 'Jimberella Hall' (both in Dajarra) and 'Jimberella House' (Mt Isa). The Dajarra school has recently been transformed in this way through the addition of artwork by local artists, including the depiction of a Dreaming Story from the Georgina. Non-Aboriginal environments are also transformed by the identification of Dajarra people with them and the layers of memories of events and experiences that occurred within them. For example, the first DAIA houses in Dajarra, seven identical masonry houses known as 'the cottages', contain the memories and experiences of over 30 years of occupation by Dajarra people.

Architectural environments 'in town' are characterised by continual transformations made in response to seasonal and diurnal changes (the movement of shade may be accompanied by the movement of furniture), changed social conditions such as changes in household numbers, and the creative responses of the 'ethno-architect' such as the redesign of a windbreak wall. Whereas external living environments are often easily and rapidly transformed in response to changed conditions, internal environments are less easily changed. Nonetheless, internal environments are also regularly transformed through the movement of furniture or the packing up of swags in the morning and the setting up of swags at night. One of the ongoing changes in the architectural environment of Dajarra is the transformation of the socio-spatial pattern of the town.

In large camps 'out bush' Dajarra people have the freedom to define socio-spatial patterns in the same way as they did in the town camp at Dajarra. For example, at the camp at the annual Urandangie rodeo Dajarra people consistently form large family camps, some of which consist of a number of sub-camps. 'In town', in Dajarra, it is less easy for people to transform socio-spatial patterns; nonetheless there are movements of family groups across the rental stock in Dajarra. Some family groups have formed large 'camps' 'in town' by gradually moving into the houses surrounding the house of a key family member. This is a slow process of social accretion that is dependent on the availability of housing stock and tenancy waiting lists. Another example of social accretion is the occupation of individual households by large extended family groups where key family members are joined by more mobile relatives. In other instances family groups operate as a large 'camp', although they occupy houses that are dispersed across the town.

Conclusion

Dajarra people are continually moving between the Georgina River and the Great Western Railway, they are continually moving between the self-constructed environments of camps 'out bush' and transformed architectural environments 'in town'. Dajarra people move between the minimalist architecture of 'travellers' camps' and 'open camps' and the transformed architecture of 'non-Aboriginal' buildings they have purchased, been supplied with and for which they have assumed responsibility.

'In town' and 'out bush' Dajarra people continue to produce and maint ain a repertoire of architectural elements and architectural environments that were first documented in the 1890s. The creative architectural transformations of Dajarra people 'in town' are an extension of these architectural traditions. The transformation of housing stock to (re)produce some of this repertoire indicates that the housing does not provide environments that totally satisfy patterns of behaviour or preferred lifestyles. There is an opportunity to develop an understanding of the preferred architectural environments of Aboriginal clients by investigating not only the architectural traditions they maintain but also the way they transform built environments to suit patterns of behaviour.

The addition of Aboriginal architecture to non-Aboriginal buildings and other transformations considered in this paper demonstrate the need for a model of architecture which is capable of encompassing a diversity of architectural transformations. To some degree this is satisfied by Memmott's definition of 'minimalist architecture', which is similar to a model of place that he developed in earlier work and which has informed the current paper. According to Memmott, places are generated and maintained through one or a combination of three types of people–environment interactions: through alterations to the natural or human-made physical characteristics of a piece of environment, through the enactment of special types of behaviour at a particular piece of environment, and by the association of knowledge properties with a particular piece of environment.[40] Rather than definitions and classifications of architecture, perhaps it is an interactive model of place such as this that is most useful in cross-cultural journeys into Aboriginal architectural environments.

The Aftermath of 'Pleasures': Untold Stories of Post-Modern Architecture in Australia

2003

PAUL HOGBEN

The 1980 conference of the Royal Australian Institute of Architects (RAIA) stands out as a critical moment in the history of architectural discourse in Australia. Held in Sydney and entitled 'The Pleasures of Architecture', this conference was devoted to exploring the pleasures and enjoyment 'found in looking at and talking about the creation of buildings, together with the formulation of architectural ideas'.[1] An announcement ran, 'Architects and students at the Convention will be examining the philosophical position taken by some of their colleagues to the development of a language of architectural form and to the relationship that the public at large has to their work.'[2]

Brian Zouch, editor of *Architecture Australia* in 1979, presented his own interpretation of the conference theme:

> For the first time in this country the public discussion of architecture by architects will turn away from social issues, away from energy conservation and environment, away from design education and away from professional practice ... Attention will be focused instead upon the joy, the poetry and the fantasy of the act of creation. For the first time architects will present the personal, intimate and private realms of their souls to public scrutiny ... Its purpose is to examine the analogies and allusions, the references, the dreams and the meanings that are a part of the way we make architecture.[3]

Perhaps not surprisingly, this was the last editorial statement Zouch was to make before being removed from the journal. The language he used was enough to stir the wrath of many Institute members and powerful figures within the profession. For those tuned into current international polemic, talk of 'fantasy' and 'dreams', 'analogies and illusions' would have sounded very much like the verbiage coming out of certain architectural circles in North America and England. The idea of devoting an entire conference to such ethereal themes also went far beyond the serious-sounding proclamations of professional identification and promotion (commitment to service, environmental concern) that usually framed this event. Andrew Metcalf, chairman of the conference organising committee, was aware of this and in an effort to create interest and calm nerves introduced the background to the conference in an evening talk on postmodernism at the New South Wales Chapter of the RAIA. Together with Alex Tzannes, Metcalf introduced the work of the three keynote speakers: Michael Graves, George Baird and Rem Koolhaas (who replaced Leon Krier). Even then there were ominous rumblings about the conference theme and the relevance of the work of these speakers to Australian architecture.[4]

The promotional lead-up to the conference was intense, with the inclusion of a competition for the completion of Engehurst, a large Georgian villa designed by the nineteenth-century architect John Verge.[5] A fragment of the villa remained buried in a property in Paddington, having been encased in subsequent additions and alterations. The brief asked participating architects to design a new house for the site that would incorporate the Verge fragment. Emphasis was on articulating a philosophical position in relation to the notion of 'completion' and what that meant in terms of heritage preservation, historical fabrication and progressing architectural ideas. Participants were free to strip back the existing building to reveal the original Verge shell on a cleared site or to take a more inclusive stance by delving into the accretionary nature of the site and its social and regional context. Twenty Australian architects took part, ranging from Ken Woolley to Norman Day, from Philip Cox to Edmond and Corrigan.[6] The range of responses to the competition brief was very diverse, and for Neville Quarry the architectural pluralism evident in the submissions was a healthy sign 'that architects, for architecture's sake, have not forgotten the value of architecture as experiment'.[7]

The conference boasted a record attendance of 560 delegates, the largest for an architectural conference in Australia ever. Officially, the event was hailed a success, as the keynote speakers and competition had provided stimulus for three days of lively debate between architects and students. However, the editors of the newly established journal *Transition* spoke in more ambivalent terms. They felt the conference had revealed alarming inadequacies in the local understanding of contemporary theory: 'It was disturbing to realise that, in comparison with the Mid-Atlantic architects, Graves, Baird, and Koolhaas, they [many of the local delegates] had not more than the barest notion of their own bailiwick.'[8] The competition had shown that Australia's architectural 'crème de la crème' had tried hard but 'with often vapid and sycophantic' results.[9] The keynote speakers were often evasive and failed to take an aesthetic position of a committed kind, with Koolhaas speaking mostly in parables.[10] Ideological relativity had proven to be a sticking point, and the editors only hoped that the embarrassment raised by the conference at the 'lack of substance' in Australian architecture would be a strong enough impetus for change.[11]

As a counterpoint to these criticisms, the international speakers were pleasantly surprised by the conference. For Koolhaas, the fact that his words were being understood in ways he could not control was 'exciting'.[12] Baird felt that, if the organisers wanted a discussion of postmodernism, they should have invited different speakers.[13] Graves saw the benefits of running a competition to provide a common focus and appreciated the ironic difference to the overall conference. He stated, 'In the US, you rarely get a conference that involves architecture. Conferences like this usually talk about pipes or money or getting clients. Calling it "The Pleasures of Architecture" would have meant that they were going to talk about making dough.'[14]

It is not difficult to understand the genesis and context of this conference. Metcalf was a local enthusiast of postmodern architecture and had written an article for *Architecture Australia* that tried to explain its various strains and sources.[15] He was part of a group of young practitioners and academics who were taking an interest in the work and writings of North American architects and architectural theorists. Several of these Australian architects had travelled overseas and studied under people like Robert Venturi and George Baird. Charles Jencks had visited Australia in October 1974 giving speeches and interviews,[16] and his books were receiving considerable press and review.[17] In her account of architecture in Australia in the late 1970s and early 1980s, Jennifer Taylor describes how interest in postmodern ideas and strategies was manifested in the work of Howroyd and Forward, Gunn Hayball, Edmond and Corrigan, Norman Day Architects, Daryl Jackson Architects, Peter Stronach of Allen Jack and Cottier, Andrew Metcalf, Alex Tzannes and Espie Dodds.[18] Buildings by these architects were attracting comment in the press as attempts to define new approaches to issues of place, context and history.[19] *Transition* had seized on the absence of a vehicle for critical discourse on architecture and started publishing academic essays that placed the rise of postmodernism in a context of social change and aesthetic upheaval.[20] 'The Pleasures of Architecture' conference can be seen as a brave attempt at introducing new themes to the general architectural profession and to find some intellectual and discursive support in Australia for what was a current area of architectural experiment and excitement internationally.

Another enthusiast was Conrad Hamann who, in a 1984 essay entitled 'Off the Straight and Narrow', tried to account for the different postmodern tendencies in Australia in the 1970s and early 1980s.[21] He noted that the widened design interests of some Melbourne architects were recent branches of a much more ingrained historical approach he called the 'inclusive method'.[22] For Hamann the inclusive method held more intellectual and interpretative interest than pastiche classicism because it was the principle behind a vigorous tradition of Australian architecture. He argued that Venturian ideas of complexity, contradiction and recognition of context could be seen operating in buildings that dated back to the Federation era, as shown in buildings by Harold Desbrowe Annear, George Sydney Jones, Roy Grounds and Frederick Romberg.[23] Because of this tradition, Australian architects, if they were prepared to read beyond Jencks, were in a good position to contribute a historical awareness to the serious issues behind the critique of International Style modernism. However, for Hamann, this potential was unlikely to be realised because in Australia a critical orthodoxy was committed to unfairly killing off the positive and generative energies of inclusivist approaches, as well as the development of valuable intellectual exchange.[24]

Hamann's account of the early 1980s is an important record of the state of debate in Australia at the time; however, it fails to explain in sufficient detail and perspective the issues of power and authority at stake. Hamann hints at but never really addresses the politics of discourse that erupted in the wake of 'The Pleasures of Architecture' conference. The conference had proven that interest in postmodern architecture, whatever it was being conceived to be, was high amongst young architects and academics, and this scenario was not welcomed by the critical orthodoxy Hamann describes.

The proponents of this orthodoxy were not going to lie down without a fight. Some, like Harry Seidler, took to arms and marshalled influential forces against the young enthusiasts. Interestingly, the aim of their attacks was not so much the functionality or the liveability of 'new style' buildings as the mechanisms through which these buildings were being given an increasing amount of legitimacy. It was the support that the RAIA, the media and schools of architecture were starting to lend to ideas about the death of modernism and the need for more meaningful architecture that really alarmed a number of established architects. They feared not for the loss of work themselves (for many were enjoying large commissions) but for the lessening of an ideological hold on the institutions of professional and aesthetic legitimisation.[25] The stakes in this battle were precisely those of ideological legitimacy and this meant that the mechanisms that controlled the appearance of ideas and images came under increased pressure at this time.

The aim of this paper is to bring into focus the real locus of anxiety and concern, that of the discourse itself: what was being published in architectural journals and what the responsibilities of architectural writers and educators were. If the direction of discourse could be controlled, then the deeper issues of power and legitimacy could be stabilised. As argued elsewhere, existing scholarship has failed to account for the unsettling ideological content of architectural discourse in Australia. This paper provides another case study in which this ideological content can be revealed.[26] By dealing with the specifics of what was said we can see the actual points of contestation and where the pressure was being applied. This enables us to develop a more nuanced understanding of this period than we currently have.

'Puerile nonsense'

The most vocal critic of postmodern architecture in Australia during the 1980s was Harry Seidler. Seidler attended 'The Pleasures of Architecture' conference and felt an immediate response was in order. He thought the conference speakers were asking the audience to 'abandon more than half a century of the evolutionary course of architectural development and change course drastically. They put to us that content and expression, use and form have no more connection in architecture than fashionable dress design, hat design or the field of advertising.'[27] He continued by saying:

> To propose that it is appropriate now to revert to a form of historicising reminiscent of the mode of 'fin de siecle' eclecticism is, to say the least, astonishing. And yet the fact that all this is being proposed, virtually unchallenged – namely that we remove from the record and reverse the entire course of the theoretical structure of rational response to environmental needs, is a sign that contemporary architecture must indeed be in crisis.[28]

In his response Seidler argued that Australia and America did not have the cultural sophistication to fully embrace and develop the ideals of modern architecture. These ideals were understood in countries like Finland, Denmark and the then West Germany, 'places where Modern Architecture has become far more an absorbed, integral part of local cultural patterns'.[29] It was to be expected that Australians would become disenchanted with modern architecture as they only had a superficial understanding of its rational aspects, its structural and constructional logic, without its aesthetic or sociological base. 'Postmodern' was a phenomenon that had not made an impact in Europe, generating no more than a 'journalistic shrug of the shoulder'.[30] Seidler stated, '[t]hey simply don't take it, or write about it, seriously'.[31] He felt architects in America and Australia were also more susceptible to commercial pressures and the media's thirst for new labels and catchphrases. This media-driven desire for the new was leading architects and students away from the real goals of architecture. Like the media-propelled 'style' movements before it, postmodernism would also fall into oblivion and be quickly forgotten. For Seidler, it was a childish attempt at being contrary and shocking, and it would not have any lasting validity and aesthetic longevity.[32]

This response became Seidler's standard line of attack. He used it again at the 1982 RAIA convention in Singapore in a speech called 'Internationalism' and also in his response to Conrad Hamann's essay outlined above. At the Singapore convention Seidler argued that the International Style (which he disassociated himself and his mentors from) was 'very low brow' and this exposed the folly of the so-called postmodernists who thought they were battling something significant.[33] As Hamann pointed out, Seidler's attacks on postmodernism were reductionist and based on a simple dichotomy of 'Modern versus Post Modern'.[34] In his speeches Seidler showed little patience with the arguments of others and was not prepared to enter into an open dialogue about new directions in architectural theory. He did not engage with specific points of contention and was guilty of what Hamann called 'the straw man approach'.[35] He used easy targets. In many ways Seidler parroted the sentiments of other anti-postmodernists such as Dutch architect Aldo van Eyck and the journal editor and critic Peter Blake. He referred to recent speeches given by these two figures in his own attacks and held up their arguments as the epitomes of reason in an era of depravity. Both van Eyck and Blake were self-proclaimed crusaders for architectural 'truth' and 'integrity' and their speeches took on a crusading zeal, lacking in rigour and solid argument. Van Eyck's speech at the 1981 annual Royal Institute of British Architects (RIBA) discourse, which Seidler admired, was full of reductive and litigious statements and his claims against postmodernism lacked a basis in any real analysis.[36]

Blake was damning of the architectural press in the United States, saying that it was populated by critics who had no experience in the design and construction of buildings, but whose livelihoods depended on discovering something new and different and therefore responded with 'effusive gratitude' when the 'marketers' of postmodernism provided them with catchy 'fodder'.[37] Seidler transferred this type of thinking to Australia, causing it to appear somewhat out of proportion and exaggerated. In 1982 he slammed two articles published in *Architecture Australia* which surveyed recent buildings in Sydney and Melbourne.[38] He saw these articles (written by Norman Day and Andrew Metcalf respectively) as being the 'childish aping of supposedly fashionable imported tendencies' and blasted the journal for subjecting its readers to such 'puerile nonsense'.[39] This outburst was unsubstantiated;

however, Seidler did supply references to an article by Blake on architectural journalism and an essay by Ada Louise Huxtable entitled 'The Troubled State of Modern Architecture' for the editor of *Architecture Australia* to read.[40] Metcalf and Day's commentaries were attempts at critiquing a diverse array of recent work in relation to a context of professional and aesthetic influences. Unlike the targets of Blake's criticisms – the large-scale corporate and leisure complexes of North America's 'nouveau riche' – the buildings described by Metcalf and Day were small-scale urban experiments mostly for community or private domestic use.

This begs the question as to why Seidler singled out these articles in such an abusive manner. It may have been due to the anxiety he shared along with Blake about the increasing coverage being given to postmodern architecture by the press. If *Architecture Australia* started publishing articles favourable to postmodern architecture and its theoretical concerns, then the discourse that lent his work so much credibility and legitimacy would be threatened. This discourse had reigned supreme throughout the 1960s and 1970s and was based on the factual description of buildings: their structural systems, function and layout. It suited the modernist pretence towards objectivity and spatial resolution through functional design very well. It allowed buildings to appear in a space of self-evident formal and technological achievement.[41] Blake's monographs on Seidler adhered to his type of description.[42] They did not enter into interpretative or critical questioning in regard to issues of legibility and meaning – topics that were foregrounded in Metcalf's and Day's reviews. Seidler may have been collapsing different critical scales, but he had clear intentions: to scare off editorial and reader support for this kind of writing.

This tactic met with some success. Metcalf was in the process of resigning from his position as contributing editor for New South Wales and Day soon loosened his connection to the journal. The journal quickly curtailed its support for postmodern architecture and, for the next three years, houses of 'postmodern' persuasion were only featured in the annual housing issue without much discussion, and interviews with anti-postmodernists were published.[43] There was a considerable swing away from the work of younger architects to that of the established profession. The journal took on a decidedly pro-Seidler appearance, publishing his current work and speeches.[44] Buildings by Cameron, Chisholm and Nicol and Edwards, Madigan, Torzillo and Briggs, firms dedicated to functional expressionist design, were given generous coverage.[45]

These changes to *Architecture Australia* cannot simply be attributed to Seidler's outburst. There were other voices and influences at play and, as the journal was a battlefield over issues of discourse, it deserves further attention here, especially in regard to the type of editorial stance that was being taken and the degree to which the journal needs to be considered as an intersection of various interests.

Heath's stance

The decision in 1980 to appoint Tom Heath as editor of *Architecture Australia* was an attempt by the RAIA to restore stability and professional credibility to its journal. Heath was well connected to the world of corporate architectural practice and brought with him a powerful array of professional contacts. His appointment as Head of the Department of Architecture at the Queensland Institute of Technology in 1979 had consolidated his position as a commentator on contemporary architecture. Heath also enjoyed the benefits of having a contributing editor from each state as well as a good relationship with the RAIA, maintained through the existence of an RAIA journal advisory committee, which for many years was headed by Professor Peter Johnson, a past employer of Heath at McConnell Smith and Johnson and a respected figure within the profession.

Heath's editorial view on the changing climate of architectural aesthetics was conditioned by his belief in the evolutionary nature of architectural knowledge and the fundamental role of scientific inquiry. Well-reasoned, historically grounded argument was his guiding motto and his editorials were devoted to clarifying a topic of concern in simple, understandable terms. For Heath, bureaucracy and 'the planning system' were the enemies of architecture and it was only through a reassertion of the role of science in architectural education and practice that architects could find the effective tools for battling externally repressive forces.[46] Initially, Heath paid some attention to the renewed interest in eclecticism and the free borrowing from history that some architects were showing,[47] as well as paying credence to the argument that over the last few decades modernist architecture had become elitist and had lost its social causes and that new forms of re-connecting architecture to the public needed to be found.[48] Not taking an outright position, his editorials were attempts to expose the blind spots and conceptual failings of both sides of the contemporary debate. In a series of editorials in 1981 and 1982 he expressed his opinions on what constituted respectable discourse, and in his view this was not to be seen in much of the writing that was currently being passed off as architectural theory by either modernist or postmodernist writers.[49] He claimed both camps were guilty of polemic. He stated,

> Polemic is propaganda or advocacy: the attempt to justify or discredit one or another style, or way of doing things, with whatever tools come to hand, from invective to argument. Theory seeks to discover by critical inquiry what actually happens, to show how things work. Polemic is interested, in the sense that it promotes certain interests; theory is disinterested and does not seek to persuade people to do this or that, though in the course of showing how things work it will certainly show that certain ways of doing things do not work, do not actually happen or do not produce the results which they are claimed to produce.[50]

According to Heath, both sides were also guilty of the 'five traps' of architectural discourse, the 'fine old fallacies of reasoning, which have been with us for millennia and show as little sign of going away as the termite, which really bring down the house of intellect'.[51] These traps were the attachment to simple definitions 'when a form of words becomes a substitute for thought'; the tendency of poetic phraseology to slip through critical thought; the objective-subjective trap; reductionism; and relativism 'the ruling intellectual error of our culture'.[52] Heath was sceptical of writers and critics who used these discursive strategies in presuming knowledge and authority in matters of art and architecture. The attention Heath paid to the misdemeanours of architectural discourse, and the merits and demerits of architectural journalism, was his attempt to tone down the hype about postmodernism and to find some middle ground through reasserting the value of calm logic.

Heath occupied an important position at a time when the established architectural orthodoxy reasserted itself in the light of new trends in discourse. *Architecture Australia* had come under attack for supporting this discourse and Heath's moderate stance helped alleviate tension. The journal could not afford to alienate Seidler and other architects of influence. It also had to remain attractive to advertisers, who were growing in number during the 1980s as the building industry started to enjoy greater prosperity and growth. It is yet to be investigated how this nexus between the journal, its audience and advertising appeal shaped the direction and critical tone it took during the 1980s.

This paper has shown that the reception of postmodern architecture in Australia occurred under fractious circumstances. There was a strong backlash against the media attention and institutional support postmodern ideas and interests were receiving, especially after 'The Pleasures of Architecture' conference. The real focus of concern was that of ideological legitimisation as it was enacted through architectural discourse and journal publication. In pointing to specific instances of response and reaction this paper presents instances that were not inconsequential or negligible to the story of postmodernism in Australia, but rather hold valuable clues that help address larger questions regarding the potentials of developing and articulating positions of theoretical difference within the profession.

The Anglo-Asian Bungalow in Australia's Northern Territory

2004

DAVID BRIDGMAN

In 1936 the Australian Government adopted a policy to upgrade housing for senior Commonwealth officers located in their northernmost tropical colony. The Canberra-based architect WT Haslam, later to become the most senior government architect in South Australia, embarked on a voyage of discovery in search of a suitable housing model for the Northern Territory tropics. He arrived in Darwin in time to experience the intense heat and humidity of the 'build-up' at the beginning of the wet season, before departing for the Dutch East Indies and then on to British Singapore. His brief was to investigate not only housing but also to look at hospitals, prisons and military installations that could act as models for the large-scale redevelopment of Darwin that was to take place in the late 1930s. The introduction of the Anglo-Asian bungalow into Darwin in 1937 was the result of Haslam's visit to South-East Asia.

The Anglo-Asian Bungalow

Darwin, on the far north coast of Australia's Northern Territory, marks the geographical limits of Australia along a north-south axis that links Canberra at one end with Darwin at the other. Beyond Darwin is Asia, historically the 'Other', the site of the unknown and hence considered threatening. The Northern Territory is also a recurring absence in Australian architectural discourse where, from the pioneering histories of Boyd and Freeland onwards, it has tended to be overlooked in favour of the more accessible and more fertile region of tropical North Queensland. Ever since the 1980s, however, there has been a growing move to rewrite the empirical history of the Territory as part of a national discourse. The story of the Anglo-Asian bungalow is one such attempt to position this unique Commonwealth housing type within a national architectural discourse.

The Anglo-Asian bungalow was introduced into Darwin in 1937 by the Works and Services Branch of the Department of Interior in Canberra and during a five-year period over 150 houses were constructed. Influenced by the vernacular and colonial architecture of Singapore and Malaysia, these strikingly picturesque bungalows are unique to Australia. As a residential style they rapidly displaced the large elevated Commonwealth officers' residences, developed from Anglo-Indian models, to become, albeit for a very brief time, a Public Works Department 'tropical style'. In the period after the Second World War they were replaced by an altogether different housing style designed to a formula and influenced by the aesthetic ideals of international modernism. The 1980s, however, saw a reappraisal of the Anglo-Asian bungalow as firms such as Troppo Architects turned towards the local vernacular for inspiration. This move towards a regional architectural vocabulary is reflected in a growing body of work undertaken by many like-minded architects in Darwin who look to historical precedent to inform their work. This paper examines events that led to the introduction of the Anglo-Asian bungalow, as a distinct housing type, into Darwin.

The bungalow as the archetypal colonial dwelling has been the subject of much research, with the story of the bungalow's diffusion around the world reasonably well known through the work of Anthony King and Clay Lancaster.[1] However, to briefly summarise: the origins of the term, if not necessarily the house type, lie in the peasant house of Bengal in northern India. By the eighteenth century the term had been adopted by Europeans living in India to describe a single-storey detached house with a large pyramid roof. This house type subsequently grew into a symbol of British colonial rule and by the nineteenth century the bungalow, initially adopted in England as a holiday house, soon spread to British colonies throughout the world as the preferred housing type for colonial administrators. By the late nineteenth century the bungalow had been introduced into the United States, where it initially developed as a holiday home in the country. However, by the early years of the twentieth century the bungalow became a suburban house type, particularly in southern California, from where it found its way to Australia as the California Bungalow. As a suburban, rather than country, house type the bungalow became a permanent residence with certain typical characteristics: it was a low-lying, single-storey, detached house generally built of wood and covered with a dominant roof.[2] While the California Bungalow in Australia dates from the early decades of the twentieth century, the colonial bungalow was introduced into Australia much earlier in its history. In fact, as King points out, in one sense the bungalow 'never went to Australia ... as it was always there from the start [of European settlement]'.[3]

The Anglo-Asian bungalow, the subject of this investigation, was introduced into Australia in 1937 and in time would come to displace the earlier Commonwealth officers' residences based on the Anglo-Indian model of central rooms and encircling verandahs. The new bungalows were small by Commonwealth standards, picturesque in design and reminiscent of the British colonies in tropical South-East Asia. Designated by a single alphabetical prefix from Type A through to Type W, they were constructed in Darwin between 1937 and 1941 in a building program unprecedented in the town's short history. Of central interest to this paper is the question of why the Public Works Department in Canberra looked towards Singapore for architectural models rather than to Australia's tropical or subtropical regions. In doing so it highlights the ambiguity of established geographical limits within a colonial system where architectural models freely circulated from one colonial station to another.

European settlement of the Northern Territory dates from 1824 when the British Colonial Office established a small military settlement in the north to protect the open coast from incursions from other European powers or from Asian migration. When the first and subsequent settlements by the British proved unsuccessful the South Australian Government pursued control of the Northern Territory 'with vigour', seeing it as a 'foreign' land waiting to be exploited. The South Australian Government had long nurtured a dream of a 'great central colony extending from the Southern Ocean to the Arafura Sea'[4] and in 1863, under South Australian rule, the Territory became 'the first internal colony within Australia'.[5] Initial attempts to establish a settlement at Escape Cliffs in 1865, however, were soon abandoned. Three years later GW Goyder, the Surveyor General of South Australia, surveyed a township on a peninsula overlooking Port Darwin. The town was founded on dreams of wealthy Asian markets and 'visions of a second Singapore'.[6]

South Australian administration, however, was not one of unprecedented success, and by 1911 they had brokered a deal with the Commonwealth that saw them relieved of their debt-ridden colony. Although its capital was Darwin, the region was now administered from Canberra some 4,000 kilometres to the south along a hot, dusty and often impassable road. The change in administration from South Australia to the Commonwealth had far-reaching implications for the built environment. By bringing government building under the control of the Commonwealth Works and Services Branch, Canberra architects would, in subsequent years, come to exercise considerable influence over the built environment of the Northern Territory. One of the first acts by the Commonwealth was to erect a number of tropical bungalows for Commonwealth officers on top of a small peninsula on the periphery of the town known as Myilly Point. These tropical bungalows, with floor areas in excess of 480 square metres were large and they were erected on 'very large blocks of land'. Based on the Anglo-Indian model popular in southern states, they comprised wide verandahs surrounding a central core of small rooms. The kitchen was usually detached and they were sometimes provided with a maid's room, although in many cases servants lived in outbuildings after the model of the Anglo-Indian colonial compound.

By the mid-1930s the population of Darwin wavered around 2,500 – 'to a black-white-yeller-feller mix' as one writer was to characterise the town's racial makeup.[7] The shortage of adequate housing had always been a problem and with the expanding military build-up in the town during the mid-1930s this reached crisis point. The inadequacies of the earlier housing had been a contentious point for many years and in an attempt to attract senior officers to Darwin the Commonwealth adopted a policy of providing new housing in 1936. The Anglo-Asian bungalow was a result of this policy decision. In 1937 a detailed report on land use 'criticised the "appalling living conditions" in Darwin, its "neglected appearance, its poor roads, unmade footpaths and evil smelling drains"'.[8] This influenced the Minister of the Interior to appoint a subcommittee to look at the re-planning of Darwin. While the focus of the re-planning was to facilitate military expansion, reports from Canberra suggested that '[c]ivil activities will provide for the reconstruction of the town according to plans considered suitable for a tropical area' with the aim to 'provide modern tropical structures'[9] in the town.

On 4 October 1936 Wilfred Thomas Haslam, Senior Architect with the Commonwealth Department of the Interior, arrived in Darwin and two weeks later left on a Qantas flight bound for the Dutch East Indies and British Singapore where he was 'to study types of buildings erected to meet similar climatic conditions to those in Darwin'.[10] In doing so Haslam was following a well-established trend at the time. His superior, Edwin Henderson, had recently returned from a trip to Europe to investigate banking facilities and had departed again for a world tour looking at broadcasting studios before designing new facilities for the recently established Australian Broadcasting Corporation. In Darwin almost every major architectural project of the late 1930s was developed following a tour by their architects to the British colonies of the tropical north: Stephenson and Turner visited Sourabaya and Singapore before designing the Art Deco-influenced Darwin Hotel; the new hospital in Darwin was the result of a similar visit resulting in an innovative cruciform plan form; extensions to the Darwin jail were based on the infamous Changi Prison in Singapore; and the Commonwealth Bank was clearly influenced by Singapore tropical Art Deco styling with a little Dutch modernism from WM Dudok thrown in for good measure. Haslam was ideally placed to investigate new housing models for tropical Australia, as his position with the Public Works Department had taken him to most states of Australia, including a lengthy period of residence in subtropical Queensland.

In December 1936, following Haslam's return, the Department of the Interior prepared two sketch designs for 'tropical type houses' that would be documented by June 1937 as the Amended Type B Residence and the Type C Residence. In total, four residences were designed in Canberra by June 1937: the Type A, B, C and D Residences with BCG Burnett signing against them in the drawing register.[11] These Anglo-Asian bungalows mark a defining moment in the architectural history of Darwin as a point of change from the tropical bungalow to a very different residential type. The Type B residence, the first of the Anglo-Asian bungalows to be built, is a large, asymmetrically planned dwelling with a highly picturesque formal composition. The interior organisation of the residence, with a clear tripartite division of space between the entry porch, the main body of the residence and the kitchen, is similar to the vernacular architecture of Singapore and Malaysia. Malay houses typically consist of three structures: an entrance or reception area at the front of the house, the main body of the house and the kitchen located to the rear of the house.

Internal spaces of the Type B residence are organised around a large verandah lounge that forms the social centre of the bungalow. While descriptive terminology is used in an attempt to differentiate internal spaces, the rooms are largely open with a hint of separation provided by screen walls. The small 'dressing rooms' are multi-functional and the 'sleeping space' is, in effect, a form of sleepout off the central verandah lounge of the residence. This central verandah has a significant place in colonial history and from the time of its adoption in British India the importance of the verandah cannot be overstated. The verandah was common in British colonies in South-East Asia where it was often enclosed with large areas of louvres, casement windows and pivoting shutters. One significant characteristic in the formal composition of the Anglo-Asian bungalow is the emphasis on the vertical axis. Elevated on short piers, with high ceilings that increase the external wall height and with a steeply pitched roof, the proportions of the Anglo-Asian bungalow differ dramatically from the long, low, tropical bungalows designed some years earlier by the Commonwealth.

I now want to provide a brief sketch – little more than a general outline – of some of the possible reasons for the introduction of the Anglo-Asian bungalow into Darwin. While the peculiarities of the local climate undoubtedly exerted some influence, a more compelling explanation can be found in the prevailing architectural currents of the metropolitan centre and the complex interaction between the metropolitan centres of Australia and Britain and the colonial peripheries of Darwin and Singapore. Nevertheless, there was a clear environmental aspect to the selection of the Anglo-Asian bungalow reflected in Haslam's repeated reference to climatic similarities between South-East Asia and northern Australia in his reports. Haslam noted: 'In October 1936 I inspected public buildings in Sourabaya, Batavia, Bandoeng, and Singapore, with the object of studying the type of architecture adopted in tropical countries.' In his preoccupation with the climate of Darwin, Haslam was responding to a long-established concern of the imperial powers about how they were to live in their tropical colonies. But he was also reflecting a growing concern, from the late nineteenth century, with the development of an architecture that was appropriate to Australian conditions, and in his quest for 'harmony with nature' he was reiterating one of the central principles of the Arts and Crafts movement. This interest in regionalism, notes Alan Colquhoun in the context of Europe, has a 'genealogy to the romantic movement'.

While architectural regionalism in Australia is often represented as a concern with national identity around the time of Federation expressed through the unique character of the Australian landscape, or as a 'local version of regional modernism' that characterised the immediate post-war period, there were a number of architects sensitive to the specificity of the Australian environment working outside of these periods. Doug Evans describes how 'a vigorous school of regional-modernist architecture emerged during the decades of the 1930s and 1940s'.[17] An intellectual position that had been developing since at least the 1930s can be found in buildings designed by architects such as Sydney Ancher and Walter Running in Sydney and by Roy Grounds and Geoffrey Mewton in Melbourne. Although Haslam's regionalism has as its area of demarcation a preoccupation with the climate as the most identifiable element of the tropics, this is not to argue the case for environmental determinism. While similarities in climate between Darwin and Singapore may have been a contributing factor in the selection of housing models, and indeed makes for a compelling argument, it is not sufficient in itself to explain why the imperial gaze was focused on South-East Asia for architectural exemplars.

By the 1930s there were any number of house types in tropical Australia that could act as models for new housing in Darwin. Over a 50-year period the Queensland house, in the popular imagination at least, had developed into an ideal, or perhaps idealised, tropical residence. In the hands of Robin Dodds it had developed into a 'highly practical positive and personal' architecture through, notes Freeland, his 'awareness of the potential of climate and environment'.[13] The many Japanese, Malays and Pacific Islanders working in the canefields, on the goldfields and as pearl divers constructed lightweight elevated dwellings reminiscent of their homelands in and around towns across the north of Australia from Cairns to Broome that could have influenced a climatically appropriate domestic architecture. Australia's involvement in New Guinea after the First World War revealed further models for tropical housing. The well-established Commonwealth officers' residences in Darwin provided an example of an Anglo-Indian bungalow adapted to life in the tropics, as did the partially elevated Broome houses with their large surrounding verandahs. The suitability of the traditional Japanese house to the relatively mild Australian climate was known, if not well advertised, since the late nineteenth century when one was built in the suburbs of Brisbane.[14] And so on.

However, Haslam's study of British domestic architecture in Singapore was not uncritical and to a parliamentary standing committee on public works in 1939 he reported: 'I found [the architecture in Singapore] different from that generally carried out in the tropical and sub-tropical portions of Australia.' It is in this 'difference' that an alternative explanation can be found: one based on cultural specificity and the political realities of colonial rule. In his exploration of 'difference' Haslam highlights the local peculiarities of domestic architecture in British Singapore:

> The British influence in Singapore is very strong, and owing to the fact that public works are controlled from the Colonial Office, and that the technicians are moved from one colonial station to another, there is a strong tendency to adhere to British practice. In these circumstances there is not the same inclination to allow for climatic conditions as there is in other countries. Their policy is more or less conservative, and sufficient allowance does not appear to be made for the climatic conditions prevailing.[15]

Haslam's initial disappointment in discovering the inherently conservative nature of British colonial housing in Singapore was replaced by a growing interest in the vernacular architecture of Malaysia. Indeed, in discussing the Anglo-Asian bungalow Haslam noted that 'in most respects we have made greater concessions than the British have made in Singapore',[16] referring firstly to the climate but secondly to the vernacular models that informed the Anglo-Asian bungalow. In the indigenous Malay house Haslam found an architecture that resonated with his metropolitan expectations – in short he discovered the 'exotic'.

From the time of Matthew Flinders' voyage around the north coast of Australia, the Northern Territory had been described as 'alien, uncomforting, uninviting, and sometimes threatening' with a 'general construction of being different, other, a place which threatens civilisation by promoting lassitude over work, and a general degeneration in social etiquette'.[17] In reworking this topos in traditional romantic terms the tropics acquired the connotations of being exotic: a place of reassuring warmth, of luxuriant growth, and of sensuality. This construct was reinforced in the work of the so-called 'landscape writers' of the 1930s and 1940s who 'concentrated on descriptive accounts of life and travel in the remote parts of Australia emphasising the heroic pioneering traditions of European settlement'.[18] Writers such as Ion Idriess, Frank Clune, William Hatfield and Ernestine Hill did much to shape the romantic image of the Northern Territory as a remote and wild frontier in the popular imagination. This is exemplified in the writing of Ernestine Hill, who describes Darwin in the following terms:

> To come into Darwin ... is to tiptoe across the bounds of possibility into an opium dream ... Government officials, immaculate in white; Larrakeahs and Wagaits, their skin gleaming like glossy black taffeta riding bicycles about under the banyan trees; Chinese ladies with pantaloons and blue umbrellas; swarthy Filipinos, Fijians fuzzy-wigged, and grave doric beauties ... these are some of the characters in Darwin's musical comedy.[19]

Stratton demonstrates the extent to which the Territory was constructed as 'different' from the rest of Australia as being 'outside the homogeneous reality of Australia'.[20] Darwin, notes Stratton, was constructed in Australian discourse as an 'insecure outpost' as opposed to the 'real' cities of Sydney and Melbourne. The transience of the white colonial population was identified as yet another instance of this insecurity, where a two-year posting was common for public servants before returning to the safety of the metropolitan centre. This was partly because of the supposed debilitating effects of the climate on Europeans, and there were no hill stations on the Indian model to provide respite from the 'torrid tropical climate'.[21] While literary fiction shaped the image of the Territory, it was the influence of academics that did much to consolidate this image. For the expanding disciplines of anthropology and sociology the Northern Territory was 'felt to be exotic because of the presence of remote and tribal peoples'.[22]

So how can we draw together these seemingly disparate elements of the discussion so far to allow space for some tentative comments on the reason for Haslam's trip to Singapore? On the one hand, there is a preoccupation with the specificities of the site, an architectural regionalism set within an emerging universal modernism. On the other hand is the discursive construct of Darwin as 'exotic', set within the romantic tradition, and as an isolated society: the colonial 'Other' to a mainstream metropolitan Australian discourse. Within these local relationships is the broader colonial relationship between Australia and Britain and it is in this relationship that the answer to the particular conditions operating at the cultural periphery of Darwin seem to lie.

Haslam came from a cultural centre in an Australian discourse that was, on the world stage, also peripheral to the cultural centres of Europe generally and Britain in particular, thus engendering an 'identity crisis' that found expression in a form of cultural insecurity. This identity crisis, notes Evans, 'resulted in a supplicant relationship between centre and periphery'.[23] Canberra was both an imperial power in its relationship with Darwin and a colonial dependency in its relationship with Britain. When Commonwealth architects in Canberra wanted to introduce a new housing type into Darwin for Commonwealth officers it was probably only natural for them to look back to Britain for guidance on how British architects dealt with housing in their own tropical colonies.

In the collective imagination British Singapore was an ideal tropical city: economically successful, populous and comfortable – at least for those in positions of power where cheap labour provided ready access to servants that allowed the colonial elite to maintain a lifestyle that was fast disappearing at home. Singapore represented the pinnacle of social and cultural sophistication for the colonial administration in Canberra and had long been held as a model for Darwin's development. In looking towards Singapore for a new series of tropical houses the Commonwealth government sought to validate the new architecture in Darwin by aligning it with tendencies occurring in

British Singapore. It is a sign of a culturally emerging Australian society and of the increasing sophistication of Australian architects in the 1930s that, when Haslam arrived in Singapore, he found the domestic architecture in the British colony somewhat conservative.

Then, in his 'plundering' of the indigenous architecture of Malaysia, Haslam was responding to an established regionalist sensibility long part of the intellectual current in the metropolitan centres of Australia. Paradoxically, he was also responding to the growing preoccupation with the functional distribution of space that was reflected in an emerging modernism. Where the earlier Commonwealth officers' residences modelled on the Anglo-Indian bungalow consisted of little more than an encircling verandah, which could be used for anything and was in fact used for everything, the Anglo-Asian bungalows contained spaces increasingly demarcated along functional lines. This functional distribution of space was to become even more marked in the post-colonial houses of the 1950s; however, between these two events lie the Anglo-Asian bungalows of Beni Burnett.

The Local and the Migrant: Limits of Mutual Recognition

2004

HARRY MARGALIT AND PAOLA FAVARO

During my formative years when I was in desperate search for the revelation, which would eventually make me understand the essence of architecture, I explored like Marco Polo as many cities as I could. Cities of temples (Athens, Rome); cities of pyramids (Paris, Cairo), dream cities (Venice), cities of churches (Orvieto), cities of markets (Verona), cities of palaces (Urbino), cities of cathedrals (Barcelona), cities of tombs (Beijing), cities of chimes (London), cities of skyscrapers (New York), cities of golden domes (Kremlin). I reached a basic conclusion: cities are not created by planners. They are created by architecture. Architecture is the real matrix of the city. I found that Sydney was a city without a matrix, a city of sprawling red roofs, with a coat hanger as a bridge and a neo-gothic and neo-classical architecture. Its matrix was not architecture but the hundreds of bays, the city of harbours. On a clear September afternoon many years ago – wattle and prunus in flower, mountains sprinkled with snow – I reached in a Fiat 500 the city of Canberra. A city without towers, without golden domes, without cathedrals, a city without a past. It was the dream of any modern architect. The nothingness was there: the silence, the music, the tabula rasa (a clean slate), the end of exploring perhaps the destination, the invisible city.

ENRICO TAGLIETTI[1]

Enrico Taglietti: A brief portrait

In 1955 Enrico Taglietti, a recent Italian architecture graduate, moved to Australia from Milan, Italy. Unlike fellow migrants who moved for economic or political reasons, Taglietti's migration was prompted by the promise of greater professional opportunities.

Taglietti's early history is bound up with Italian colonial ambitions. In 1938, with Enrico aged twelve, the Taglietti family moved to Asmara in Eritrea, East Africa, an Italian colony since 1860. The intent of the move was to expand the family's hardware concern, which embraced both production and, until the move, European distribution of its products. The move proved a success, and the elder Taglietti succeeded in diversifying the industry within the Ethiopian colonies.[2]

The advent of the Second World War changed the family's fortunes. In April 1941 Italian civil authorities in Asmara surrendered to British forces, delivering some 40,000 prisoners of war into Allied hands.[3] The Taglietti family, as part of the Italian civilian contingent, were kept confined in the city. From 1941 to 1948 Taglietti experienced confinement in Asmara, his mobility restricted to a radius of ten kilometres, limited by curfew, and dominated by military presence.

In 1948 Taglietti returned to Milan to study architecture at the Polytechnic. During his studies from 1948 to 1954 he witnessed Italy's post-war reconstruction, with its attendant social and political conflicts and debates over architectural education. In parallel with the general political debate, the period was marked by a growing conflict of ideas in the traditionally conservative academy of the architectural schools.

The political milestone of the period was the national referendum of 2 June 1946, which transformed Italy from a monarchy to a republic. In the educational context, a strong debate was encouraged by ALSA (Free Society of Architecture Students).[4] This in effect promoted new 'rationalist' leftist ideas in opposition to the conformist principles prevailing in traditional education. This rupture allowed inter-war modernism into the academies and created an opening for the organic tendencies, with Wrightian overtones, promoted by Bruno Zevi and the School of Rome.

After graduating in 1954, Taglietti commenced his career as an architectural consultant by designing the St Erasmo Theatre, various residential and commercial developments in Milan and Zurich and in an association with the International Exhibition of Decorative and Industrial Arts and Modern Architecture of the Milan Triennale. The Triennale exhibition of design and *Domus* architectural design magazine were two established means of raising the profile of architecture and design in Milanese circles.

Taglietti's role as curator of foreign entries at the Triennale, and his involvement in promoting part of the Triennale as an Italian exhibition in Sydney, brought him to Australia. While in Sydney the Italian Ambassador commissioned him to search for a suitable site for the Italian Embassy in Canberra. The consequence of this series of fortuitous events was Taglietti's adoption of Canberra as his home.

From 1955 to the present he has designed, within his private architectural practice, a broad range of private and public buildings. His major works include the Italian Embassy, the Town House Motels in Wagga Wagga and Canberra, the Dickson Library in Canberra and St Kilda Library in Melbourne, the War Memorial repository in Canberra and St Anthony's Church, Sydney, all built in the period from the early 1960s to the late 1970s. Subsequent projects from the 1980s and 1990s include the Giralang Primary School and Forrest day care centre. Taglietti continues to practise from his office in Canberra, and has entered built work in the Royal Australian Institute of Architects (RAIA) Chapter Awards as recently as 2002.

Taglietti in the international and Australian architectural context in the 1960s and 1970s

In 1979 Taglietti was invited to participate in the international exhibition titled *Transformations in Modern Architecture* held at the Museum of Modern Art (MoMA) in New York. The intent of the exhibition was to identify particular directions within International architecture in the period 1959–79 through 400 images of selected buildings. The examples were grouped in seven categories and 22 subcategories that exhibited similar characteristics. From sculptural form to structure, from hybrids to elements, vernacular and historicising, these categories invited a direct comparison of about ten images of architectural projects in the same group.

This exhibition and the book published by MoMA described how Taglietti fitted into the international architectural context in the late 1970s. Taglietti's selected project, the Town House Motel in Wagga Wagga, New South Wales (designed in the early 1960s and opened in 1964) was included in the category of 'Elements: Parapets' as an example of a building designed in the Wrightian manner. The Wagga Wagga Town House Motel was compared to Paul Rudolph's New Haven Parking Garage (1963) and Luigi Moretti's 'San Maurizio' condominium apartment block in Rome (1965). According to the exhibition curators these projects emphasised a horizontality through the play of cantilevered planes, horizontal roofs, parapets and terraces. Their images were compared to Frank Lloyd Wright's Fallingwater to denote, according to the catalogue, how their 'cantilevered terraces seem to float in the air and have the effect of "demolishing the box" as Wright put it, because their varying projections obscure the continuity of the wall plane'.[5] The curator of the exhibition, Arthur Drexler, noted that: 'Enrico Taglietti's motel in Australia has rectilinear terraces cantilevered at all sides, but where the parapets meet the corner is chamfered and extended visually with a projecting beam like a downspout. The sloping corners emphatically terminate the horizontals and evoke Oriental pagodas, because each floor can be read equally well as a roof.'[6]

Taglietti's use of concrete in projects such as the War Memorial repository or the Giralang School of the late 1970s resonates with the sculptural forms of the vaulted shapes of Eero Saarinen's TWA Terminal at Kennedy Airport (1962) and Joern Utzon's Sydney Opera House (1973), as well as having an affinity with the elements of post-war Japanese architecture, in particular Kenzo Tange's Kurashiki Town Hall (1960) and Kuyio Mayekawa's Festival Hall in Tokyo.

The inclusion of the Wagga Wagga Town House Motel in the exhibition is significant in that the exhibits were chosen for their thematic affinity with each other. It is worth noting that Taglietti's motel and the Sydney Opera House were the two projects selected to represent Australian architecture.

Within the Australian architectural community recognition was also forthcoming for Taglietti's designs. Architectural merit awards from the

Australian Capital Territory Chapter of the RAIA were awarded to the Paterson House in Aranda, ACT in 1969 and the Apostolic Nunciature (the Vatican Embassy) in Canberra in 1979. The Philip District Oval grandstand and the Forrest Early Childhood Centre in the ACT were both recipients of the award in 1992. In 1997 the Apostolic Nunciature was entered in the Register of the National Estate by the Australian Heritage Commission (n. 101288). The 1977 Canberra Medallion of the ACT Chapter of the RAIA was awarded to the Giralang Primary School. The school also received a 25-year award for sustained architectural excellence from the ACT Chapter in 2000. Another Taglietti project, the Dickson District Library (opened in 1969), received the same award in 1995. In 2001 national recognition from RAIA in form of a Life Fellowship certificate was conferred on Enrico Taglietti and Romaldo Giurgola.

Despite the fact that Taglietti's projects had received numerous architectural RAIA awards, and his work had been published in numerous European architectural journals, the acknowledgment of his work by Australian architectural historians has been limited until 1985. This was the year when his residential projects were mentioned, albeit briefly, by Jennifer Taylor in her article 'Beyond the 1950s' in *The History and Design of the Australian House* compiled by Robert Irving.[7] Notable omissions in Australian historiography include JM Freeland's *Architecture in Australia: a History*[8], published in 1968, as well in the Harry Sowden's polemical *Towards an Australian Architecture*,[9] published in the same year or in the Ian McKay edited *Living and partly living*.[10]

Meanwhile the Town House Motels in Wagga Wagga and Canberra were published in *Architettura: Cronache e storia* in 1962, in *Deutsche Bauzeitung* in 1964 and in the journal *Architecture d'Aujourd'hui* in 1966, and his residential projects were published in *Domus* in 1964. The first project of Taglietti's acknowledged with an article in the journal *Architecture in Australia*[11] was the Conference Centre for the Associated Chambers of Manufacturers of Australia in 1968. His work appears occasionally from 1961 in the journal *Cross-section*, published by the Department of Architecture of the University of Melbourne. In 1961 the Town House Motel in Canberra was featured; in 1962, the Wagga Wagga Town House Motel in 1963, the Italo-Australian club in Canberra and in 1964, two houses in Canberra. St Anthony's Church, Marsfield appears in 1970 with the Dickson Library and the Sundown Drive-in Theatre, and in 1971 the Paterson House is presented.

Architecture in Australia acknowledged Taglietti in 1970 with the publication of the Dickson District Library in Canberra and St Anthony's Church, Marsfield. In 1981 the journal presented the Apostolic Nunciature for the Vatican diplomatic representatives, comprising a residence and offices.

The special issue of *The Architectural Review* in September 1978 devoted to Australia states, in a generally favourable review of the Giralang School, that it was 'designed by "a new Australian" Dr Enrico Taglietti from Italy, and applies a genial expressionism to the libertarian fabric of Australian Primary Education'.[12] Although published in the UK, the wording seems an astonishing inflection on the career of an architect by then resident in Australia for nearly a quarter of a century, the currency of the term 'new Australian' notwithstanding.

Despite wide publication in journals, Taglietti's work remains thinly represented in books. In 1989 his conference centre for the Associated Chamber of Manufacturers of Australia (1967) in Canberra was included in the chapter on 'Late Twentieth-century Organic Architecture' in Richard Apperly's *Identifying Australian Architecture*.[13] It is not until 1990 that Jennifer Taylor draws attention to Taglietti's work with a series of projects including the Italian Embassy, St Anthony's Church and the Dickson Library in her book *Australian Architecture Since 1960*.

Locating Taglietti

The recognition of Taglietti's work in the professional arena thus proceeded from international exposure to local acknowledgment of the strength of his work. A recent article in the *Canberra City News* quotes architect and academic Roger Pegrum thus: 'Canberra architecture was at that time (1960s) a bit dull. He brought a lot of things with him. His style was and is very strong, simple, and dynamic. He made buildings that people found interesting and they then started to take an interest in architecture.'[14] The central issue, however, is the persistent difficulty of local historiography in assimilating Taglietti's work into prevailing schemata. The dilemma is aptly expressed by Jennifer Taylor:

> Italy also contributed to the fashioning of Australian sculptural architecture of the 1960s and 1970s with the work of Enrico Taglietti. The exuberance and formal play of Taglietti's architecture has no parallel in the country. It strangely combines the gaiety of much Italian, free-form construction with the sobriety of the heavy forms of Japan's post-war architects: it is an architecture fashioned for mood and visual delight.[15]

In a similar vein, Richard Apperly states: 'Outside the realm of domestic architecture, the more dramatic and spectacular aspects of organic architecture were to be seen in the idiosyncratic designs of Enrico Taglietti.'[16] Even the architectural journal *Cross-section*, an early vehicle for his work, observed in 1970: 'It is impossible to place the work of Enrico Taglietti in a convenient stylistic basket marked "FLW" or "Scarpa", although in the meticulous handling of detail one can detect a leaning towards recent Italian work.'[17] The same journal states: 'The architecture of Taglietti of Canberra displays masterful handling of a highly personalised style.'[18] An earlier edition had prefaced his work with similar sentiments: 'These two houses were recently completed in Canberra by arch. Dr Enrico Taglietti, whose highly personal style remains outside the main streams of current Australian architecture but is nonetheless invigorating and adaptable. It is an architecture of exaggeration, but within its own idiom, consistently controlled.'[19] These statements can be contrasted with the observations on his work made by the curators of the 1979 *Transformations in Modern Architecture* exhibition at MoMA. The singularity of Taglietti's work was no barrier to the affinities it held to other modern work, a point that underpinned the presentation at the exhibition.

Taglietti's career intersects a number of historical dynamics: issues of migrancy, style and professional opportunity are laid over prevailing architectural and historiographic concerns. The inability of local historians to place Taglietti is clearly symptomatic of particular constructions of identity and their sharp limits.

Architecture and migration

William Jordy[20] (1972) and Siegfried Giedion[21] (1982) have written extensively about the impact of the post-1930s emigration of European architects on American architecture, and questioned the nature of the evolving dialogue of the imported European modernism and the American architectural environment. On the other hand, the study of migrant architects is a relatively new field in Australian architectural history.

It is not until 1997 with the volumes *The Europeans: Émigré artists in Australia 1930–1960*[22] and *Building, Dwelling, Drifting: Migrancy and the limits of architecture*[23] that artists and architecture in general have been considered in relation to their connection with migration. *The Europeans* acknowledges the impact of the post-1930s emigration of European artists. Roger Butler argues in the introduction that 'Australian life and culture was transformed by the many European émigrés who settled here in the period between 1930 and 1960'.[24] Contributors to the publication generally agree that 'Little is known of the contribution by European-trained migrants who arrived after 1930'.[25] Among the artists who contributed to the development of contemporary Australian sculpture, graphic arts, jewellery, textile art and design, and photography, one architect is mentioned: the Swiss-trained Frederick Romberg in an article by Conrad Hamann.

This limited attention paid to the work and influences of continental European migrant architects on Australian architecture has been recently noted by architect and academic Mirjana Lozanovska. In the introduction to the April 2002 issue of the journal *Architect* (Victoria), she editorialised that 'this issue of *Architect* begins to explore the effects of migration on architecture and urbanisation in Melbourne'.[26] With the notable exception of Harry Seidler and Frederick Romberg, Lozanovska notes that 'histories of architects who migrated from places other than England and Ireland such as Ermin Smerkar and Enrico Taglietti are still to be written'.[27]

The career of Frederick Romberg has garnered attention from Conrad Hamann and Harriet Edquist. The latter notes in the introduction to the publication *Frederick Romberg: The Architecture of Migration 1938–1975* that the history of Australian architecture from the 1940s to the present includes very little of his work, and his projects have at times been mentioned with inaccurate attribution and inadequate recognition even from his practice partner, Robin Boyd.[28] Conrad Hamann concludes one of his articles with the following exhortation, which could equally apply to Taglietti's work:

> There is now a real chance for historians and critics of Australian architecture to reap full benefit from architects such as Frederick Romberg. This means responding more to architecture outside of the beguilingly teachable mainstream, as Romberg's so clearly was: outside the stylistic exemplar. It means going beyond what Australian architecture wanted European authenticity to be, and instead looking at both the full diversity of European culture, and the real transformation that this diversity would undergo in Australia.[29]

The recent volume *Drifting: Architecture and Migrancy*[30] presents a number of views of architecture and migrancy in the broadest sense. Of particular relevance to the issues raised above are observations made by Paul Carter in his chapter titled 'Mythforms: Techniques of migrant place-making'. Indeed, the fit between Taglietti's history and Carter's observations on placism are neat enough to undermine Carter's broader argument through a simple literal correspondence, although the relevance goes deeper. Carter writes:

> Only against the background of the pervasive placism which white settler ideology takes over from its colonial origins, can the distinctiveness of migrant place-making be measured. Otherwise, there would be nothing to distinguish the migrant's arrival from any act of colonisation. Yet, the difference of his arrival is well established, residing precisely in his refusal to repress the traces of his mobility – by contrast, in white settler foundationalist myths, it is axiomatic that the people were always there, and that without them the land was nothing.[31]

The origins of the problem are not hard to find. Most Australian historiography betrays its naturalist or placist origins, where placism holds that 'every place had its own individual spirit, which it was the artist's task to paint, describe or, in the jargon of the time, "capture"'.[32] Freeland states in the preface to *Architecture in Australia* that 'Every building records, describes and explains the time and place in which it was built'.[33] Writing some years later, Jennifer Taylor is more aware of the ironies implicit in the formulation of Australian architecture, yet an overarching national framework remains in her work. The first line of her preface to *Australian Architecture Since 1960* reads 'This book tells of one part of the saga of the making of Australia'.[34] The issue persists; Philip Goad's text for the recent *New Directions in Australian Architecture* is constantly concerned with pinning down commonalities across a range of work nationwide.[35]

It is Taglietti's very success in holding on to the traces of his mobility, to use Carter's term, that renders his work opaque to attempts at an 'Australian' historiography. In sketching out a solution Carter offers that 'the placist myth, that stories are made after the place, has to be reversed: places are made after the story'.[36] Yet he warns of the possible resulting 'picturesque multiculturalism, in which every story has a place, and where no history is allowed to leave a mark'.[37]

In the case of architecture, though, the 'story' is not quite as passive. This allows for further reflection: architectural pieces exhibit a self-awareness that, in the strongest cases, issues a challenge. In the case of Taglietti's work, this challenge has been sufficient to allow his works to be valued for their experiential power, whilst still leaving the nationalist question hanging: how might these formal attributes be useful to evolving representations of place?

For Taglietti, this second question has been one of accommodation. He has engaged with it where he saw fit, but the accidents of historical ideology – what defines the unfolding identity of place – have passed him by. Yet the closeness of that passing has its own fascination. What factors determine that Bruce Rickard or Ian McKay's Usonian-inspired houses become allied to a regional identity, when Taglietti's own Wrightian influences fail to resonate at a local level? The answer to this and related questions clearly involves a critical stance towards the placist mythologies that sustain these judgments.

Yet the impression remains that one could write about Taglietti's work and its historical place by simply circumventing the demands of a coherent Australian history. In this way, quite literally, the story would precede place with little loss of coherence. The perplexity of desiring a nationalist consistency seems the domain of those who have most heavily invested in its existence. For others (especially migrants), the opportunity to build, to transpose their story, is firmly taken alongside a wry awareness of the largely symbolic nature of the placist angst. In this it is somewhat akin to flying the flag at primary school: a point of identification, but hardly necessary for the conducting of classes.

Notes

Introduction

1 For an account of the Society's early history, see Julia Gatley, 'SAHANZ: The First 20 Years, 1984–2004', *Fabrications: The Journal of the Society of Architectural Historians, Australia and New Zealand* 13, 2, 2003, pp. 63–87. SAHANZ was formally incorporated in South Australia following a meeting in Sydney in 1985.

2 JM Freeland, *Architecture in Australia*, Cheshire, Melbourne, 1968; Peter Shaw, with Robin Morrison, *New Zealand Architecture, from Polynesian Beginnings to 1990*, Hodder & Stoughton, Auckland, 1991.

3 David Saunders, 'Preface', in *Architectural History Papers, Australia and New Zealand: Papers Delivered or Circulated at the Conference 'Architectural Historians in Australia', Adelaide, 11–13 August 1984*, Department of Architecture, University of Adelaide and SAHANZ, Adelaide, 1985, p. 5.

4 Derek Linstrum, 'The Uses of Architectural History', in Paul-Alan Johnson (ed.), *SAHANZ 1987: Papers, Fourth Annual Conference, Adelaide, 9–10 May 1987*, SAHANZ, Kensington, NSW, 1991, p. 11.

5 Stanislaus Fung, 'Introduction', in Stanislaus Fung & Timothy Turner (eds), *Australian Studies in Architectural History: Papers from the Fifth Annual Conference of the Society of Architectural Historians, Australia and New Zealand, 1988*, SAHANZ, Belconnen, ACT: SAHANZ, 1990, p. vii.

6 Ibid., p. viii.

Charting Shifting Views of Port Arthur and Associated Methodological Problems

1 Philippe Boudon, *Lived-in Architecture: Le Corbusier's Pessac Revisited*, translated by Gerald Onn, Lund Humphries, London, 1972 (1969).

2 Marcus Clarke, *His Natural Life*, George Robertson, Melbourne, 1874.

3 Ibid., ch. XX.

4 Marcus Clarke, 'Port Arthur Visited, 1870', in *A Marcus Clarke Reader*, edited with an Introduction by Bill Wannan, Angus & Robertson Ltd, London, 1964, p. 148.

5 Ibid., p. 141.

6 William Senior, *Travel and Trout in the Antipodes: An Angler's Sketches in Tasmania and New Zealand*, Chatto and Windus, Piccadily, London, 1880, pp. 73–4.

7 Haywood, 1885–6.

8 Walch, c. 1900.

9 Ibid.

10 *Tasmanian Mail*, 1887. The author quotes four lines from Lovelace's poem 'To Althea, From Prison' (1649).

11 *Tasmanian Mail*, 1889.

12 JW Beattie, *Port Arthur, The British Penal Settlement in Tasmania: glimpses of its Stirring History*, compiled from authentic sources by JW Beattie, Oldham, Beddome & Meredith Pty Ltd, Hobart, c.193?, p. 2.

13 Ibid.

14 *Mercury*, 11 March 1889.

15 *Mercury*, 30 July 1926.

16 Ibid.

17 *Mercury*, 31 September 1926.

18 *Mercury*, 31 July 1926.

19 *Field Naturalists Club*, 1926.

20 M Hookey, *The Romance of Tasmania*, The Bookshelf, Hobart, 1921.

21 Weetman, 1 May 1935.

22 Parker, 1937.

23 Bryant, 1 August 1943.

24 *Mercury*, 5 August 1926.

25 Clive Lord, 1926.

26 Ibid.

27 Ibid.

28 Ibid., quoting Voltaire.

29 Ibid.

30 Ibid.

31 Ibid.

32 Ibid.

33 Ibid.

34 B Coultman-Smith, *Shadow Over Tasmania*, J Walch & Sons, Hobart, 5th edn, 1947 (1941), p. 9.

35 Robert Cosgrove, 'Foreword to the First Edition', in Smith, *Shadow Over Tasmania*, p. 2.

36 Smith, 1948.

37 Ibid.

38 E Graeme Robertson, *Early Buildings of Southern Tasmania*, 2 vols, Georgian House, Melbourne, 1970, vol. 2, p. 368.

39 Ibid., p. 376.

The 'Sydney School'?

1 Research for this paper was carried out as part of a BSc (Arch) honours project in the School of Architecture, University of New South Wales. The author would like to thank Dr Peter Proudfoot and Associate Professor John Ingleson for their supervision. This paper was written with the support of a University Postgraduate Research Award from the University of Sydney.

2 Peter Muller, pers. comm., 1984.

3 Milo Dunphy, 'The Growth of an Australian Architecture', *Hemisphere*, August 1962, pp. 19–20.

4 Robin Boyd, 'The State of Australian Architecture', *Architecture in Australia*, vol. 56, June 1967, p. 459.

5 David Saunders, 'Australian Architecture', *Process: Architecture*, no. 22, March 1981, p. 20.

6 Philip Cox, 'Housing in the past 10 years', *Architecture in Australia*, vol. 62, October 1973, p. 55.

7 Jennifer Taylor, 'Australia', in Warren Sanderson (ed.) *International Handbook of Contemporary Developments in Architecture*, Warren Sanderson (ed.), Greenwood Press, Westport, Conn, 1981, p. 112; Taylor, manuscript circa January 1984, to be published in *Developments in Architecture in Australia, 1950–80* (forthcoming), 1st paragraph. I am grateful to Professor Taylor for kindly making available to me her unpublished manuscripts and other materials. In the following discussion, 'The Sydney School' shall refer to a hypothetical group of architects alleged to have shared common aims and attitudes unless otherwise indicated. I use the label purely as a terminological device, and do not in any way wish to imply that the existence of a Sydney School can be or has been established in any of the senses the term has been used so far.

8 Taylor, *An Australian Identity: Houses for Sydney 1953-63*, University of Sydney, Dept. of Architecture, Sydney, 1972, p. 16. A second edition is now available, but my notes refer to the first edition.

9 Dunphy, 'The Growth of an Australian Architecture'. This article also appeared in *Architecture, Building, Structural Engineering*, vol. 47, October 1969, pp. 17, 19, 21. I have not referred to a third version in *Architect* (Perth), vol. 6, September 1963, pp. 28–34. My notes refer to the pagination in *Hemisphere*.

10 Dunphy, 'The Growth of an Australian architecture', p. 18.

11 Ibid., p. 19.

12 My discussion is based on discussions with Mr Muller and Professor Kollar in 1984. On Muller, see Andrew Poulos, 'The Private House: Architect-designed Houses

Between 1950 and 1960,' BArch thesis, University of New South Wales, 1983, p. 110. Both Kollar and Muller were interested in the writings of René Guénon and Ananda K Coomaraswamy. On these two writers, see Seyyed Hossein Nasr, *Knowledge and the Sacred: the Gifford Lectures*, Edinburgh University Press, New York, 1981, Chapter 3. For further references, see my 'Second Thoughts on "The Sydney School",' BSc(Arch) honours thesis, University of New South Wales, 1984, p. 8, n. 23. The lasting influence of Coomaraswamy on Muller can be seen in his statement in *Art and Australia*, June 1971, p. 38.

13 Jack, pers. comm., 1984.

14 Boyd, 'The State of Australian Architecture'. Boyd's views are put forward earlier in April 1967, and published as an article 'Architecture in Seclusion' in *Journal of the New Zealand Institute of Architects*, vol. 34, September 1967, pp. 270–5.

15 Ibid., p. 454.

16 Ibid., p. 459.

17 Ibid., pp. 454, 459.

18 Ibid., p. 463

19 Ibid., p. 459.

20 Ibid.

21 Ibid.

22 Boyd, 'Architecture in Australia', *RIBA Journal*, vol. 78, January 1971, pp. 12–20.

23 Ibid., p. 19.

24 Ibid.

25 Ibid.

26 *Cross-section* (Melbourne), no. 179, 1 September 1967, p. 1.

27 Ibid.

28 David Saunders, 'Sydney', *Architect*, Melbourne, vol. 3, no. 4, September–October 1969, pp. 20–1.

29 Ibid., p. 20.

30 Ibid.

31 Ibid.

32 Ibid.

33 Saunders, 'Australian Architecture', pp. 9–22.

34 Ibid., p. 20.

35 Phillip Cox, 'The Development of Domestic Architecture in Australia' in *Etruscan*, vol. 21, March 1972, pp. 18–22. Cox's use of the term 'vernacular' as a style-label has been criticised as 'sloppy and silly' by Joan Kerr in *Art and Australia*, vol. 17, no. 2, December 1979, p. 134. Dr Kerr has elaborated her view in a paper entitled

'Why Architects Should Not Write Architectural History' (1984, also published in this volume).

36 Cox, 'The Development of Domestic Architecture in Australia', p. 22.

37 Cox, 'Housing in the past 10 years', p. 55.

38 See note 8 above.

39 Taylor, *An Australian Identity*, pp. 25–73.

40 Ibid., p. 67.

41 Ibid., p. 79.

42 Ibid., pp. 25–71.

43 Ibid.

44 Ibid., p. 79.

45 Ibid., p. 74.

46 Ibid., pp. 28–9.

47 Ibid., p. 31.

48 Ibid., p. 31ff.

49 Ibid., p. 44.

50 Ibid.

51 Ibid.

52 Ibid., pp. 48ff.

53 Ibid., p. 52.

54 Ibid., p. 53.

55 Ibid., p. 56.

56 Ibid., p. 64.

57 Ibid.

58 Ibid., p. 67.

59 Ibid., p. 74.

60 Ibid.

61 Ibid., p. 58.

62 Dunphy, 'The Growth of an Australian Architecture', p. 18; Taylor, *An Australian Identity*, pp. 15–16, 44, 63–4, 79.

63 Taylor, 'Looking at the Sydney School', *Transition*, vol. 1, no. 2, November 1979, pp. 4–8.

64 Ibid., p. 7.

65 Ibid.

66 Ibid., p. 8.

67 Taylor, 'Australia', in *Developments in Architecture in Australia, 1950–80*; 'Beyond the 1950s', in Robert Irving (ed.), *History and Design of the Australian House*, Oxford

University Press, Sydney, 1985, pp. 145–167; and 'Postscript 1983' in *An Australian Identity*, 2nd edn.

68 E.g. in Taylor, 'Australia', p. 112.

69 See James S Ackerman, 'Art History and the Problems of Criticism', in Gyorgy Kepes (ed.) *The Visual Arts Today*, Wesleyan University Press, Middletown, Conn., 1960, pp. 257–67; George Kubler, *The Shape of Time: Remarks on the History of Things*, Yale University Press, New Haven & London, 1962, p. 2ff; Thomas Munro, 'Do the Arts Evolve? Some Recent Conflicting Answers', *Journal of Aesthetics and Art Criticism*, vol. 19, 1960–61, pp. 407–17.

70 Joyce Brodsky, 'Continuity and Discontinuity in Style: A Problem in Art Historical Methodology', *Journal of Aesthetics and Art Criticism*, vol. 39, no. 1, Fall 1980, p. 27.

71 Munro, 'Do the Arts Evolve?', pp. 407–9.

72 Ackerman, 'Art History and the Problems of Criticism', p. 259.

73 E.g. Lance Wright, 'A coming-of-age', *Architectural Review*, vol. 164, 1978, p. 198; William JR Curtis, *Modern Architecture Since 1900*, Phaidon, Oxford, 1982.

Attitudes and Evidence: The View from the Government House Verandah

1 See Helen Proudfoot, 'The First Government House, Sydney, and the subsequent History of the Site after 1845', Study for the Department of Environment and Planning, Sydney, March 1983.

2 The archaeological investigation was carried out by Anne Bickford and her team for the Department of Environment and Planning.

3 John Skinner Prout and John Rae, *Sydney Illustrated*, T Bluett, Sydney, 1843.

4 J Henniker Heaton, *Australian Dictionary of Dates and Men of the Time*, Sydney, G. Robertson, Sydney,1879, p. 115.

5 James Houison, 'Address to the Society, 15 March, 1901', *Australian Historical Society Journal*, vol. 1, pt. 2, 1902, pp. 13–14.

6 *Sydney Morning Herald*, 11 March 1899, p. 11, c. 7.

7 Anne Toy, pers. comm., 1983.

8 *Sydney Morning Herald*, 18 March 1899, p. 8 c.7–8.

9 WC Wentworth, *A Statistical, Historical, and Political Description of the Colony of New South Wales*, G & WB Whittaker, London, pp. 18–19; JD Lang, *An Historical and Statistical Account of New South Wales*, Cochrane and M'Crone, London, 1834; John West, *The History of Tasmania*, Henry Dowling, Launceston, 1852. Geoffrey Bolton and Neville Meaney drew attention to these attitudes in their papers at the Australian Historical Association Conference, 1988.

10 JP McGuanne, 'Old Government House, Sydney', *Australian Historical Society Journal* vol. 1, pt. 5, 1902, pp. 73–82.

11 Norman Selfe, 'A Century of Sydney Cove and the Genesis of Circular Quay', *Royal Australian Historical Society Journal*, vol. 1, pt. 4, 1901/2, pp. 55–71; 'Sydney Past, Present and Possible', ibid., 1, pt. 12, 1905, pp. 239–60; 'The Quays. Wharves and Shipping of Port Jackson', *Proceedings of the Engineering Association of New South Wales*, vol. 23, 1908, p. 105.

12 Captain WAB Greaves, 'Recollections of Old Sydney', *Royal Australian Historical Society Journal*, vol. 3, pt. 9, 1916, pp. 403–28.

13 *Art and Architecture*, vol. 4, 1907. Frank Walker extended this in a later article, 'Vice-Regal Residences of New South Wales', *Royal Australian Historical Society Journal*, vol. 4, pt. 9, 1919, pp. 456–68.

14 Percival Serle, *Dictionary of Australian Biography*, Angus & Robertson, Sydney, 1949.

15 DR Hainsworth, *The Sydney Traders*, Cassell Australia, Melbourne, 1971.

16 George Mackanness, *Admiral Arthur Phillip*, Angus & Robertson, Sydney, 1937; M Barnard Eldershaw, *Phillip of Australia*, Harrap, London, 1938; HV Evatt, *The Rum Rebellion*, Angus & Robertson, Sydney, 1938; MH Ellis, *Lachlan Macquarie*, Angus & Robertson, Sydney, 1947 and *John Macarthur*, Angus & Robertson, Sydney, 1955. Ellis also wrote the first biography of an Australian architect: *Francis Greenway*, Angus & Robertson, Sydney, 1953.

17 Brian Fitzpatrick, *British Imperialism and Australia 1788–1833*, G Allen & Unwin, London, 1933.

18 Morton Herman, *The Early Australian Architects and Their Work*, Angus & Robertson, Sydney, 1954; JM Freeland, *Architecture in Australia: A History*, Cheshire, Melbourne, 1968.

19 Bernard Smith, 'Architecture in Australia', *Historical Studies* vol. 14, no. 53, October 1969, pp. 85–92.

20 KW Robinson, 'Sydney: 1820–1952, A Comparison of Developments in the Heart of the City', *The Australian Geographer*, vol. 6, no. I, June 1952, pp. 6–12; GP Walsh 'The Geography of Manufacturing in Sydney. 1788–1851', *Business Archives History*, vol. 3, no. 1, 1963, pp. 20–52; N Edwards, 'The Genesis of the Sydney Central Business District 1788–1856', in Max Kelly (ed.), *Nineteenth Century Sydney*, Sydney History Group, Sydney, 1978, pp. 37–53.

21 Robert Irving, (ed.), *The History and Design of the Australian House*, Oxford University Press, Melbourne, 1985.

The Spanish Scene: Some Houses of the Thirties by Marshall Clifton (1903–75)

1 ARL Wright, 'RIAWA Presidential Address', *Building and Construction*, 28 July 1927, pp. 14–18.

2 In addition to the architects specifically mentioned, many of Perth's important designers such as FGB Hawkins, AB Kreitmayer, Richard Spanney and Howard Bonner were involved with the 'Spanish style' during the thirties.

3 Ian Molyneux, *Looking Around Perth: A Guide to the Architecture of Perth and Surrounding Towns*, RAIA, Perth, 1981, p. 63. Probably the only case of a clearly identified model for a local work is St Columbia's Roman Catholic Church, South Perth, dating from 1936 by E le B Henderson, which was a copy of a Spanish Mission Revival Church at 624 North Rossmore Avenue, Hollywood.

4 *Building and Construction*, 30 November 1928, p. 6. This was Professor Wilkinson's interpretation of the Hackett Memorial Buildings at UWA. Alsop described them as Georgian and a University of Western Australia academic of the day termed the buildings as Spanish Sicilian. In this case I can only assume that Wilkinson possessed a wry sense of humour.

5 Ian Molyneux, *Looking around Perth*, p. 55. In October 1932, a local committee awarded the RIBA Gold Medal to the Hackett Memorial Buildings, so it is evident that they were indeed valued by Western Australian architects. Marshall Clifton, on the other hand, had little regard for Alsop's Hackett Memorial Buildings and commented in a letter to his family in June 1932 that 'he [Alsop] doesn't seem to have made the most of that style of architecture'.

6 Professor Wilkinson was initially invited to Perth by the Vice Chancellor of the University of Western Australia, Professor HE Whitfeld (a graduate of Sydney University, Whitfeld was impressed by the work that Wilkinson had undertaken for the University) to advise on the preparation of a master plan for the University of Western Australia. Wilkinson subsequently drafted the competition conditions for the Hackett Memorial Buildings and with the University Chancellor, Dr Saw, and ARL Wright, acted as an adjudicator for the competition. The competition was won jointly by Rodney Alsop and Conrad Sayce with a design established as being by Sayce. In the competition conditions stress was placed upon a 'climate and setting which may perhaps be best described as Mediterranean'.

7 Rodney Alsop did not have as great an impact on Perth's domestic architecture as has been supposed. In the early years during the construction of the Hackett Memorial Buildings (1927–31) he was frequently out of the state for long periods meeting his continuing eastern states obligations and he died in October 1932.

Two or three houses are presently attributed to him, but one of the most notable, the McKellar-Hall house, is now tentatively supposed to have been undertaken by Reginald Summerhayes from a sketch by Alsop.

8 ASC Strempel, 'What is Period Architecture?', *Building and Construction*, 13 February 1931, pp. 19 & 23.

9 Margaret Pitt Morrison and John White (eds), *Western Towns and Buildings*, UWA Press, Perth, 1979, p. 135.

10 Given Western Australia's environmental conditions, this Janus-like double interpretation is only possible if a hot-dry climate building model is selected. It would be equally possible to propose other stylistic models, such as the Arts and Crafts, as a basis, but given this choice, the interpretation could not hope to be sustained.

11 Wright, 'Presidential Address'. Italics added.

12 'Modernism on an International Basis: The "Manifesto of Sarraz"', *Building and Construction*, 1 November 1929, p. 1. The number of references to modern architecture in this journal during the late twenties and thirties would be too numerous to list here.

13 Clearly defined in that the works reflect the stylistic criteria identified in articles published in *Building and Construction* during 1927 and are not later attributions. George Herbert Parry and Monsignor John C Hawes designed buildings in WA during the early twenties that may well have influenced the 'Spanish style', but these works were not houses.

14 R Summerhayes in association with AR Baxter Cox was also to build the next important sequence of buildings at UWA based upon the Alsop and Sayce model in 1933.

15 These drawings are held in the archives of the firm Summerhayes Way & Associates, 940a Hay Street, Perth.

16 'A New Design in Architecture for WA', *Building and Construction*, 22 December 1927, pp. 10 & 13. Italics added. It cannot be established with certainty that R Summerhayes was the president responsible for either of the drawings that illustrate this article or even that the drawings represent a specific design proposal or just an illustration of stylistic characteristics. However, Summerhayes's obsessive concern for colour blended 'Spanish' tile roofs is well established and the link between these articles and the work of Summerhayes is reinforced by subsequent reports in *Building and Construction* discussing the Forbes and Summerhayes houses.

17 Ibid.

18 Strempel. 'What is Period Architecture?', pp. 19 & 23.

19 *Building and Construction*, 21 December 1934, p. 8.

20 'A New Design in Architecture for WA', p. 13.

21 This Wilkinson connection has yet to be explored and remains at present as conjecture. A possible explanation is that, during the twenties, some of the major projects undertaken by the PWD were large high schools in country towns such as Northam, Bunbury and Albany. Given this building type, Professor Wilkinson's example could hardly be ignored.

22 This study has focused upon 'Spanish style' houses; however, R Summerhayes had undertaken other works using Spanish precedent. An excellent example is the Karrinyup Golf Club house, now demolished.

23 Marshall Clifton, 'In Soviet Russia', *West Australian*, 13 March 1933, p. 5.

24 Ibid. In 1933, Professor EG Asplund was reported in *Building and Construction* as stating that 'the so-called functionalism must acquire more psychology and human feeling'.

25 'Return of Melbourne Architect from Europe', *Building and Construction*, 13 May 1932, p. 10.

26 Duncan Richards, 'Puzzles and Problems: The Architecture of Marshall Clifton', *Fremantle Arts Review*, vol. 2, no. 12, December 1987, pp. 10–12.

27 'Home Plan Series No. 114', *Building and Construction*, 2 January 1931, p. 5; 'Home Plan Series No. 116', *Building and Construction*, 16 January 1931, p. 5. These are essentially local house forms with 'Spanish features' superficially added.

28 Molyneux, *Looking around Perth*, p. 62.

29 'RIAWA Presidential Address', *Building and Construction*, 4 August 1933, p. 34. In his address the RAIWA President, WJ Waldie Forbes remarked on *the value of precedent* in the development of an Australian architecture and the value of travel as a means of understanding what precedent may offer. Marshall Clifton was in the audience that night and was circumspectly mentioned and commended by the President.

Kenneth Frampton and the Fiction of Place

1 Alan Colquhoun, 'Modern Architecture and the Liberal Conscience', in Kenneth Frampton (ed.), *Modern Architecture and the Critical Present*, Architectural Design, London; St Martin's Press, New York, 1982, p. 47.

2 Kenneth Frampton, *Modern Architecture: A Critical History*, 2nd edn, Thames and Hudson, London, 1985, p. 7.

3 Ibid., p. 327.

4 For a critical account of Frampton's interpretation of Heidegger's 'Building, Dwelling, Thinking', in *Poetry, Language, Thought*, translated by Albert Hofstadter, New York, 1971; see Ignasi Sola-Morales, 'Weak Architecture', *Quadems d'arquitectura i urbanisme*, no. 175, 1987, pp. 80–1.

5 Kenneth Frampton, 'Towards a Critical Regionalism: Six Points for an Architecture of Resistance', in Hal Foster (ed.), *The Anti-Aesthetic: Essays on Postmodern Culture*, Bay Press, Port Townsend, WA, 1983, p. 25.

6 Ibid., p. 28.

7 Robert Venturi, *Complexity and Contradiction in Architecture*, Museum of Modern Art, New York, 1966; Robert Venturi, Denise Scott Brown & Steven Izenour, *Learning from Las Vegas: The Forgotten Symbolism of Architectural Form*, revised edn, MIT Press, Cambridge, Mass., 1977; Frampton, *Modern Architecture*, pp. 290–1.

8 Ibid., p. 311.

9 Frampton, 'Towards a Critical Regionalism', p. 21.

10 Kenneth Frampton, 'The Need for Roots: Venice 1980', *GA Document*, no. 3, 1980, p. 14.

11 Frampton, 'Towards a Critical Regionalism', p. 27.

12 Susanne K Langer, *Feeling and Form: A Theory of Art Developed from Philosophy in a New Key*, Routledge & Kegan Paul, London, 1953, p. 95.

13 Frampton, *Modern Architecture*, p. 312; 'The Need for Roots', p. 18; 'A Note on Photography and Its Influence on Architecture', *Perspecta*, no. 22, 1986, pp. 40–1.

14 Frampton, *Modern Architecture*, p. 327.

15 Kenneth Frampton, 'Seidler at Riverside: A Retrospective Synthesis', in *Riverside Centre*, Horwitz Grahame, Cammeray, NSW, 1988, p. 10.

16 Frampton, 'Towards a Critical Regionalism', p. 17.

17 Frampton, 'Seidler at Riverside', p. 10.

18 Frampton, *Modern Architecture*, p. 327.

19 David Dunster, 'Maid in USA', in Frampton (ed.), *Modern Architecture and the Critical Present*, p. 51.

20 Frampton, 'The Need for Roots', p. 14.

21 Kenneth Frampton, 'The Japanese New Wave', in *A New Wave of Japanese Architecture, September 25, 1978 to November 14, 1978*, Institute for Architecture and Urban Studies, New York, 1978, p. 8; Kenneth Frampton, 'Poesis and Transformation: the Architecture of Alvaro Siza', in Alvaro Siza, *Poetic Profession*, Electa, London & Milan, 1986, p. 15; 'The Johnson Wax Buildings and the Angel of History', in Jonathan Lipman, *Frank Lloyd Wright and the Johnson Wax Buildings*, Rizzoli, New York, 1986, p. xiv.

22 These papers were in order, published in: Foster (ed.), *The Anti-Aesthetic*; *Perspecta*, no. 20; *RIBA Transactions*, no. 3; *Modern Architecture*; Chris Johnson (ed.), *The City in Conflict*, The Law Book Company, Sydney, 1985; *Center*, no. 3; Scott Marble et al, (eds), *Architecture and Body*, Rizzoli, New York, 1988.
23 In Paul Ricoeur, *History and Truth*, translated with an introduction by Charles A Kelbley, Northwestern University, Evanston, Ill., 1965.
24 Michael Starenko, 'The Politics of Interpretation', *Afterimage*, vol. XI, no. 6, 1984, p. 14.
25 Craig Owens, 'The Discourse of Others: Feminists and Postmodernism', in Foster (ed.), *The Anti-Aesthetic*, pp. 61–2.
26 Frampton, *Modern Architecture*, pp. 321–2.
27 Ibid., p. 313.
28 Ibid., p. 319.
29 Frampton, 'Prospects for a Critical Regionalism', p. 149.
30 Kenneth Frampton & John Knesl, 'Cultural Resistance in the Postmodern Condition' (interview), *Precis*, no. 6, 1987, p. 117.
31 Frampton, 'Prospects for a Critical Regionalism', p. 162. Emphasis added.
32 See the interview between Frampton and Knesl that appeared in *Precis*, no. 6. In response to Frampton's offering the canton as a model of local political control, Knesl responds that the cantons 'do not necessarily resist or even impede the all penetrating commodifying thrust of global capitalism' (p. 115).
33 Thomas Schumacher, 'Regional Intentions and Contemporary Architecture: A Critique', *Center*, no. 3, 1987, p. 55.
34 Jacques Derrida, 'Sending: On Representation', *Social Research*, vol. 49, no. 2, 1982.
35 Frampton, *Modern Architecture*, p. 313.
36 Alan Colquhoun, 'Regionalism and Technology', in *Modernity and the Classical Tradition Architectural Essays, 1980–1987*, MIT Press, Cambridge, Mass., 1989, pp. 207–8.

The Imperial Technology Cringe

1 *Builder*, vol. 12, 579, 11 March 1854, p. 127.
2 A Karman & H Egli, 'Vernacular Approaches to Passive Cooling in Hot Arid Zones', *Passive Cooling*, International Passive and Hybrid Cooling Conference held at Miami Beach, November 1981, Newark, NJ, 1981, p. 242.

3 Anthony D King, *The Bungalow: The Production of a Global Culture*, Routledge & Kegan Paul, London, 1984, p. 34.

4 James Broadbent, 'Aspects of Domestic Architecture in New South Wales 1788–1843', PhD thesis, Australian National University, 1985, vol. 2, p. 419, ref. unpaginated sketchbook with Scott plans, Mitchell Library ML *D64.

5 Francis White, reported in the *Australian Builder*, 24 December 1859, p. 409.

6 Victorian patent no. 193 to Thomas William Badham, 12 January 1859; also reported in the *Australian Builder*, 22 January 1859, p. 24.

7 ML Gardam, *The Bishop's Lodge*, Hay, NSW, 1993, p. 10, quoting *Riverina Grazier*, 2 April 1879, p. 2.

8 42 inches or 1.07 m wide, by 1½ inch or 38 mm mesh of 17 gauge or 1.4 mm wire.

9 Tom Cartwright of Rockhampton, letter of 21 March 1994.

10 Mortlock Library S.RG.104, processed and unprocessed records of the Adelaide Club.

11 Information and inspection courtesy of Kate McDougall & Liz Vines, and of the club, 1991.

12 King, *The Bungalow*, p. 34.

13 TJ Maslen, *The Friend of Australia*, Hurst, Chance, and Co, London, 1830, p. 272.

14 Charles Tomlinson, *Rudimentary Treatise on Warming and Ventilation*, John Weale, Architectural Library, London, 1850, p. 181.

15 Ray & John Oldham, *George Temple-Poole: Architect of the Golden Years, 1885–1897*, UWA Press, Nedlands, WA, 1980, p. 14.

16 Michael Cannon, *Life in the Cities*, Thomas Nelson, West Melbourne, 1975, p. 117, citing *Australasian Ironmonger*, May 1900.

17 FN Barker, *Station Life in New Zealand*, Golden Press, Auckland, 1973 (1883), p. 49.

18 Morton Herman, *The Early Australian Architects and their Work*, Angus & Robertson, Sydney, 1954, p. 4.

19 Peter Cunningham, *Two Years in New South Wales*, Colburn, London, 1827, vol. 2, p. 165.

20 Robert Irving, 'The First Australian Architecture', MArch, University of New South Wales, 1975, p. 187.

21 John Fitchen, *Building Construction Before Mechanisation*, MIT Press, Cambridge, Mass., 1986, pp. 136–7.

22 GF Train, letter of 23 June 1853 in the *Boston Post*, 20 October 1853, reproduced in GF Train, *A Yankee Merchant in Goldrush Australia: The Letters of George Francis Train 1853–55*, edited & with an introduction by ED & A Potts, Heinemann, London, 1970, p. 25.

23 CB Mayes, *The Australian Builders' Price-Book*, Sands & McDougall, Melbourne, 1862, p. 107.
24 *Builder*, vol. 3, no. 137, 20 September 1855, p. 456.
25 *Mechanics Magazine*, vol. 33, no. 894, 26 September 1840, p. 349.
26 Wyatt Papworth (ed.), *The Dictionary of Architecture*, Longman, Brown, Green & Longmans, London 1853–92, sv Nail.
27 [Francis Young], *Every Man His Own Mechanic*, London, c 1882, §328, p. 138.
28 Papworth, *Dictionary*, sv Nail.
29 [Young], *Every Man His Own Mechanic*, p. 138.
30 This nail has been given to me by Ms Nada Brozel, who assisted in the dismantling of the cottage in the 1960s. Although the cottage had a chequered history, it had been moved bodily from site to site, and the later accretions had been stripped by the time the National Trust brought it back to Melbourne. Thus the nail came from the original section and, being so large, is likely to have been from the basic structure.
31 Miles Lewis, 'Pontville' (typescript report to the City of Doncaster & Templestowe, Melbourne 1994).
32 Hardwicke Knight & Peter Coutts, *Matanaka: Otago's First Farm*, Dunedin, 1975, p. 29. The nail is illustrated, though not identified, and it is implied that it is from the original structure.
33 Miles Lewis, *370 Malvern Road, Prahran*, Melbourne, 1989, p. 14.
34 Mayes, *Australian Builders' Price-Book*, p. 107.
35 Charles Mayes, *The Australian Builders' Price-Book*, 5th edn, Melbourne, 1886, advertisements, p. xix.
36 Joseph Gwilt, in Wyatt Papworth (ed.), *An Encyclopaedia of Architecture*, London, 1899 (1842), §2257b, p. 720, refers to Cordes' patent rose, flat points, 1¼, 1½, 1¾, 2, 2½, 3 and 6 inches long.
37 For example Miles Lewis, quoted by Anne Bickford in *Kalori Quarterly Newsletter*, vol. 3, no. 76, September-October 1976, pp. 15–16.
38 George Kubler, 'The Machine for living in 18th-Century West Africa', *Journal of the American Society of Architectural Historians*, vol. 4, no. 2, April 1944.
39 John Martin Robinson, *The Wyatts, An Architectural Dynasty*, Oxford University Press, Oxford, 1979, pp. 36–9.
40 Irving, 'The First Australian Architecture', pp. 483–7.
41 Though there is some doubt even as to his name. Gilbert Herbert, in *Pioneers of Prefabrication*, consistently cites him as 'John' Manning, but his advertisements uniformly refer to 'H Manning', and the *Post Office Directory* shows Henry Manning at the appropriate address, 251 High Holborn.

42 John Stacpoole, *William Mason*, Auckland University Press, Auckland, 1971, p. 32, ref. *Bell's Weekly Messenger*, London, 28 December 1839.

43 *Nelson Examiner*, 22 July 1843, where he claims twenty years' experience in furnishing supplies to emigrants, quoted in Stanley Northcote-Bade, *Colonial Furniture in New Zealand*, AH & AW Reed, Wellington, 1971, p. 21.

44 JC Loudon, *Encyclopaedia of Cottage, Farm and Villa Architecture and Furniture, &c*, Longman, Brown, Green, and Longmans, London, 1846 (1833), p. 256.

45 *Nelson Examiner*, 22 July 1843, quoted by Northcote-Bade.

46 Information provided to me, and marriage certificate kindly obtained for me, by David Hutchison, then Curator of History at the West Australian Museum, 1976.

47 Manning, 'Portable Cottages for the use of Emigrants and Others', in JC Loudon, *Encyclopaedia of Cottage, Farm and Villa Architecture and Furniture*, pp. 251–7.

48 Photograph of AH Stone, 1861, in an AH Stone album at the West Australian Museum. This seems to have been the house of Thomas Helms, who came to Perth in the 1830s, which stood in Irwin Street between Hay and Murray Streets, The photographer is annotated 'Grandpa', apparently in reference to the figure on the steps, and the photographer AH Stone was married to Helms's daughter. Information from David Hutchison, as above.

49 Information from Ian Molyneux, Fremantle, and Charles Staples, Perth, 1990.

50 Information from John White of Gingin, 1990.

51 My information is from Mrs Anne Marchant of Christchurch, who investigated the building with colleagues and students of the Draughting Course, Christchurch Polytechnic. The work has been published as Anne Marchant (ed.), *The Pegasus Building: Research Report 1993*, Christchurch Polytechnic, Christchurch, NZ, ?1994.

52 CB Mayes, *The Victorian Contractors' and Builders' Price-Book*, Melbourne, 1859, p. viii.

53 Victorian patents no. 291 to James Doulton, 3 December 1859; no. 232 to James Doulton, 28 January 1864. Both were presumably extensions of British patents, the latter presumably that of 1847 which would under normal circumstances have already expired in 1861: *Builder*, vol. 5, no. 254, 18 December 1847, p. 607.

54 *The Lysaght Century 1857–1937*, nd.

55 *John Lysaght (Aust.) Ltd, The Referee*, 12th edn, Sydney, 1921, p. 7.

56 *Lysaght's Works Ply. Ltd., Lysaght's Silver Jubilee*, Sydney 1946, p. 16.

57 *Post Office London Directory 1889*, London, 1889, p. 139.

58 James Davies, *Galvanized Iron: Its Manufacture and Uses*, E & FN Spon, London, 1899, p. 16.

59 *Lysaght Venture*, Sydney 1955, p. 2.

60 Ibid.

61 *Australasian Builder and Contractor's News*, 8 October 1887, p. 348.

62 *Lord & Hughes' Monthly Circular*, Melbourne, 2 June 1884, p. 5.

63 *Lysaght's Silver Jubilee*, p. 16.

64 *Australasian Ironmonger*, vol. 1, no. 7, 1 October 1886, advertisements p. xv.

65 Gilbert Herbert, *Pioneers of Prefabrication*, John Hopkins University Press, Baltimore, 1978, p. 144, quoting *Longland's Transvaal and Rhodesia Directory*, 1903, p. 11.

66 *Lysaght's Silver Jubilee, 1921–1946*, Sydney, 1946, p. 17.

67 James Smith (ed.), *Cyclopedia of Victoria* (3 vols), The Cyclopedia Company, Melbourne, 1903, 1904, 1905, vol. 1, pp. 534–5.

68 *Lysaght Venture*, Sydney, 1955, pp. 3–5. See also Ambrose Pratt (ed.), *The National Handbook of Australia's Industries*, Specialty Press, Melbourne, 1934, pp. 138–9.

69 *Lysaght's Referee*, 1938, p. 4.

70 'Esperance: Description etc. of Designs of Proposed New Public Office: Brisbane', 1883, (transcript held by the Historic Buildings Branch, Brisbane).

71 Joseph Gwilt in Wyatt Papworth (ed.), *An Encyclopaedia of Architecture*, London, 1899 (1842), § 2278k, p. 742.

72 Robert Boyle & Co, *A Sanitary Crusade through the East and Australasia*, Boyle, London, 1892 – not yet sighted by the present writer.

73 Elfrida & Ross Jensen, *Colonial Architecture in South Australia: A Definitive Chronicle of Development 1836–1890, and the Social History of the Times*, Rigby, Adelaide, 1980, p. 91, quoting an obituary in the *Australian Ironmonger*, 1 June 1894.

74 ML Holbrook, *Dr Holbrook's American Cookery ... with an Australian Appendix*, Melbourne, 1888, advertisement, reproduced in Terence Lane & Jessie Serle, *Australians at Home: A Documentary History of Australian Domestic Interiors from 1788 to 1914*, Oxford University Press, Melbourne & New York, 1990, p. 210.

75 Robert Haddon, *Australian Architecture: A Technical Manual for all those Engaged in Architectural and Building Work*, Melbourne, nd.

76 GAT Middleton, *Modern Buildings: Their Planning, Construction and Equipment* (6 vols), London, nd. Haddon's 'Australian Planning and Construction' is a substantial section in vol. 5, pp. 141–97.

Heavenly Groundings: Missionary Architectural Practice in Nineteenth-Century New Zealand

1 Rev. R. Taylor 'Ruapehu: Source of the Wangaehu' [185–], *Sketchbook 1839–86* (typescript), 88b, Alexander Turnbull Library, Wellington (hereafter ATL).

2 Simon Schama on Ruskin and mountain climbing points out that '[p]roper inspection actually revealed the mountaintops to be what Ruskin preferred to call "crests"'. *Landscape and Memory*, AA Knopf & Random House, New York, c.l995, p. 509.

3 Rev. Richard Taylor, *Sketchbook 1839–65*; 'Mangakino April 27 1847', ATL no. 50697 and 'Sketch, (Maowhango River)', ATL no. 50631 1/2, ATL.

4 Rev. Richard Taylor, *Journal*, 5 August 1843, vol. 2 (typescript), pp. 274–75.

5 Rev. Richard Taylor, *Journal*, 13 October 1851, vol. 7 (typescript), p. 233.

6 Rev. Richard Taylor, *Journal*, 1 February 1846, vol. 3 (typescript), pp. 211–12.

7 'I was sorry to find ... part of the church wall which had been moved out of its place by the earthquake of 55 had been blown down into the church and pressed down one side of the flooring and raised up the other, about thirty feet had fallen.' Taylor, Rev. R, *Journal*, Pipiriki, 28 July 1859, vol. 11 (typescript), p. 12.

8 Description in Ernst Dieffenbach, *Travels in New Zealand*, vol. 1, 1843, (reprint Capper Press, Christchurch, 1974), p. 103.

9 Account in Joan Maclean, 'Casualties of History: Waikanae's Lost Buildings', *Otaki Historical Society Historical Journal*, vol. 13, 1990, pp. 30–6.

10 Rev. Richard Taylor, *Journal*, 27 August 1843, vol. 2 (typescript), p. 277.

11 A more complete description of the church by GA Selwyn can be found in *New Zealand. Part 111, A Journal of the Bishop's Visitation Tour through his Diocese, ... December 1843–March 1844*, printed for the Society for the Propagation of the Gospel, London, 1849.

12 Octavius Hadfield, 'The people at Waikanae have built a very beautiful church, ... They have been engaged nearly two years at it, & have worked well & altogether gratuitously.' Letter to his mother, 1 September 1843, *Papers*, ATL.

13 JF Lloyd, Letter to Editor, *New Zealand Spectator and Cook's Strait Guardian*, 3 November 1849, p. 2.

14 Eric Ramsden, *Rangiatea: The Story of Otaki's Maori Church, its First Pastor and its People*, AH & AW Reed, Wellington, 1951, p. 60.

15 See letter from O Hadfield to Octavia, April 23 1848, *Papers*, ATL.

16 Ramsden, *Rangiatea*, p. 122.

17 WC Carkeek, *The Kapiti Coast: Maori History and Place Names*, AH & AW Reed, Wellington, 1966, pp. 83–4.

18 B Wells, *The History of Taranaki: A Standard Work on the History of the Province*, Mullon, New Plymouth, 1967, p. 140.

19 Rev. Richard Taylor, *Journal*, 4 April 1848, vol. 5 (typescript), p. 203.

20 Carkeek, 1966, p. 84.

21 Godley, JR (ed.), *Letters from New Zealand by Charlotte Godley 1850–1853*, Whitcombe & Tombs Ltd., Christchurch, 1951, p. 106.

22 Rev. Richard Taylor, *Journal*, 29 December 1844, vol. 3 (typescript), p. 203.

23 Rev. Richard Taylor, *Journal*, 4 April 1856, vol. 8 (typescript), p. 174.

24 A copy of this drawing was made by William John Swainson [Maori Pa], ATL ref. no.156571/2. ATL.

25 William Swainson made several drawings of the Waikanae area in 1849. Because his drawings were copied by his son and then redrawn by William Swainson, authorship of these works is assigned with difficulty.

26 Paul Carter, *The Lie of the Land*, Faber & Faber, London, 1996, p. 293.

27 Carkeek, 1966, p. 89.

28 See discussion in C & J Maclean, *Waikanae Past & Present*, Whitcombe Press, Waikanae, 1988, p. 28.

29 Carkeek, 1966, p. 89.

30 GA Selwyn, *Documents of the Central Committee of the New Zealand Mission*, 1847–54 (typescript), ATL.

31 Bishop Selwyn's description of the construction of Waikanae church is similar to later descriptions of the building of Rangiatea. GA Selwyn, *New Zealand. Part I, Letters from the Bishop to the Society for the Propagation of the Gospel, together with extracts from his Visitation Journal, from July 1842, to January 1843*, printed for the Society for the Propagation of the Gospel, London, 1847, p. 52. His later description of the Waikanae church could well be a description of Rangiatea. GA Selwyn, 27 & 28 December 1843, *New Zealand. Part III, Journal of the Bishop's Visitation Tour, from December 1843, to March 1844, including an account of his Visit to the Southern Island*, printed for the Society for the Propagation of the Gospel, London, 1851, ch. 1.

32 Pers. comm. Mike Austin.

Larrikins Abroad: International Account of the New Zealand Architects in the 1970s and 1980s

1 HW Harper, *Letters from New Zealand, 1857–1911*, H Rees, London, 1914, p. 123. Cited in HW Orsman (ed.), *The Dictionary of New Zealand English*, Oxford University Press, Auckland, 1997, p. 438.

2 Astragal, 'Notes and Topics: Fuss Over Frognal', *Architects' Journal (AJ)*, vol. 83, 28 May 1936, p. 793. He is referring to the controversy over the design of semi-Detached houses at Ruislip two years earlier. The *Architects' Journal* supported the architects in this earlier case. In this later notice, Astragal observed that, given the proximity of Maxwell Fry's sun house in the vicinity, the opposition to the proposed

design was bound to fail. Nevertheless, the architects wrote to the journal taking exception to the 'loose statement' that 'we are in trouble again' suggesting that 'Connell, Ward and Lucas are being troubled again' would have been a more appropriate statement. Connell, Ward & Lucas, 'Letters from readers: The Hampstead Case', *AJ*, vol. 83, 11 June 1936, p. 902.

3 'No. 66 [Frognal] by *Connell, Ward, & Lucas*, 1937, in the extreme idiom of the day, somewhat dated now, since the design was perhaps originally a little too much concerned with *épater le bourgeois.*' Nikolaus Pevsner, *Buildings of England: London except the Cities of London and Westminster*, Penguin, Harmondsworth, 1952, p. 199. Ward disputed this writing, 'We were very serious and quite uncompromising in approach to the work we did and I hope it does not sound too priggish to say we sacrificed a good deal personally in being so. A less compromising course might well have brought us more commissions.' Basil Ward, 'Connell, Ward and Lucas', in Dennis Sharp (ed.), *Planning and Architecture*, Barrie and Rockliff, London, 1967, p. 83. See also Dennis Sharp 'Radical heroes in a concrete age: Connell, Ward and Lucas and English Modernism of the 1930s', in Dennis Sharp (ed.), *Connell, Ward & Lucas: Modern Movement Architects in England 1929–1939*, Book Art, London, 1994, p. 9.

4 Their work was featured in the architectural press, mostly in the *Architect and Building News* and in the *AJ*. Significantly, in New Zealand their achievement was ignored. Apart from reports of their winning the Rome Prize and the Henry Jarvis Medal in 1926, the *Journal of the New Zealand Institute of Architects* did not acknowledge the achievement of Connell and Ward in the 1930s.

5 John Summerson, 'Introduction', in Trevor Dannat, *Modern Architecture in Britain*, Batsford, London, 1959, p. 14. Cited by Michael Findlay, 'Barbarians at the Gate: Expatriate New Zealand Architects and the Problem of Ultra-Modernism', *Regional Responses: Papers and Proceedings of the Eight Annual Conference of the Society of Architectural Historians of Australia and New Zealand, Christchurch, New Zealand, 1991*, SAHANZ, Christchurch, 1995, p. 136. Findlay also notes that Summerson later in 1980 made disparaging comment on the contribution made in the 1930s by the 'Colonials'. I am grateful to Findlay for discussion of this part of the paper.

6 'New Zealand Vernacular', *Architect and Building News*, vol. 197, 9 June 1950, p. 585.

7 Alistair Best, 'The Architecture of Ebullience', *AJ*, vol. 168, 8 November 1978, pp. 881–91.

8 He suggested that Walker's response was 'to up-date the New Zealand Pioneer Home *circa* 1800'. This may have been a typographic error.

9 Best, 'The Architecture of Ebullience,' p. 884.
10 Ibid., p. 894.
11 Tony Hutchinson, 'Cry for Freedom?' (letter), *AJ*, vol. 168, 22 November 1978, p. 973.
12 Astragal, 'New Zealand Standards,' *AJ*, vol. 168, 8 November 1978, p. 867. This is ironically the same column where the criticism of Connell, Ward and Lucas appeared in 1936.
13 'Pionierre in Patria', *Architettura*, vol. 25, February 1979, pp. 110–11.
14 Russell Walden, 'Walker's Double Code', *AJ*, vol. 169, 21 February 1979, p. 361.
15 Russell Walden, 'N.Z. audacity: the Work of Roger Walker', *Architectural Review*, vol. 169, February 1981, pp. 91–7, and cover.
16 *Dominion*, 11 February 1981, p. 13.
17 Alistair Best, 'Franchising Architects', *AJ*, vol. 174, 28 October 1981, pp. 854–5.
18 The house at Milton Keynes is still occupied by the original owners. They continue to send Walker Christmas cards which annually feature artist's drawings of the home.
19 Charles Jencks, *Current Architecture*, Academy Editions, London, 1982, pp. 160, 325. Roger Walker is featured a lengthy paragraph which includes quotations from the *AJ* article by Best and from the letter following by Walden. In the biographical notes, Jencks apparently confuses Walker with Peter Beaven, erroneously stating that he authored the 1972 text, *New Zealand Architecture 1820–1970*.
20 Mary Mountier, 'Kiwi Concrete', *Design*, vol. 312, December 1974, p. 29. Like many writers on Athfield and Walker, Mountier is from Wellington.
21 Athfield's scheme was for 5 hectare development for 3500 people in walled villages (barangays) of 500 people. The homes would be built by the owners, out of corrugated iron and plaster over perforated metal. The proposed scheme incorporated mills, recycling and the use of windpower.
22 Ian Hogan, 'Habitat', *Royal Institute of British Architects' Journal* [*RIBA Journal*], vol. 83, August 1976, p. 318.
23 Boyce Richardson, 'Athfield under attack', *New Zealand Listener*, 17 July 1976, p. 15.
24 Ian Hogan, 'Habitat', p. 318.
25 Peter Murray, 'Architecture in the Antipodes', *RIBA Journal*, vol. 91, no. 2, February 1984, p. 26.
26 W Alington, 'Ian Athfield' in Muriel Emanuel (ed.), *Contemporary Architects*, Macmillan, London, 1980, pp. 52–53.
27 It is also apparent in such events as the publication of the magazine, *Oz*, in the nineteen-seventies, and the success of antipodean films such as Bruce Beresford's *The Adventures of Barry Mackenzie* (1971) and Geoff Murphy's *Goodbye Pork Pie* (1981).

28 Alistair Best, 'Highgate Down Under', *AJ*, vol. 175, 12 May 1982, pp. 40–2 and cover. Also see 'Highgate Studios: Tile Kiln Lane, Highgate, London N6', *Concrete Quarterly*, vol. 134, 1982, pp. 2–6.

29 K Coates, 'London Gets a Look at Kiwi Architecture and Building', *The Press*, 30 December 1980, p. 11.

30 Beaven wrote, 'Roger Walker's and Ian Athfield's work have both been in colour on the cover of the *Architectural Review*. Miles Warren's Chancery has been described as one of the best mannered buildings in Washington. Ted McCoy's houses have been published in the *RIBA Journal* … The Chateau Commodore Hotel by my office in Christchurch was one of the first Post Modern style buildings published in the *Architectural Review* in 1976.' Peter Beaven 'The post colonial world', *New Zealand Architect*, no. 2, 1982, p. 6.

31 Peter Beaven, 'Beaven on Europe: a Post New Zealand Perspective', *New Zealand Architect*, no. 2, 1983, p. 8.

32 Peter Murray, 'Architecture in the Antipodes', *RIBA Journal*, vol. 91, no. 2, February 1984, p. 26. When Murray went to Australia, Peter Corrigan took him to an Australian Rules game to explain the nature of the hybridity of Australian architecture.

33 Ibid., p. 26.

34 Walden, 'N.Z. Audacity', p. 95.

35 Eartha Post, 'At home in Hutt', *Architectural Review*, vol. 190, no. 1141, March 1992, p. 56. For some reason the New Zealanders are often described in French terms, which further reinforces a sense of exoticism.

36 'Have you ever made a study of the hooligan of the Antipodes, our own binging, leary, larrikin.' *New Zealand Truth*, 2 September 1905, p. 7. Cited in Orsman, *The Dictionary of New Zealand English*, p. 438.

37 Karl Johaentges, 'Neuland Neuseeland: Neue Architekturwelle in Neuseeland Wohnhäuser am anderen Ende der Welt', *Deutsche bauzeitung*, vol. 119, no. 1, January 1985, pp. 10–39, 113, 114, 119.

38 Gerald Melling, 'Beach house that Caricatures some Fashionable Icons: Omaha Beach House by Roger Walker', *Architecture*, vol. 74, September 1985, p. 119.

39 Frances Fitzgerald, 'Architecture: Ian Athfield: a Residence for Vintners in Hawkes Bay', *Architectural Digest*, vol. 44, January 1987, p. 82.

40 Ian Athfield, untitled section of 'New Zealand in America', *New Zealand Architect*, no. 1, 1987, p. 14.

41 Roger Walker, 'Fear and Loathing on the Lecture Trail: USA trip April 1986', *New Zealand Architect*, no. 1, 1987, p. 28. That week Reagan had bombed Gaddafi's home in Libya. It looks like this was a great trip.

42 John Blair, untitled section of 'New Zealand in America', *New Zealand Architect*, no. 1, 1987, p. 45.
43 Clare Melhuish, 'Laughter Lines', *Building Design*, no. 1083, 5 June 1992, p. 16.
44 A special issue devoted to the work of Athfield architects, New Zealand and Aasen • Athfield + Co International, *World Architecture Review*, vol. 37, 1993–4.
45 Clarence Aasen, 'The Architecture of Ian Athfield', *World Architecture Review*, vol. 37, 1993–4, p. 6.
46 Ibid., p. 6.
47 Ibid., p. 8.
48 Hugh Meller, 'Drogo Down Under: Designs by Lutyens in New Zealand', *Apollo*, vol. 143, April 1996, p. 44.
49 Meller's supposition was not challenged. There was no response from New Zealand.

Post-European and Indigenous Architectural Histories in Aotearoa New Zealand

1 Pei Te Hurinui Jones, *Mahinarangi: A Tainui Saga*, JC Ekdahl, Hawera, 1946; Leo Fowler, *Te Mana o Turanga*, New Zealand Historic Places Trust, Auckland, 1974.
2 Elsdon Best, *Maori Storehouses and Kindred Structures*, AR Shearer, Wellington, 1974, first pub. 1916; Hirini Moko Mead, *Te Toi Whakairo: The Art of Maori Carving*, Reed Publishing, Auckland, 1995, first pub. 1986; Roger Neich, *Painted Histories*, Auckland University Press, Auckland, 1993; WJ Phillipps, *Carved Homes of the Eastern Districts of the North Island*, Harry H Tombs, Wellington, 1944; WJ Phillipps, *Maori Houses and Foodstores*, RE Owen Government Printer, Wellington, 1952; WJ Phillips, *Carved Maori Houses of the Western and Northern Areas of New Zealand*, RE Owen Government Printer, Wellington, 1955; David Simmons, *Whakairo: Maori Tribal Art Styles*, Oxford University Press, Auckland, 1994, first pub. 1985; David Simmons, *Ti Whare Runanga*, Reed, Auckland, 1997.
3 Apirana Ngata, 'The Origin of Maori Carving', *Te Ao Hou*, vol. 22, 1958, pp. 30–7, vol. 23, 1958, pp. 30–4; Ranginui Walker, 'Marae: A Place to Stand', in Michael King (ed.), *Te Ao Hurihuri: Aspects of Maoritanga*, 1992, Reed Books, Auckland, pp. 15–27.
4 Michael Austin, 'Polynesian Architecture in New Zealand', PhD thesis, University of Auckland, 1976.
5 Allan Hanson, 'The Making of Maori: Culture Invention and its Logic', *American Anthropologist*, vol. 91, no. 4 December 1989, pp. 890–902.
6 Steven Webster, *Patrons of Maori Culture*, Otago University Press, Dunedin, 1998, p. 230.

7 M Jolly, 'Spectres of Inauthenticity', *The Contemporary Pacific*, vol. 4, 1992, pp. 49–72; R Keesing, 'Reply to Trask', *The Contemporary Pacific*, vol. 3, 1991, pp. 168–71; J Linnekin, 'Text Bites and the R-Word: The Politics of Representing Scholarship', *The Contemporary Pacific*, vol. 3, 1991, pp. 172–7; HK Trask, 'Natives and Anthropologists: A Colonial Struggle', *The Contemporary Pacific*, vol. 3, 1991, pp. 159–67.

8 Jeffrey Sissons, 'The Traditionalisation of the Maori Meeting House', *Oceania*, vol. 69, September 1998, unpaginated.

9 Ibid.

10 Ibid.

11 Ibid.

12 Hamilton was the Director of the Dominion Museum in Wellington (now known as Te Papa Tongarewa – The Museum of New Zealand) and the author of *Maori Art*, Ferguson and Mitchell, Dunedin, 1896. See also Roger Neich, 'Historical Change in Rotorua Ngati Tarawhai Woodcarving Art', MA thesis, Victoria University of Wellington, 1977.

13 Sissons, 'Traditionalisation'. Sissons regards the writings of Elsdon Best, Te Rangi Hiroa (aka Peter Buck) and Apirana as being important texts in the traditionalisation process.

14 Deidre Brown, 'The Architecture of the School of Maori Arts and Crafts', *Journal of the Polynesian Society*, vol. 108, no. 3, September 1999, p. 245.

15 Sissons, 'Traditionalisation', not paginated.

16 Toon van Mejil, 'Historicising Maoritanga: Colonial Ethnography and the Reification of Maori Tradition', *Journal of the Polynesian Society*, vol. 105, no. 3, September 1996, pp. 339–40.

17 Bill McKay & Deidre Brown, 'The Buildings of the Morehu', *Interstices*, no. 2, 1992, pp. 113–33; Deidre Brown, 'Morehu Architecture', PhD thesis, University of Auckland, 1997.

18 Klaus Neumann, Nicholas Thomas & Hilary Ericksen, *Quicksands: Foundational Histories in Australia and Aotearoa New Zealand*, UNSW Press, Sydney, 1999, p. xvii.

19 See Anne Salmond, *Hui: A Study of Maori Ceremonial Gatherings*, Reed, Wellington, 1975; *Two Worlds*, Viking, Auckland, 1991; and *Between Worlds*, Viking Auckland, 1997; see also James Belich, *The New Zealand Wars*, Penguin Books, Auckland, 1986; and *Making Peoples*, Viking, Wellington, 1996.

20 Neumann, Thomas & Ericksen, *Quicksands*, p. xvii.

21 Salmond, *Hui*, p. 47.

22 See Neich, *Painted Histories*, p. 129, and Walker, 'Marae', pp. 21–2.

23 Fairburn in Michael King, 'A Fraction too Much Friction', *Mana*, vol. 32, March 2000, p. 32.
24 Ibid.
25 Sutton n.d., in Webster, *Patrons*, p. 245.
26 Ibid., pp. 245–6.
27 Ibid., p. 245.
28 Neumann, Thomas & Ericksen, *Quicksands*, p. xvii.
29 Deborah Bird Rose, 'Hard Times: An Australian Study', in Neumann, Thomas & Ericksen (eds), *Quicksands*, p. 9.
30 The critically acclaimed *Te Maori* exhibition of customary Maori art opened at New York's Metropolitan Museum of Modern Art in September 1984, and after returning from North America it toured institutions in Aotearoa New Zealand. Nicholas Thomas, 'A Second Reflection: Presence and Opposition in Contemporary Maori Art', *Journal of the Royal Anthropological Institute*, vol. 1, no. 1, March 1995, unpaginated.
31 Ibid.
32 Many of the Maori artists who became part of Gordon Tovey's Maori art advisory service, within the Education Department, in the late 1950s and 1960s went on to have highly successfully careers as artists. They include Paratene Matchitt, Cliff Whiting, Arnold Wilson, Selwyn Wilson, Katarina Mataira and Cath Brown amongst others. See Jonathan Mane-Wheoki & Luit Bieriga, *Tovey and the Tovey Generation*, Porirua Museum, Porirua, 1999; and Carol Henderson, *A Blaze of Colour: Gordon Tovey, Artist and Educator*, Hazard Press, Christchurch, 1998.
33 Deidre Brown, 'Nga Whare Matauranga Maori', in Richard Blythe and Rory Spence (eds), *Thresholds: Proceedings of the 16th Annual Conference of the Society of Architectural Historians, Australia and New Zealand*, SAHANZ, Launceston, 1999, pp. 23–4.
34 Thomas, 'A Second Reflection'.
35 Stephen Turner, 'Settlement as Forgetting', in Neumann, Thomas & Ericksen (eds), *Quicksands*, p. 20.
36 Ibid., p. 23.
37 Ibid., p. 21.
38 Jonathan Lamb, 'The Idea of Utopia in New Zealand', in Neumann, Thomas & Ericksen (eds), *Quicksands*, p. 80.
39 Webster, *Patrons*, p. 226.
40 Margo Neale 'Beyond Objects: Defining and Communicating Cutural Relativity in New Zealand', in Jonathan Wheoki, *Communicating Cultures*, Museums Australia, Brisbane, 1995, p. 19.

41 See Ruth Frankenberg, *Displacing Whiteness*, Duke University Press, Durham, NC, 1997.

Polynesian Influences in New Zealand Architecture

1 Russell Walden, *Voices of Silence: New Zealand's Chapel of Futuna*, Victoria University Press, Wellington, 1987, p. 145.

2 S Hurst Seager, 'Architectural Art in New Zealand', *RIBA Journal*, vol. VII, no. 19, 29 September 1900, p. 490.

3 'The Papuan covers with tattoos his skin, his boat, his paddle, in short anything within his reach. He is not a delinquent but the modern man who tattoos himself is a delinquent or a degenerate.' Adolph Loos, 'Ornament and Crime', 1908, translated by Michael Bullock, in Ulrich Conrads (ed.) *Programs and Manifestos on 20th Century Architecture*, MIT Press, Cambridge, Mass.1975, p. 20.

4 Cyril Knight, *1840 and After*, Auckland University College, Auckland, 1940, pp. 180–1.

5 Paul Pascoe & Humphrey Hall, 'The Modern House', *Landfall*, vol. 1, no. 2, June 1947, p. 124.

6 Walden describes John Scott as 'a relaxed New Zealander' in *Voices of Silence*, p. 58.

7 Robin Skinner, 'Macaulay's Revisitor: A Traveller from a Modern Land', *Proceedings of Building Dwelling Drifting: Migrancy and the Limits of Architecture, The 3rd Other Connections Conference*, Melbourne, 1997, pp. 312–18.

8 Peter Shaw & Peter Hallett, *Art Deco Napier: styles of the thirties*, Craig Potton Publishing, Nelson, 1987, pp. 46–8.

9 Nikolaus Pevsner, 'The Ingratiating Chaos', *The Listener*, 20 November 1958, p. 825.

10 Peter Shaw, *New Zealand Architecture: From Polynesian Beginnings to 1990*, Hodder & Stoughton, Auckland, 1991, p. 10.

11 Peter Sargisson, 'Architectural Truths', *Islands*, vol. 2, no. 3, Spring 1973, pp. 303–4. The two buildings illustrated are Rangiatea Church at Otaki and Major Fox's house, which has a small Gothic storehouse alongside – and to which the text gives more significance. John Stacpoole & Peter Beaven, *New Zealand Art: Architecture 1820–1970*, AH and AW Reed, Wellington, 1972, p. 34.

12 John Stacpoole, *Colonial Architecture in New Zealand*, AH & AW Reed, Wellington, 1976, p. 8.

13 Specifically over a crucial event that took place in Queen Charlotte Sound. Gananath Obeyesekere, 'British Cannibals: Contemplation of an event in the death and

resurrection of James Cook explorer', in Gilles Bibeau & Ellen Corin (eds), *Beyond Textuality, Asceticism and Violence in Anthropological Interpretation*, Mouton de Gruyter, Berlin, 1995, p. 145.

14 Vanya Steiner, '(Mis)appropriation in New Zealand Architecture; an incriminating cite', *Interstices no. 4*, Auckland University (CD ROM), 1996. Lloyd Jenkins argues that Maori images were being used by designers since before the turn of last century. Douglas Lloyd Jenkins, 'Avis Higgs and the Maori Motif Textile', *The Pumpkin Soup Papers*, Research Papers in the School of Design UNITEC, Auckland, 1996.

15 David Mitchell & Gillian Chaplin, *The Elegant Shed: New Zealand Architecture since 1945*, Oxford University Press, Auckland, 1984, pp. 93–94; Gerald Melling, *Joyful Architecture: The Genius of New Zealand's Ian Athfield*, Caveman Press, Dunedin, 1980; Gerald Melling, *Positively Architecture: New Zealand's Roger Walker*, Square One Press, Dunedin, 1985.

16 Justine Clark & Paul Walker, *Looking for the Local: Architecture and the New Zealand Modern*, Victoria University Press, Wellington, 2000, p. 31.

17 Keith Stewart, 'Living through art', *Architecture New Zealand*, July–August 1999, p. 50.

18 Although it is admitted that: 'His lifestyle owes much to Polynesian values'. Walden, *Voices of Silence*, p. 58.

19 Ibid., p. 134.

20 Stacpoole & Beaven, *New Zealand Art*, p. 92.

21 Walden, *Voices of Silence*, p.147.

22 Ibid., p. 20.

23 Sarah Treadwell, 'European Representations of the architecture of Rangiatea', PhD thesis, University of Auckland, 1995.

24 Shaw, *New Zealand Architecture*, p. 22.

25 'Bishop Hadfield provided the inspiration for Rangiatea but it was built under the supervision of Samuel Williams.' Stacpoole & Beaven, *New Zealand Art*, p. 16.

26 Christine McCarthy, 'The Maori House, Te Pa and Captain Hankey's House: Bicultural architecture in New Zealand at the turn of the century', *Fabrications*, vol. 11, no. 1, July 2000, pp. 62–78.

27 Roger Neich, *Painted Histories: Early Maori Figurative Painting*, Auckland University Press, Auckland, 1993. 'The totality of Maori meeting houses, therefore constitutes a particular genre of art production, over a particular historical phase in the course of Maori history (in many ways a glorious period, which contemporary Maoris recall with pride), which can be considered "coherent" in the sense we require.' Alfred Gell, *Art and Agency: An Anthropological Theory*, Clarendon Press, Oxford, 1998, p. 251.

28 As documented by Bernard Smith in *European Vision and the South Pacific*, Yale University Press, New Haven, 1985. The Polynesian words 'taboo' and 'tattoo' were discussed by Freud and Loos respectively in significant modernist texts. Mike Austin, 'Taboo and Tattoo: Freud Loos and South Pacific Practices', in Maryam Gusheh (ed.), *Double Frames: Proceedings of the First International Symposium of the Centre for Asian Environments*, University of New South Wales, Sydney, 2000, pp. 33–42.

29 Examples are the Auckland War Memorial Museum and the Wanganui Post Office. Shaw, *New Zealand Architecture*, p. 122.

30 Shaw & Hallett, *Art Deco Napier*, pp. 46–8.

31 Bill McKay, 'The Whare face of Modernism', *FIRM(ness) commodity DE-LIGHT: Questioning the Canons, Proceedings of the Annual Conference of the Society of Architectural Historians, Australia and New Zealand*, Melbourne, 1998, p. 262.

32 Shaw, *New Zealand Architecture*, p. 154.

33 *Architects' Journal*, March 1951, quoted in Bill McKay, 'The Whare face of Modernism', p. 260; and 'New Zealand Vernacular Architecture', *The Architect and Building News*, 9 June 1950, p. 585, quoted In Robin Skinner, 'Larrikins Abroad: International Account of New Zealand Architects in the 1970s and 1980s' (published in this selection), p. 302.

34 George French Angas, *Savage Life and Scenes in Australia and New Zealand*, 1847, vol. 11, Smith, Elder & Co., London, 1847, pp. 88–9.

35 David Pearson, *A Dream Deferred: The Origins of Ethnic Conflict in New Zealand*, Allen and Unwin, Wellington, 1990, p. 39.

36 'It must be confessed that the huts built by them [Maori] were much superior to those of our handywork.' Henry William Petre, *An Account of the Settlement of the New Zealand Company*, Smith Elder and Co., London, 1842, p. 11.

37 James Belich, *Making Peoples: A History of the New Zealanders from Polynesian Settlement to the End of the Nineteenth Century*, Allen Lane, Auckland, 1996.

38 Mike Linzey, 'Te Kooti Architect', *Architecture New Zealand*, September–October 1989, pp. 90–95.

39 The 'Anytime' conference which focused on the temporal in architecture, failed to look at this double architectural process where buildings respond to the crisis of the present by constituting protensions and pretensions. Cynthia Davidson (ed.), *Anytime*, MIT Press, Cambridge, Mass., 1999.

40 Owen Jones, *The Grammar of Ornament*, B Quaritch, London, 1868, p. 13 ff.

41 John Scott & Ming Ching-Fan, 'Of Woolsheds, Houses and People', *Islands*, vol. 2, no. 3, Spring 1973, p. 291.

42 This building uses the colonial style which is identified with Maori Meeting houses much as Maori ritual life seems to operate with a nineteenth century missionary version of Christianity.

43 Bruce Biggs, 'The Maori language Past and Present', in Eric Schwimmer (ed.), *The Maori People in the Nineteen Sixties*, Blackwood and Janet Paul, Auckland, 1968, pp. 447–54.

44 Hugh Kawharu, 'Urban Immigrants and Tangata Whenua', in Schwimmer (ed.), *The Maori People in the Nineteen Sixties*, pp. 174–86.

45 Derek Kawiti, Paper to NZIA, July 2000.

46 Walden criticised architects for using 'totem poles'. Walden, *Voices of Silence*, p. 145.

47 Steiner, '(MIS)appropriation in New Zealand Architecture'.

48 Ibid.

49 'Maori Battalion Memorial: A Distinguished Building by a Gifted Architect', *Te Ao Ho The New World* (The Maori Magazine), June 1964, pp. 32–34.

50 Glen Jowitt & Peter Shaw, *Pacific Island Style*, David Bateman, Auckland, 1999; Herbert Ypma, *Pacific Island*, Thames and Hudson, London, 1996.

A Myth in its Making: Federation Style and Australian Architectural History

1 The authors wish to thank Bernard Smith and Ann Stephen for their comments on early versions of this paper.

2 For example, Trevor Howells & Michael Nicholson (eds), *Towards the Dawn: Federation Architecture in Australia 1890–1915*, Hale & Iremonger, Sydney, 1989; Ian Evans, *The Federation House: A restoration guide*, Flannel Flower Press, Sydney, 1986.

3 Alastair Service, *Edwardian Architecture: A handbook to building design in Britain, 1890–1914*, Thames & Hudson, London, 1977, pp. 42–3.

4 David Saunders, 'Domestic styles of Australia's Federation period: Queen Anne and the Balcony Style', *Architecture in Australia*, vol. 58, no. 4, August 1969, pp. 655–62.

5 Ibid., p. 662.

6 For example, Martin Boyd described Queen Anne as 'having as much resemblance to the sober dignified houses of the early eighteenth century, as a modern chorus girl to a mid-Victorian Duchess' and that he wanted to 'hold the type up to as much hatred, ridicule and contempt as is possible'. Martin Mills [Boyd], 'Domestic Architecture in

Australia: Past Mistakes and Future Possibilities', *The British Australian and New Zealander*, July 1927, pp. 18–19, as quoted in George Tibbits, 'An Emanation of Lunacy', in Howells & Nicholson (eds), *Towards the Dawn*, p. 82; Katrina Place, in her paper 'Arts and Crafts Architects in Melbourne: Utopian and Practical' for the SAHANZ conference (2000), notes extensive criticism of the term Queen Anne by architects in the 1890s and 1900s.

7 Saunders, 'Domestic styles of Australia's Federation period', p. 655.

8 Bernard Smith, 'Architecture in Australia', *Historical Studies*, vol. 14, no. 53, October 1969, p. 90.

9 Ibid., p. 91.

10 Bernard & Kate Smith, *The Architectural Character of Glebe Sydney*, University Cooperative Bookshop, Sydney, 1973, pp. 107–19.

11 Ibid., p. 107.

12 Ibid.

13 Ibid., p. 119.

14 Howells & Nicholson (eds), *Towards the Dawn*, p. 9.

15 Trevor Howells, 'In Search of a Grand National Style', in Howells & Nicholson (eds), *Towards the Dawn*, p. 13.

16 Tibbits wrote of an Australian Queen Anne. Despite all the uncertainty in the use of 'Queen Anne' or 'Queen Anne Revival' to describe late nineteenth-century architecture, Girouard's *Sweetness and Light* has now given the term credence and it is no longer confused with the 'real' Queen Anne of the eighteenth century.

17 Interview with George Tibbits by Julie Willis and Philip Goad, August 2000.

18 Stuart Macintyre gives a brief discussion of this side of Federation in *The Oxford History of Australia*, vol. 4, *The Succeeding Age 1901–1942*, Oxford University Press, Melbourne, 1993 (1986), pp. 122–25.

19 Richard Apperly, Robert Irving & Peter Reynolds, *A Pictorial Guide to Identifying Australian Architecture: Styles and Terms from 1988 to the Present*, Angus & Robertson, Sydney, 1989, pp. 99–147.

20 Service, *Edwardian Architecture*.

21 Conrad Hamann, 'The Federation City', in Philip Goad, *Melbourne Architecture*, Watermark Press, Sydney, 1999, p. 78.

22 Ibid.

23 Smith & Smith, *The Architectural Character of Glebe Sydney*, p. 107.

Between the Georgina and the Great Western Railway: The Transformation and Maintenance of Aboriginal Architecture in North-West Queensland

1 Paul Memmott & Carroll Go-Sam, 'Australian Indigenous Architecture: Its Forms and Evolution', *Thresholds: Papers of the Sixteenth Annual Conference of the Society of Architectural Historians, Australia and New Zealand*, SAHANZ, Launceston & Hobart, 1999, p. 233.

2 Examples are drawn from the author's PhD fieldwork concerned more broadly with cultural heritage and the people–environment interactions of the Dajarra community.

3 Dajarra has a high Indigenous population (around 85%), which is unique for a town in Queensland where similar population characteristics are only to be found in discrete, self-governed Aboriginal settlements on community title land. See Australian Bureau of Statistics, *Population Distribution, Indigenous Australians*, Australian Bureau of Statistics, Canberra, 1997, pp. 35–6.

4 P Memmott, P Kelleher, R Stacy & S Long, 'South-West Queensland to Mt Isa Gas Pipeline. Social Impact Assessment–Aboriginal Sector (Central and northern Components)', Report prepared for Australian Gas Light Company (AGL), Aboriginal Environments Research Centre, Department of Architecture, University of Queensland, Brisbane, January, 1997, pp. 25, 93.

5 Australian Bureau of Meteorology, 'Climate Averages for Australian Sites: Averages for Urandangie', www.bom.gov.au/climate/averages/tables/cw_037043.shtml, 2001. Australian Water Resources Council, *Review of Australia's Water Resources 1975*, Australian Government Publishing Service, Canberra, 1976, p. 144.

6 These trade routes extend from the south of Australia, along the Georgina, through Cape York and into Papua New Guinea via the Torres Strait Islands. See Walter Roth, *Ethnological Studies Among the North-West-Central Queensland Aborigines*, Government Printer, Brisbane, 1897, pp. 132–8; Frederick McCarthy, '"Trade" in Aboriginal Australia, and "Trade" Relationships with Torres Strait, New Guinea and Malaya', *Oceania*, vol. 9, 1939, pp. 405–38.

7 G Sutherland, *Pioneering Days: Thrilling Incidents in the Early Sixties, Across the Wilds of Queensland with Sheep to the Northern Territory*, WH Wendt & Co. Ltd Printers, Brisbane, 1913, pp. 8–13; E Favenc, *The History of Australia: Exploration from 1788 to 1888*, Turner & Henderson, Sydney, 1967, pp. 229–30.

8 Henry Reynolds, *The Other Side of the Frontier: Aboriginal Resistance to the European Invasion of Australia*, Penguin Books, Ringwood, Victoria, 1995 (1981), p. 106; Roth, *Ethnological Studies Among the North-West-Central Queensland Aborigines*, pp. 120–5.

9 Paul Memmott, 'Draft History Manuscript for Wakaya-Alyawarre Land Claim Book', Aboriginal Data Archive, University of Queensland, Brisbane, 1985.

10 Letter from Alex Gordon to Home Secretary's Office, Brisbane, received 8 February 1900, Letter No. 01894, Home Secretary's Office Correspondence and Records and Printed Papers Relating to Queensland Aborigines 1900–1902, Col/145 M1636 Z1613, Queensland State Archives.

11 HG Lamond, 'Contraband Chinese', *The Bulletin*, 24 June 1953, p. 4.

12 J Kerr, *Triumph of Narrow Gauge: A History of Queensland Railways*, Boolarong Publications, Bowen Hills, Qld, 1990, p. 125.

13 M Hunt, *My Life, Mary Hunt*, The Hand-in-Hand Press, Wellington, 1999, p. 31.

14 Queensland Government, *The Queensland Statutes 1910*, Government Printer, Brisbane, c.1910, pp. 10128–32.

15 Cattle were brought from as far west as the Kimberley. In its prime Dajarra was renowned as the largest cattle trucking centre in the southern hemisphere. See Paul Memmott, 'From the Curry to the "Weal": Aboriginal Town Camps and Compounds of the Western Back-Blocks', *Fabrications*, vol. 7, August 1996, pp. 1–50.

16 A major migration from the Georgina to Dajarra occurred in 1965 following the transferral of the responsibilities of the 'Protector of Aborigines' from Urandangie to Dajarra. B. Rosser, *Dreamtime Nightmares*, Penguin, Melbourne, 1987, p. 35.

17 Other Aboriginal groups occupied camps at other locations along Carbine Creek and on the edge of town.

18 Memmott, 'From the Curry to the "Weal"', p. 16.

19 Roth, *Ethnological Studies Among the North-West-Central Queensland Aborigines*, pp. 105–6.

20 Although Roth's description of these shelter types applies to his 'Boulia district', his description and those of Waluwarra informants indicate that similar types were built in the vicinity of Roxborough and elsewhere on the Georgina River. Other types of architecture produced on the Georgina include structures accompanying ceremonies and corroborees, tree-burial platforms and various hunting structures. Ibid., pp. 105–6, 165, 168, 171–2.

21 The cold weather shelter had an internal height of approximately 1.7 metres. Ibid., p. 106.

22 Trees with low limbs or angled trunks were also used as primary support structures for shades. Ibid., p. 106.

23 See for example Cathy Keys, 'Warlpiri ethno-architecture and applied Aboriginal architectural design: Case study material from Yuendumu', *People and Physical Environment Research*, no. 55–56, 2000, p. 58.

24 Roth, *Ethnological Studies Among the North-West-Central Queensland Aborigines*, pp. 105–7.
25 Ibid., p. 106.
26 Ibid., p. 134.
27 Paul Memmott, 'Socio-spatial structures of Australian Aboriginal Settlements' [m/s], p. 7; 'The Way it Was: Customary Camps and Houses in the Southern Gulf of Carpentaria', in Peter Read (ed.), *Settlement, A History of Australian Indigenous Housing*, Aboriginal Studies Press, Canberra, 2000, p. 32.
28 Memmott, 'From the Curry to the "Weal"', pp. 1–18.
29 Gidgee wood (*Acacia georginae* and *A. cambagei*) is the preferred firewood of Dajarra people; it is slow burning, it produces very hot coals which are long lasting and it produces very little smoke. Gidgee wood is also used as in the manufacture of artefacts and structures.
30 Memmott, 'From the Curry to the "Weal"', pp. 11–18.
31 Ibid.
32 Memmott & Go-Sam, 'Australian Indigenous Architecture', p. 237.
33 The use of shade trees as an architectural element or type has been documented amongst other groups. See Keys 'Warlpiri Ethno-architecture and Applied Aboriginal Architectural Design', pp. 58–9.
34 Memmott & Go-Sam, 'Australian Indigenous Architecture', p. 237.
35 Ibid.
36 See for example 'RAIA Gold Medallist 2002', *Architecture Australia*, March–April 2002, pp. 80–5.
37 See for example M Heppell, *A Black Reality: Aboriginal Camps and Housing in Remote Australia*, Australian Institute of Aboriginal Studies, Canberra, 1979; Paul Memmott, 'Aboriginal Housing, the State of the Art (or the non-State of the Art)', *Architecture Australia*, June 1988, pp. 34–47; C Keys, 'The Architectural Implications of Warlpiri "Jilmi"', PhD thesis, University of Queensland, 1998.
38 The flat roofed post and beam bough-sheds produced today differ from the curvilinear forms of the bough-sheds described by Roth.
39 Despite the significance of external living environments some architects fail to consider them in the design of houses for Aboriginal clients. While budget constraints and the dynamic nature of external living environments make it difficult for a consultant to design them this is not an excuse to avoid considering them in the design of a 'house'. See Paul Memmott & Catherine Chambers, 'Spatial Behaviour and Spatial Planning at Galiwin'ku. New Insights into Aboriginal Housing', *Architectural Review Australia*, Residential, vol. 2, 2002, p. 92.

40 Paul Memmott & Stephen Long, 'Place Theory and Place Maintenance in Indigenous Australia', *Urban Policy and Research*, vol. 20, no. 1, 2002, pp. 39–40.

The Aftermath of 'Pleasures': Untold Stories of Post-Modern Architecture in Australia

1 'RAIA Conference 1980', *Architecture Australia*, vol. 69, no. 1, February–March, 1980, p. 66.
2 Ibid.
3 Brian Zouch, 'Editorial', *Architecture Australia*, vol. 69, no. 2, May 1980, p. 25.
4 Chris Johnson, 'Talks Report: Andrew Metcalf and Peter Kollar', *Bulletin*, June 1980, p. 7.
5 Engehurst was built between 1832 and 1835 as a house for Frederick Augustus Hely, Principal Superintendant of Convicts. See James Broadbent, *The Golden Decade of Australian Architecture: The Work of John Verge*, Sydney, David Ell Press in association with Elizabeth House Trust, Sydney, 1978, pp. 56–59.
6 For a list of invited architects see *Architecture Australia*, vol. 69, vol. 2, May 1980, p. 39.
7 Neville Quarry, 'Verge'n on the Absurd', *Architecture Australia*, vol. 69, vol. 2, May 1980, p. 77.
8 'Editorial', *Transition*, vol. 1, no. 4, October 1980, p. 3. Author's bracketed insertion.
9 Ibid.
10 'The Pleasures of Architecture Conference, 1980: The Interviews', *Transition*, vol. 1, no. 4, October 1980, p. 4.
11 'Editorial', *Transition*, vol. 1, no. 4, October 1980, p. 3.
12 'Rem Koolhaas', *Transition*, vol. 1, no. 4, October 1980, p. 3.
13 'George Baird', *Transition* vol. 1, no. 4, October 1980, p. 19.
14 'Michael Graves', *Transition* vol. 1, no. 4, October 1980, p. 6.
15 Andrew Metcalf, 'On the Waterfront: An Appraisal of Birkenhead Point', *Architecture Australia*, vol. 68, no. 6, December–January 1980, pp. 56–57.
16 See 'AA Interview: Charles Jencks', *Architecture Australia*, vol. 64, no. 1, February 1975, pp. 50–59.
17 See Michael Jorgensen's review of *The Language of Post-Modern Architecture* by Charles A. Jencks, Academy Editions, London, 1978, in *Architecture Australia*, vol. 68, no. 5, October–November 1979, p. 65. Also, Michael Jorgensen, review of *Late Modern Architecture* by Charles Jencks, Rizzoli International Publications, 1980, in *Architecture Australia*, vol. 70, no. 3, July 1981, pp. 29–31.

18 Jennifer Taylor, *Australian Architecture since 1960*, 2nd edn, RAIA National Education Division, Canberra, 1990, pp. 192–222.

19 See, for instance, Norman Day's commentaries in *Age* in the late 1970s, including 'Exorcism of the Modernist Spirit', *Age* 23 March 1978, p. 2; 'Primary Forms Top the Class,' *Age*, December 12 1978, p. 2; 'Council's Take On US Look', *Age*, 28 November 1978, p. 2; 'Chapel Hides An Alter Ego', *Age*, 10 April 1979, p. 2; 'A Valuable Land Deal for the Elderly', *Age*, 27 June 1979, p. 2.

20 Philip Drew, 'Mannerism in Contemporary Architecture', *Transition*, vol. 1, no. 1, July 1979, pp. 4–10; 'Post-Modern: The Renewal of Style in Architecture', *Transition*, vol. 1, no. 3, March 1980, pp. 9–16; Neville Quarry, 'First Past the Post-Modernism: An Exercise in Metaphor', *Transition*, vol. 1, no. 4, October 1980, pp. 24–28.

21 Conrad Hamann, 'Off the Straight and Narrow', *Architecture Australia*, vol. 1, no. 4, October 1980, pp. 24–28.

22 Ibid., p. 61.

23 Ibid., pp. 65–66.

24 Ibid., p. 61.

25 Legitimisation refers to the actions and processes through which something is granted authenticity and the right to be regarded as genuine and admissible.

26 See Paul Hogben, 'Nationalism in Australian Architectural History, 1890–1920: A Discourse Analysis,' *Architectural Theory Review*, vol. 5, no. 2, November 2000, pp. 94–111; 'Maintaining an Image of Objectivity: Reflections on an Institutional Anxiety', *Architectural Theory Review*, vol. 6, no. 1, April 2001, pp. 63–75.

27 Harry Seidler, 'Principles in the Mainstream of Modern Architecture', *Bulletin*, August 1980, p. 18.

28 Ibid.

29 Ibid.

30 Ibid.

31 Ibid.

32 Ibid., p. 19.

33 Harry Seidler, 'Internationalism', *Architecture Australia*, vol. 71, no. 5, September 1982, pp. 58–60.

34 Hamann, 'Response to Harry Seidler's reply', *Architecture Australia*, vol. 73, no. 4, June 1984, p. 70.

35 Ibid., p. 71.

36 Aldo van Eyck, 'Rats Posts and Pests', *RIBA Journal*, vol. 88, no. 4, April 1981, pp. 25–28.

37 See Peter Blake, *No Place Like Utopia: Modern Architecture and the Company We Kept*, Alfred A Knopf, New York, 1993, p. 311.

38 See Norman Day, 'Sydney's haut gout: the high flavoured taste', *Architecture Australia*, vol. 71, no. 1, January 1982, pp. 26–33; Andrew Metcalf, 'Some Notes on Recent Melbourne Architecture', *Architecture Australia*, vol. 71, no. 1, January 1982, pp. 34–43.

39 'Letters: Puerile Nonsense', *Architecture Australia*, vol. 71, no. 3, May 1982, p. 35.

40 Ibid. The Huxtable article was published in *Architectural Design*, vol. 51, nos. 1–2, 1981, pp. 8–17.

41 For an analysis of the discursive practices behind building reviews see Hogben, 'Maintaining an Image of Objectivity', pp. 63–75.

42 Peter Blake was one of Seidler's favoured commentators. See Peter Blake, *Architecture for the New World: The Work of Harry Seidler*, Horwitz, Sydney, Wittenborn & Co, New York, 1973; Peter Blake, *Harry Seidler, Australian Embassy = Ambassade d'Australie Paris*, Horwitz, Sydney, 1979.

43 See for instance, 'Architectural Forum: Dr. Neville Gruzman', *Architecture Australia*, vol. 73, no. 5, July 1984, pp. 68–69.

44 'Castle Cove', *Architecture Australia*, vol. 71, no. 5, September 1982, pp. 48–49; 'Kooralbyn', *Architecture Australia*, vol. 71, no. 5, September 1982, pp. 50–57; Harry Seidler, 'Internationalism', *Architecture Australia*, vol. 71, no. 5, September 1982, pp. 58–60; 'Mid City Centre', *Architecture Australia*, vol. 72, no. 1, January 1983, pp. 48–53; 'Apartments, Broadbeach', *Architecture Australia*, vol. 72, no. 6, November 1983, pp. 42–3; 'Ringwood Cultural Centre', *Architecture Australia*, vol. 73, no. 2, March 1984, pp. 44–7.

45 'Education Centre', *Architecture Australia*, vol. 71, no. 5, September 1982, pp. 40–7; 'Forestry Headquarters', *Architecture Australia*, vol. 72, no. 6, November 1983, pp. 68–9; 'Cameron Chisholm and Nicol: RAIA Gold Medal', *Architecture Australia*, vol. 73, no. 6, September 1984, pp. 38–67. See issue devoted to Colin Madigan and the National Gallery of Australia, *Architecture Australia*, vol. 71, no. 7, November 1982.

46 See Tom Heath, 'If that is the answer, what is the question?' *Architecture Australia*, vol. 69, no. 3, July 1980, p. 25; 'Architectural Education: evolution or revolution?' *Architecture Australia*, vol. 70, no. 1, March 1981, p. 25; 'The universe is out to get you', *Architecture Australia*, vol. 70, no. 4, September, 1981, p. 27; 'Architectural Theory', *Architecture Australia*, vol. 70, no. 5, November 1981, p. 29.

47 Tom Heath, 'The eclectic horseman,' *Architecture Australia*, vol. 69, no. 5, November 1980, p. 23.

48 Tom Heath, 'Towards a popular architecture?' *Architecture Australia*, vol. 71, no. 1, January 1982, p. 1; 'Panic and desperation', *Architecture Australia*, vol. 71, no. 5, September 1982, p. 15.

49 See Heath, 'Architectural Theory', p. 29. In this editorial Heath expressed his opinion about the quality of the writing that was appearing in large quantity in the architectural press. He stated, 'It becomes increasingly difficult to view the present upturn with enthusiasm as successive journals deliver yet more masses of bad prose, worse reasoning, and trivial designs, buttressed by random references to half-understood historical examples.'

50 Ibid. Heath's italicisation.

51 Tom Heath, 'Five traps of architectural discourse', *Architecture Australia*, vol. 71, no. 2, March 1982, p. 17.

52 Ibid.

The Anglo-Asian Bungalow in Australia's Northern Territory

1 See Antony King, *The Bungalow: Production of a Global Culture*, Routledge & Kegan Paul, London, 1984; Clay Lancaster, *The American Bungalow 1880–1930*, Abbeville Press, New York, 1985.

2 See King and Lancaster for a detailed history of the development and dissemination of the Colonial Bungalow. See also B. Giberti, 'The Chalet as Archetype: The Bungalow, the picturesque tradition and vernacular form', *Traditional Dwellings and Settlement Review*, vol. 3, no. 1, 1991, pp. 54–64, for a summary of this process and from where this description was taken.

3 King, *The Bungalow*, p. 224.

4 RA McInnis, *A Town Planning Scheme for the Town of Darwin, Northern Territory of Australia*, Commonwealth Government Printer, Canberra, 1940.

5 See J Martinez, 'Plural Australia: Aboriginal and Asian Labour in Tropical White Australia, Darwin 1911–1940', PhD thesis, University of Woolongong, 1999, p. 45; A Powell, *Far Country: A Short History of the Northern Territory*, Melbourne University Press, Carlton, 1982, pp. 73–4.

6 Powell, *Far Country*, p.101. In 1843 attempts were made to attract 'white or coloured settlers' and advertisements were placed in such places as Singapore. 'Asiatics', notes Powell, were also encouraged to settle in the region but most declined. See also C Doran, 'Colonising the Territory', *Northern Perspective*, vol. 13, no. 2, 1990.

7 See P Harris, 'In Defence of Tent: The top-ender as analogue for the minimal house', in P Freeman & J Vulker (eds), *The Australian Dwelling*, RAIA Education Division, Red Hill, 1991, pp. 59–64.

8 WL Payne & JW Fletcher, *Report of the Board of Inquiry appointed to inquire into the Land and Land Industries of the Northern Territory of Australia*, Commonwealth Government Printer, Canberra, 10 October 1937.

9 Reported in the regional newspaper, *Northern Standard*, 1 October 1937 and 21 December 1937. Emphasis mine.

10 Letter RH Weddell (Administrator of the NT) to the Colonial Secretary, Singapore FMS. Dated 17 October 1936 (National Archives NAA CRS F1 1937/673).

11 National Archives, NAA A12428, 2002/04/998306.

12 D Evans, 'Centre and Periphery: Melbourne Regionalism and Global Context in the 1950s and 1960s', in *Universal versus Individual*, Proceedings of the International Conference on the Research of Modern Architecture, Jyvaskyla, Finland, 30 August–1 September 2002, www.aalvaralto.fi/conferences/universal/papers, p. 3.

13 JM Freeland, *Architecture in Australia: A History*, Cheshire, Melbourne, 1968, pp. 238, 247.

14 See WH Carr, 'The Japanese House', *Architecture in Australia*, December 1964, pp. 98–100. The house was built for GW Paul in a Brisbane suburb in 1887 by 'an English contractor using three Japanese carpenters and two Japanese plasterers' and 'it was dismantled in 1962'.

15 WT Haslam, *Parliamentary Standing Committee on Public Works: Minutes of Evidence relating to the proposed erection of Administrative Offices at Darwin*, NT, 2 August 1939, Commonwealth Government Printer, Canberra.

16 Ibid.

17 J Stratton, 'Deconstructing the Territory', *Cultural Studies*, vol. 3, no. 1, 1989, p. 50.

18 M Dewar, 'In Search of the "Never-Never": The Northern Territory metaphor in Australian writing 1837–1992', PhD thesis, Northern Territory University, 1993, p. 86.

19 Ernestine Hill, *The Territory*, Angus & Robertson, Sydney and London, 1951, pp. 136–7.

20 Stratton, 'Deconstructing the Territory', p. 42.

21 See Taylor, 1918; Breinl & Young, 1920; Barrett, 1925; Elkin, 1947. Cilento, 1925, argued against this construct suggesting that climate was no impediment for the colonization of the tropics by Europeans. Ellsworth Huntington (1925, 1929) from a climatic determinist position argued that climate was an impediment and many agreed with him.

22 Dewar, 'In Search of the "Never-Never"', p. 88.

23 Evans, 'Centre and Periphery', p. 1.

The Local and the Migrant: Limits of Mutual Recognition

1 Peter Robinson, 'Visions of reality through the building of dreams', *Canberra Times*, 20 October 2001, pp. 4–5.
2 Heather Rusden, interview with E Taglietti, National Library of Australia, Oral History section, ORAL TRC 2263, March 1988.
3 Paul Ginsborg, *History of Contemporary Italy Society and Politics 1943–1988*, Penguin Books, London, 1990.
4 Vittorio Gregotti, *New Directions in Italian Architecture*, George Braziller, New York, 1968, p. 40.
5 Arthur Drexler, *Transformations in Modern Architecture*, The Museum of Modern Art, New York, 1979, p. 124.
6 Ibid.
7 Jennifer Taylor, 'Beyond the 1950s' in Robert Irving (ed.), *The History and Design of the Australian House*, Oxford University Press, Melbourne, 1985, p. 155.
8 JM Freeland, *Architecture in Australia: A History*, Penguin, Ringwood, Vic, 1972.
9 Harry Sowden, *Towards an Australian Architecture*, Ure Smith, Sydney, 1968.
10 Ian McKay, Robin Boyd, Hugh Stretton & John Mant, *Living and Partly Living*, Nelson, Sydney, 1971.
11 'Conference Centre, Canberra, ACT, for the Associated Chambers of Manufacturers of Australia', *Architecture in Australia*, vol. 57, no. 7.
12 Lance Wright & Kenneth Browne (eds), *The Architectural Review*, September 1978, pp. 156–7.
13 Richard Apperly, Robert Irving & Peter Reynolds, *A Pictorial Guide to Identifying Australian Architecture*, Angus and Robertson, Sydney, 1989.
14 Jehane Sharah, 'Making designs in Canberra', *Canberra City News*, 17 September 2003.
15 Jennifer Taylor, *Australian Architecture since 1960*, RAIA National Education Division, Canberra, 1990, p. 89.
16 Apperly, Irving & Reynolds, *A Pictorial Guide to Identifying Australian Architecture*, p. 236.
17 *Cross-section*, no. 212, 1 July 1970.
18 Ibid.
19 *Cross-section*, no. 159, 1 January 1966.
20 William Jordy, *The Impact of European Modernism in the Mid-Twentieth Century*, Volume 5 of the series *American Buildings and their Architects*, Oxford University Press, New York, 1972.

21 Sigfried Giedion, *Space, Time and Architecture*, Harvard University Press, Cambridge, Mass., 1982.

22 Roger Butler (ed.), *The Europeans: Émigré artists in Australia 1930–1960*, National Gallery of Australia, Canberra, 1997.

23 Stephen Cairns & Philip Goad (eds), *Building, Dwelling, Drifting: Migrancy and the Limits of Architecture, Papers from the 3rd 'Other Connections' Conference*, University of Melbourne, 26–29 June 1997.

24 Butler (ed.), *The Europeans*, p. 7.

25 Margaret Vine, 'Jewellers and Jewellery: European trained, made in Australia,' in Butler (ed.), *The Europeans*, p. 192.

26 Mirjana Lozanovska (ed.), 'New Australian Architecture', *Architect*, April 2002, pp. 4–6.

27 Ibid.

28 Harriet Edquist, 'Introduction,' in Edquist (ed.), *Frederick Romberg: The Architecture of Migration, 1938–1975*, RMIT University Press, Melbourne, 2000, p. 11.

29 Conrad Hamann, 'Frederick Romberg and the Problem of European Authenticity,' in Butler (ed.), *The Europeans*, p. 55.

30 Stephen Cairns (ed.), *Drifting: Architecture and Migrancy*, Routledge, London, 2004.

31 Paul Carter, 'Mythforms' in Cairns (ed.), *Drifting*, p. 85.

32 Ibid., p. 82.

33 Freeland, *Architecture in Australia*, preface.

34 Taylor, *Australian Architecture since 1960*, preface.

35 Philip Goad & Patrick Bingham-Hall, *New Directions in Australian Architecture*, Pesaro Publishing, Sydney, 2001.

36 Carter, 'Mythforms', p. 92.

37 Ibid.